I Walk Alone

Geoffrey Eldridge

I Walk Alone

I Walk Alone
ISBN 978 1 76041 653 9
Copyright © Geoffrey Eldridge 2018
Cover: Geoffrey Eldridge

First published 2018 by
GINNINDERRA PRESS
PO Box 3461 Port Adelaide 5015
www.ginninderrapress.com.au

Contents

Preface	7
Part One	**9**
Get-out Clauses	11
Important facts of life	11
Summit Talks 1	16
Who or what am I?	16
All at sea (and no place to go)	18
Summit Talks 2	30
Why write a book when I prefer to walk the talk?	30
Summit Talks 3	40
Dark days in the Dark Peak	40
Summit Talks 4	57
Becoming a peak-bagger – with hiccups	57
Summit Talks 5	80
All abroad and thrill-seekers explained…or exposed perhaps	80
Summit Talks 6	107
I walk alone	107
Summit Talks 7	122
There has be reckoning	122
Summit Talks 8	132
Too many demands on my time	132
Summit Talks 9	153
The winter of discontent	153
Intermission	**159**
Comfort Break	161

Part Two	**167**
Summit Talks 10	169
On the dark side	169
Summit Talks 11	180
What's a foot?	180
Summit Talks 12	188
The TGOC debacle	188
Summit Talks 13	211
Credibility regained	211
Summit Talks 14	218
The Cape Wrath Trail with the big ask	218
Summit Talks 15	251
Done and dusted	251

Preface

The TV was on in one room and I was cooking dinner in another when my attention was caught by the closing line of an advert that I heard, 'You do not have to climb a mountain to feel on top of the world.' I was taken aback because I most certainly do. I was trying to climb one thousand of them and, at the time I heard this, I was 99.92% done! After all my efforts to reach this target, I was going to feel pretty peeved when AN Other, feeling elated about not climbing one thousand mountains, set out to write a book about their virtual achievement.

This could well be why me and the TV share different rooms. We don't get on very well together. Which in itself could be deemed an odd arrangement, because I live on my own.

I also climb the vast majority of my mountains alone.

Geoff Eldridge

Part One

Get-out Clauses

One step taken into the world of adventure without a robust sense of humour is already one step too far. – The Aimless Rambler

On 3 November 2017, I reached the summit of my one thousandth different UK big hill or mountain.

This story won't be a chronological account or even a list of those peaks attained, but instead it's tales about some of the trials and tribulations that form the catalogue of misadventure that has to accompany such an endeavour.

Before I can begin to recount any of this, like all trips that I embark upon, there are some technicalities that have to be dealt with first.

Important facts of life

For your health and safety, and the continued goodwill of others, please read the following carefully and act accordingly.

Travelling with me is as simple, or as difficult, as you want it to be. You get what you see and I'm prone to both having a laugh at your misfortune and going up more hills than you may have expected. Lots of hills, and that is often over and over again. Choose to make it any more difficult for me and I'll dump you as a potential companion for any future trip as soon as we get back. I don't have time enough left to make allowances beyond that initial opening gesture of amenability and continue to enjoy the reputation that people tend to only walk with me once. If you can't get a grip on that as the basis for a walk with me, then you could well have difficulties reading about them also.

The reason why I say this is because you could well be featured. Which, of course, could explain why I spend so much time walking alone. If that's the case, then no worries. It's my problem to sort and quite frankly I can't be bothered. I no longer give much of a damn and will more than likely walk away rather than get tied up in all that nonsense that's currently being used to try and replace common sense and decency. If I do stick around, it's only for any humour that may be milked from the beast. I have been walking alone for most of my life and have no intention of changing my ways at this late stage into the journey just to suit this new and supposedly better world that is being sought by so many pressure groups.

My world is by no means perfect but it's a lot better than what I see before me as it rapidly declines into a maelstrom of doom and gloom. The current formula has always worked for me. Nobody is deliberately being hurt or offended, so there is no need to fix it. Importantly you should note the use of the words 'nobody is deliberately' in that last sentence…and remember them.

There are no other warnings of my indifference to the threatening menaces of those Prophets of Gloom who seek to blight my world of both adventure and humour. They are Health and Safety Executive, Equal Opportunities and Political Correctness. Accidents in adventure and humour happen. This is what my computer's dictionary has to say on the subject but they are all more or less the same if you wish to check elsewhere.

Accident – An event that happens by chance or that is without apparent or deliberate cause.

Adventure – An unusual and exciting or daring experience associated with danger or the taking of risks.

Humour – The quality of being amusing or comic, especially as expressed in literature and speech. The ability to amuse other people.

And there you have it. That's what I work with. Take it or leave it.

Political Correctness? Nah, I haven't got the patience either for it or for justifying my complete indifference to any champions of such petty causes. Equal Opportunities are not really relevant to loners such as I, but anyone is welcome to make a fool of themselves with me for a while and be dumped with equal rapidity if they get touchy about their status. No preferential treatment for anyone – that's equal enough for me.

So, and I'm being quite serious here, if you can't accept that, as the status quo, there is no real malice in me or my work then you had best be off. Yes, go. Now. There is nothing here for you and you could well spoil it for others if you remain.

It's another fact of life that as soon as you write something down with the thought of publishing it somewhere, or perhaps putting a picture into the public arena, there are a bunch of wannabe critics and experts sitting out there poised to pass critical judgement. If you're one of those, then you'll also need that tough sense of humour, because I don't have a lot of time for people like you either. If you do try to get too serious about what I – a pretty harmless, self-styled lone adventure-seeker – have to say, then you're far too sad a person to be looking any further into my aimless ramblings. So it'd be better for us both if you went on your way as well.

It's a pound to a penny that says there will still be some miserable sod out there who will have ignored those warnings and still feel the need to take adverse issue with the contents of my lifelong hobbies. In good faith, I hope it's not going to be you after such clear and precise warnings. So please exercise the joys of your free choice and put it down just as soon as you start to feel aggrieved rather than wasting my time with grievances. Remember – if you're offended, you're not actually hurt… Only warned.

Next, we ought to sort out what is a mountain. I wouldn't normally bother, because you will never get agreement on such definitions, but since I have taken to writing about them, some form of explanation is needed.

John and Anne Nuttall in their guidebook *The Mountains of England*

and Wales, felt that to qualify as a mountain it needed to be 2,000 feet or above and must rise above all its surroundings by at least 50 feet. Which invites scorn from the Scottish because they have 284 Munros alone, and to qualify they have to be over 3,000 feet with a 500-foot drop between it and any other 3,000-foot top. Which wouldn't even rate as a foothill to the Alpinist. Thousands of people are living higher than most UK mountains in towns like Chamonix in the Alps before they get out of bed in the morning.

Timing is also relevant. In today's attention-seeking world and the habit of generating exaggerated fear and drama out of everything, what we would have hardly noticed as a hill forty years ago is now likely to be someone's Everest. Ticking off the highest point of London Boroughs is a case in point and there are those who do it.

So to make it absolutely clear, they are my mountains. They are what I decide qualifies but I wouldn't try justifying any of them as such, under any circumstances, to anyone because I'm one of those people who would cross the street to avoid an argument. In saying that, I tend to use the generalisation 'a thousand mountains' because it is so much easier than trying to explain what I'm really doing. That is to more or less go up any lumpy bit that I see and if that features in some list or another, then it counts…on the proviso that I deem it worthy. (I lived in London for a while and none of its summits have ever appeared in my list. I looked them up out of curiosity and got lost in the question – is it the highest piece of dirt or the concrete that is sitting on it that you have to stand on to tick the box?)

Even with that, it's still not straightforward. For an example, some people will try to climb every top listed in the Wainwright *Lake District Guides* (214) but to me, and I have done them all, some are not worthy, whereas some other hills that I have surmounted are, but don't feature in anyone's list when they ought to. One such hill is near my home. It is even called Great Hill and it has no paths or easy ways to reach it. This isn't counted in my total either, because I only include peaks off other people's lists. I am satisfied that those who really know me also know just how much big-hill walking I do. None of it is easy for reasons that may become clearer as it unfolds within these pages. Who knows, if I did get famous for any reason, one day people may be doing Geoff's List if they can find it.

So, when I say one thousand mountains, they have to be in the UK and not something that I could be ashamed of, and they are only counted once. Along with enough complications and anomalies to add the shades of grey necessary to generate sufficient material to write a book about.

Like mountains, a book without risk of conflict is dull.

Now, if you're still coming with me, please read on with a clear understanding that this is neither manual nor guide. Whatever else it may turn out to be, I intend it for entertainment purposes only and you must make of it what you will. After all, it's my life that we're talking about here and I have been encouraged enough by previous reactions to parts of it for me to share it with others, like yourself, in a little more depth.

Oh, and I nearly forgot. Any similarities to a real person, living or dead, can't be attributed to my writing skills, because I'm not that clever. So if you think you recognise yourself in a detrimental manner, don't fret. It's a coincidence.

Summit Talks 1

It would seem when I listen to interviews with celebrities that they all come from a poor background – so there might still be some hope for me yet. – The Aimless Rambler

Who or what am I?

Who – or, perhaps more importantly, what – am I? I am a cartoonist. Not by trade. Just a hobby. I also write a bit and a few decades ago I enjoyed an enviable success rate at both to supplement my meagre wages. My humorous style has now fallen out of favour with the world of magazines where they were being published but rather than adapt to the new demands of their glossy approach, safe from the adverse reactions of the nit-picking minority, I stayed loyal to myself and walked away.

Now I offer the following preamble to anything that I would draw or write:

> Hi. I am The Aimless Rambler and I have just happened down your way. Which means one, or both, of us is undoubtedly lost. So until we get back on track let's share a few drinks, tell some tall tales and have a bit of a chuckle about it all… Then move on before we get called to account. Life is too serious. What I do in the mountains is too serious. There has to be a release. Humour in adversity does it for so many. The British are renowned for it and I'm proud to sit amongst those that can receive and deliver that gritty wit in good faith.

What on earth was I thinking of when I came up with The Aimless Rambler? Like it or not, I'm stuck with it now because I really did make it up as an alternative name to use as a front to my art and writing. For most of my life, I have had this notion to write a witty book, using my cartoons to illustrate it, about the ups and downs of life in the mountains with a family and low budget. Others may now be using the title Aimless Rambler, for one reason or another, and where they got it from is of no interest to me because I've been using it for close on forty years. I can honestly say with my hand on my heart and wallet that when I came up with it as a pseudonym, I'd never seen or heard of anyone else using it.

I had no access to any kind of internet in those days to check if The Aimless Rambler lived elsewhere so it was a bit of a shock when I searched about a year ago and saw the number of other hits besides mine. Mind you, I used to do cartoons and sign them off as 'The Aimless Rambler' in the Alpine Hut's visitor's books when staying overnight – so anyone could have seen them. If, perchance, some disgruntled person or persons feels that I've pinched Aimless Rambler from them, then along with the above as an explanation and an articulated version of 'sod off' they will need to note my version is The Aimless Rambler. If they still don't like it then I would change it to Another Aimless Rambler and so on. When I say I don't care, in this instance, I really mean it. I am The Aimless Rambler just as I am Geoffrey Eldridge. I can't change that even if some smooth-talking lawyers said I had to.

To support my claim to originality, I am providing the full history of its roots in this chapter and suggest that you be cautious of anyone who would claim that I stole it from them. Either directly or indirectly.

Short version: I'm aimless and tend to ramble a bit. Both on foot and on paper.

Long version: it stems from 'The Rime of The Ancient Mariner' by Samuel Taylor Coleridge and illustrated by Gustave Doré. I bought a copy of this book around 1980. Why I did so is quite important. Ever since I had acquired a tape cassette of Richard Burton reciting this classic work a few years earlier and since his rendition brought so much life, and colourful death, into those two-hundred-year-old words, it has always been part of my life. As a poem about misadventure without the usual war, women and wine, it struck me as a tale of ordinary folk just trying to cope with whatever Fate threw at them. You shoot a bloody albatross and the world goes mad. Who'd have thought it two hundred years ago?

When I saw this unabridged book version in a second-hand bookshop, I had to have it. I have endured enough misfortunes of my own to identify with it as well as having a short history of messing about on boats. However, it was the illustrations that clinched it.

Gustave Doré's drawings are a tad more serious than mine but the similarity is close enough to see my connection. A search on the internet would turn up endless examples of his without cost or copyright difficulties and some of mine could be found with a little more exploring on the search engines. (Try Aimless Rambler on Facebook.) We had too many similarities to let things go, so… Well, now my work is on the cover. Enough said. Incidentally, I was both drawing and writing long before I discovered this works and you would have to go back to the *MAD* magazines of the sixties to find what first inspired me.

The even longer version, condensed from around forty years to a few pages, happened like this.

We begin a mountaineering book by going to sea.

All at sea (and no place to go)

While my true calling was already to the wild country where terra firma of some kind was under at least one of my feet, during those early adventure-seeking years of mine I took to the sea when the opportunity presented itself. It was largely to keep the family talking to each other after my wife Diane and I moved from London and the Home Counties on a two-hundred-mile exodus to live in the hilly bits between Lancashire and Yorkshire. A thinly disguised emotional shanghai for which I didn't even get the Queen's five pence. (We had just been decimalised.)

Married but before kids, and I used to go sailing around the Solent and English Channel with her father in his twenty-eight-foot, four-berth yacht. In nautical terms, that meant swinging cats was not to be an evening's entertainment unless you stayed 'up on top'. (A nautical term for outside.) These terms were to become crucial, so please bear with me on their usage.

Our crewing duties were limited, because the captain liked to do everything himself so that it was done right. I had spent too much of my time throwing up over the leeward side to become competent in anything practical. Diane, being the only female on board, was allowed, under supervision, to do a bit of cooking and dangle a buoy over the side as we came alongside something or other. However, I did learn a bit about boats. Primarily that I didn't like them.

The freedom of the seven seas was nothing more than a fairy tale. For me, it was a prison. I like to consider myself as a very ordinary person so with my claims to adventure-seeking perhaps already sounding too boastful, it is time to burst the first bubble.

I can't swim. Babies can. I can't.

I have no idea why not and don't want to know. Nor do I have any intention of learning. Move on and play your strengths elsewhere. Except on a boat you can't. My motto of running away when the going gets tough can't be applied. It has to be seen through to the journey's end with no guarantee of shore leave when you get there either.

If the marina (boat park) is full, you could end up offshore lying at anchor or tied (moored) to a mooring buoy. (A big floaty thing attached by hawsers to a couple of tons of concrete lying on the seabed. Not to be confused with a ship's buoy, the ship's boy, a channel buoy, a hazard buoy or the plastic bottle marking the local fisherman's lobster pot.) These were the days of communication by semaphore, signal flags and half a hundredweight of ship's radio. I'm not even sure if *Star Trek* was around in those days to show us a preview of our lives with a mobile phone because I didn't watch telly much then either.

To go ashore (land) would mean taking the tender (rubber dingy) but that would leave the rest of the crew stranded out there until you got back. So the alternative was for one of them to take you ashore in it and then take it back to the boat. Which, when your shoreside excursions had been completed, left you stranded on land with your berth (bed) still out at sea until you are jumping up and down on a crowded shoreline, frantically waving your arms, while shouting 'Ahoy' ('Over here, you deaf bastards') to attract the crew and you were spotted. No wonder the Ancient Mariner shot that albatross to relieve his frustrations.

I think this can be best summed up in the captain's log of one trip to Devon. 'Geoff walked back.' No, Jesus was the guy walking on the water looking for disciples. I could only mutineer. After a day of calling for Uncle Hughie, as we rounded some headland in a squall, we called into a small harbour for a look around and resupply. While on shore I, for the first time that I can recall, walked away. I refused to get back on board and instead walked along the cliff paths to their next port of call. My sailing days were over.

But all of that was spread over three or four years and enough experiences to spot some discrepancies in 'The Rime Of The Ancient Mariner' and realise that Samuel Taylor Coleridge and I had many things in common. We were both frauds for starters. When I say I climb mountains, I am walking up them and not doing the Chris Bonnington thing, while, judging by the terminology, the nearest STC had been to sea was more likely to be in a rowing boat trip around Windermere with his mate Wordsworth's sister, Dotty.

Let's just have a quick look to see if I can show you why. Long before that fatal shooting and the hanging of the carcass around the bird-killer's neck, you will find this verse.

> The sun came up upon the left,
> Out of the sea came he!
> And he shone bright and on the right
> Went down into the sea.

No sailor, be they ancient or modern, ever talks like that. They talk salty gibberish, unknown to anyone outside of the sailing fraternity, with words like fore an' aft, port and starboard, laced with a generous dose of rum and more rum. It should read something like:

The sun came up o'er port-side rail.
Out of yon briny came he.
And he shone bright o'er poop deck 'n' m'ns'l,
Afore dipping down to starboard bow 'n' t' sea.

I had a bit of trouble with my poetry there because the obvious rhyme to rail was sail but sailors don't use them. The have spinnakers, jibs and the like. I'm not a good enough poet to write the stuff that doesn't rhyme so I went for the phonetic sailor from Lancashire's version of mainsail. I will give another slightly clearer example. One seemingly innocent line that could be likened to the 'red rag to a bull'. (Before they discovered that cattle are colour-blind, that is.)

The mariners all gan work the ropes,

'Mariners' is OK, better than sailors for poetry anyway; 'gan' is quaint. A bit of Olde English never hurts to give it character but 'ropes'! Surely not! That is outrageous. Jolly Jack Tars never, ever, use ropes. They are lines, springers, painters and halyards, to name but a few. If really pushed, they will resort to hemp, but rope shows a shameful ignorance of their nautical prowess. You certainly don't get to be ancient with such a poor grasp of the jargon.

Anyway, methinks, 'Is it that difficult?' I can write, I can draw a bit and I'm somewhat experienced at roughing it with the elements. Yep, I can do that. I will write and illustrate a book. All my own work. *The Trail of The Aimless Rambler* was born…and died. But more of that later. For now, it is enough to know that's how I came to be The Aimless Rambler. I can't dump it because it's part of me now. Although a more accurate title, if I had stuck to that same honesty, would have been, *The Trail of The Starts Off With Good Intentions But Is Easily Distracted Person Who Does a Lot of Things*.

Moving on, I am good at some of those things and average at most but when it comes to the really useful skills in the marketplace, I am abysmal. I have to be, otherwise I would be a success at something other than a failed trier at everything. One of life's 'also rans' in the great race for fame and fortune. ('Baulked at the first fence' as my father might have put it as he scanned the racing page.)

No, to be fair, that's a not quite the way of it. At one significant milestone in my life around the time of the miners' strikes, after years of working overtime to try, unsuccessfully, to make ends meet, I made the conscious decision to no longer compete in the race for any kind of success at all.

I had a young family and a sick wife who I wanted to share my time with. They were far more important to me than the production targets of an ever-demanding employer. From that day, I would work to live and not vice versa by doing just enough to earn my wage fairly and nothing more. For the first time in my life, I showed what I was really made of and all my energies would be directed at making the most of what we had as a family. When the going got tough, I walked away with the arse hanging out of my trousers but my conscience was clear.

I would rather bodge and dodge with what I had than compare my lot to that of my contemporaries. I have been doing that rather successfully ever since. I'm not quite one of the drop-outs of the hippy sixties, because I never had much to drop out from, but I'm certainly a Thatcher victim of the eighties. If you can't beat them and don't want to join them, then there isn't much left to do but kick, squeal and bitch…and then take to the rough country with the kids for a healthy dose of R&R.

Voila! And what you end up with is me. A stress-free anti-hero with the gifts of tenacity, imagination and creativity that can make something special, out of nothing more than the ordinary.

Those hills that I wander now begin on my doorstep. If the Pennines are regarded as the backbone of England, then for the majority of my life I have lived in one of the cushiony parts between the vertebrae. I rode a mountain bike over them to get to and from work – winter and summer alike with no let up for bad weather or darkness. For over thirty years, I made commuting a twice-daily endurance event. The bit in between was just a job that almost paid the bills. Nothing more, nothing less.

And to make life at work a little easier and certainly more interesting, I discovered that one of the things that I was particularly good at was being a 'management problem'. I was the spanner in their works. The proverbial pain in the arse. A level-headed trade union representative who had the gift of popularity and competence. As with my adventure and art, I took my humour with me and used it as both shield and weapon. I was the oddball who could get away with thumbing my nose at the established order. That slightly freaky wild card who everyone was watching because it was a good source of entertainment in an otherwise mundane environment – but too risky to try and emulate or eradicate. By the time I was reaching retirement age, my reputation had spread far enough for it not to be unusual to find me representing senior managers, way above my own station, at hearings of alleged misconduct or inefficiency. I really was that good; or, as is more likely, the opposition was particularly bad.

There is a price to pay for that, though, and it's called by the economists 'the lower income bracket'. The slippery career ladder that others were frantically trying to climb to escape the low pay and tedium was always going to be nothing more than a token gesture on my part. Just another experience to bleed for humorous content. I think I nailed it on about my eighth of thirteen attempts at promotion when the comments in the failed box read, 'Refreshingly honest. Not suitable for management grade at this stage.'

On the plus side, the low income meant that there were no short cuts to honing my skills on the hills. Every lesson had to be self-taught, every trip had to be maximised to justify any expenditure and the off-road commuting by bike had made me a formidable endurance athlete. It is perhaps worth mentioning that I didn't make up that formidable endurance athlete description. A cycling magazine described me as one of those. That's along with all the other podium finishers, in a round-up of the event that they were covering. That was a big WOW.

Probably the biggest because I stopped competing soon after that. Like my walking, people only rode with me once and you needed two for a team in that particular event.

For my deepest taproot, here is a blog (tweaked a little to make it more suitable for inclusion here) that I wrote about my childhood. It was subsequently published a few years ago by Ginninderra Press in a chapbook titled *From Humble Beginnings*.

> Life, for me, began from humble beginnings and has been pretty much downhill ever since.
>
> Of course this is written in jest. An opener designed to catch attention and, if looked at closely, could be interpreted to have opposite meanings. The obvious is the pessimistic line of going from bad to worse, whereas optimism suggest that it was easy from that point on as a downhill ride.
>
> Whichever way you wish to take it is up to you but rarely will you hear of a celebrity saying that they had an advantageous start in life. It would appear, according to them, that you would have to have your roots in poverty to expect any hope of success. Next comes the arguments about one man's poverty being another man's riches. Followed by the differing levels of hardship and one person's perception of it against another's. It's all relative. What it is relative to then also becomes subjective and so the circle turns.
>
> I'm no celebrity but my life did start from humble beginnings. Well, not so much humble – more like downright bloody hard. Today, by the celebrity reckoning, I should be a millionaire or have worldwide fame but, alas, I think it's safe to say that I took the less risky, pessimistic, route. It's perhaps important to mention here that my older brother, from exactly the same start, took the optimistic approach and for him, in terms of material gain, it has paid off. I do have two other siblings of whom I would suggest that my sister would probably say she went my way and my younger brother (with almost a generation gap between us) as a child of the sixties went completely off on his own and differing tangent.
>
> I was born, a month after the Welfare State was created, on a working farm in Buckinghamshire. There was a king on the UK throne, the Olympics were in London, Everest had not been climbed, food was still rationed, there were no motorways

or national parks, and it hardly ever rained. Our home had no electricity, no phone, no mains sewer connection, no central heating and was three hundred years old. Complete with all the associated problems and livestock resulting from negative maintenance. Candles for light and baths by the fire were a way of life.

There is even photographic evidence that shows me as barefoot child! Can you possibly get any better qualifications for the road to fame or fortune than that? Of course you can and I had that as well. Jumping forward a bit…wait for it…I left school to start full-time work at just fourteen years old. Absolutely true. I could legally work a nine-hour day but not have sex.

I was probably one of the last legal school-leavers of that era to leave at fourteen and the less informed may well claim that it is a lie for exaggeration purposes. It is not. In 1963 you could leave school at the end of the term in which you reached your fifteenth birthday. My birthday was during the last week of August and the summer term was deemed to end on the 31st of that month. It also meant I was always battling the rise to manhood with the constant niggles of being the youngest, but one of the toughest, in the class.

Take that lot as my opening gambit in the bid for glory.

It's essential that this home is examined in the correct context here, because using today's assumptions that accompany living in what was to become a listed building may lead people to think that I am from a privileged background but trying to play it down. At the time, before any renovation or extensions, it was, to put it simply, crudely basic. The house went with my father's job. We did not own or rent it. He was perhaps a living-in farm foreman; while his boss, a property speculator of some sort, lived in a neighbouring, but much posher, farm just over a mile away. Therefore no job equalled no home. Why it is so important to my journey, is that in 2012, forty years after I had left it, the house that I was born in went on the market for two and a half million quid!

It's only as adults that we can look back and decide if we had a hard initiation into life because at the time it was, whatever it may have been, the normal state of affairs for us as kids. We grew up with whatever hand Fate had dealt our parents at the time. Rather than say I had an upbringing built on poverty and hardship, I would prefer to say that life on the farm moulded us from foundations fashioned from a rudimentary bodge and dodge policy into practical and hardy characters that are not easily phased by hardship. It certainly worked that way for me.

Okay, so now I have an MBE, but it was not for my art, writing or mountaineering skills. Not directly anyway, but the characteristics that enabled me to shine in those strengths may have been a useful contribution towards it. At the time of nomination as well as being a trade union representative I was an office magazine editor and also had the unenviable job of dealing with customer complaints – all for, by its various names over successive governments, the social security department. (Part of that welfare state that shared the year of my birth as its beginning. In comparison today I think I may be fairing better of the two.) The MBE was awarded for nothing more than making sure that the voices of people less fortunate than myself were getting heard and having a fair hearing. It seems that I was particularly good at it and could be relied upon to always keep my sense of humour under duress and still give the task at hand my best shot – which turned out to be a lot better than that of my contemporaries and many of the opposition that would seek to prove me wrong.

I see my MBE as a thank you for thirty years of fighting to retain my integrity and individuality in a system that is notorious for its conformity, back-stabbing and arse-kissing under a top-heavy, dog eat dog management structure. A lot of people secretly wanted to be a wild card like me but successful careers do not allow such luxuries. Since the award of the MBE, my social status has been elevated to a position where I am no longer a mere nutter but can now lay claim to the much sought-for 'eccentricity' without fear of accusations claiming that I am acting above my station.

I never set out to do this. It just unfolded that way as Fate dealt me that next hand and I adapted my lifestyle to suit. Which, I suspect, is also what most people do. We have a vague notion of what we would like and try to steer in that direction, although I would be lying if I said that I ever had a long-term plan. Today is, and always has been, too important as it may be my last. Build a camp, make a rope bridge, shoot vermin and chase the dream. I am so easily distracted from any set course, as my grasshopper mind takes me from one interest to another, that I have rarely finished anything to my complete satisfaction.

This could well stem from growing up on the farm where there was always work to do and the only difference between that work and play was that we got paid for the latter. Adventure was everywhere around us. The guns were real, sharp knives and a stout stick were tools never to be without and baths were on Saturdays.

We didn't carry that other obligatory item for adventure and exploration, string, because it was a farm and therefore held together by baling twine. It was everywhere that you looked because as a multi-purpose commodity it was never thrown away and my memories of it are from the days before nylon replaced the sisal. When the bale was broken, the two strings were automatically coiled up and tied in a single knot and put in a sack or they were left hanging loosely from a convenient hook, nail or door handle. If there was nowhere to hang it, then it was often tied around a gate post or other timber – along with years of the stuff growing fragile with age. We even plaited strands together to make ropes.

From my earliest memory, we always had to try and be self-sufficient. We roamed the fields, orchards and woods on a whim. The guidelines and rules were vague. Use your common sense, don't shoot if you can't see where a missed shot is going to safely end and always cut with the sharp edge going away from you.

Amongst my clearer early memories I have this vivid picture of a steam train passing close by in the dark during a windy snow storm. The glow and sparks of an open firebox, carriage lights and the rattle of wheels on the track joints right beside me were all adding drama to a wild night. I was on a steep railway embankment helping to herd sheep back through the gap where the fence had been broken, allowing them to stray. Then on another occasion looking for black cows at night in a wood after they had been reported straying on to a nearby lane. I also remember loading dead and maimed sheep, victims from a frenzied dog attack, onto the back of the farm lorry and taking them down to the slaughterhouse to be finished off. It was a Sunday and nobody was working so the manager had opened it up for us and we did the job ourselves with a bolt gun. A teacher, at school the next day, more or less accused me of making it all up when she heard me telling my friends that there were twenty-three. I wasn't.

Most of my memories, though, are less extreme and just snippets of everyday farm life, while I can hardly recall primary school at all. Except the enormous, wooden, dentist chair and the treadle-driven drill that put the fear of hell and damnation into us kids quicker than any priest ever could. We also had to pass our cycle proficiency test first time so that we could bike to school on our boneshakers. It was a mile and a half of pathless country lanes to walk each way until we did.

My apprenticeship for life was the stuff of boyhood dreams. With hindsight, I don't think I ever really grew out of it. Instead I took it into adult life with my outdoor pursuits. And I am so fortunate that my own kids [Simon, James and Claire] came with me and the adventures continue into my autumn years. However…it has also taught me, perhaps more so during this latter part of my life, that if the notoriously fickle whims of Fate did deal me the hand necessary for major recognition, I would probably have to fold it unseen.

I simply abhor this twenty-first century's obsession with the celebrity cult and all its spin-offs. The hype and drama of TV that is now creeping down into the ordinary people, who are making extremely hard work of doing exactly the same ordinary things that I do. It makes me seethe with inner rage. It has all become a noisy clamour for attention that has no part in the world of adventure. Except of course when you are hanging by your fingertips on a rocky mountain side and haven't got a piece of string to start the recovery process with.

And as for those humble beginnings:– that farm I grew up on has become a luxury mansion. The stable where we kept pigs has become the drawing room, the tractor shed is part of a visitors' suite and the kitchen extension, built on the runner bean patch and coal shed is bigger than my current house. The muddy farmyard of oil slicks, sheds, TVO tanks, water troughs, tractors, machinery and endless piles of string played a very small part of today's immaculate forecourt.

There are very few photographs of that era to help boost my

memories because photography in those days was expensive and saved for the summer holiday at the seaside. However, as with most adults, there are memories of my childhood that I will take to the grave, which can be imagined by others but not wholly shared. You had to be there.

We should always be careful when looking back. We may not like what we see.

Back to today. I'm now old, widowed with a grown-up family that have all left home. I'm retired with no commitments or ties until about five years ago, when I targeted myself to climb a thousand UK summits before I was seventy. To that end, I can walk all day and into the night if needed but the grandchildren can exhaust me in an hour. I drink too much red wine, try to steer clear of loud people, avoid gratuitous swearing but recognise that sometimes nothing else fully fits the occasion, and I probably harbour a whole a host of faults that you can pick out for yourself as you read on. Caught in that trap between being good but not quite good enough to be recognised at anything, the rest of it is all about padding and crap jokes to add a rosy glow to that sense of well-being when playing in the harsh demands of the rough country.

Summit Talks 2

The trouble with getting old is there are so many young people that know better than me. Just as I did when I was their age. You couldn't tell me then and I can't tell them now. It's shit getting old.
– The Aimless Rambler

Why write a book when I prefer to walk the talk?

Having established that I am old school when it comes to responsibility, a likeable rogue in the workplace and can draw if the fancy takes me, it's now time to address my reasons for writing this lot. *The Trail of The Aimless Rambler* is all very well in theory but it has already been written and dumped by me at least three times since its conception. The point at which it got tough was when I would have to show it to others and I would then shove it back in to the battered box under the bed instead. I don't need the hassle. I suppose it could be having that chapbook recently published in Australia that rekindled the spirit, but this time I think it is largely due to two other stronger influences: Age and Achievement.

It was the former that started me thinking more about what I have done and, with some continued degree of good fortune, what I'm still capable of doing. I'm constantly reminded that for my age, and in comparison with others coming to terms with the debilitating factors that normally come with it, I remain a considerable force to be reckoned with. I'm still capable of covering some incredible distances and ascents in my quest for summiting as many peaks as I can before turning up the front points of my crampons.

Taking the website that I use to find and record such summits as indicative of the peak-bagging community, then I sit amongst the UK's top ten per cent. Certainly very few will pass me on the uphills or can match the distances that I'm asking of myself. Those who do are usually a lot younger. Not all of them, though. There are a lot more of us old geezers up there than you would perhaps imagine. Any Monday to Friday, when the weekend crowds are at work, I will rarely get a day on the hills without seeing at least one similar upland traveller on some mission of his own. It's marked with a respectful nod and a grunt as we pass as shadows of each other.

To those who are going to say women do this as well, I have no argument. It's a simple fact that I very rarely see them where I go and when I do they usually come in twos or more. When I do see a single woman coming the other way, one of my biggest fears of solo travel in the mountains kicks in. That is, a single bloke without a dog is deemed guilty of something, be it just the capability of doing something that they do not like, until proved innocent. Leastwise, that is how I am made to feel these days. But is there really any logic to a prowler roaming such remote places looking for a target when finding one is likely to buy him serious trouble? Any woman who can handle that country on their own is never going to be an easy target and it's more than likely that his manhood, if he was indeed capable of rising to such in the extremes of the nine-month winter of the mountains, is likely to find itself fencing with a trekking pole or on the receiving end of a very angry boot bent on continuing the owner's walking progress. Yet the curse of the lurker lingers on. (A lurker being a stalker without portfolio.)

Another niggling little factor that irritates me now and again is that I'm actually looking to guess, in my head, the ages of those others out there and doing a comparison. I remember walking with a friend who had actually asked how old people were by sentence four of any conversation on a chance meeting in the hills. He was in his mid-seventies at the time and now I can see a whole lot more clearly why he was doing it. It's not to boast but to check: yep, I have still got it. Okay, so it's true to say that it could all come to an end quite suddenly as those age factors play their joker, but I have had an exceptionally good run of luck so far. If it ended tomorrow, I'd have no right to be disappointed in any way. I will be, of course, but that's beside the point.

It was while brooding on all this that it occurred to me that a childhood hero of mine had sneaked up on me. With a generous helping of gratuitous satisfaction, and perhaps a short dose of mild shock, I reached the conclusion that in my own way I have become the mountain man of the comic book Westerns that I read as a kid.

I really am the loner who is capable of roaming the high country, that others may hold in awe or dread, with a bold confidence fashioned from forty-five years' experience of traversing hostile terrain. I am that dishevelled, lonesome, stranger who comes down out of the hills for short periods and then disappears off back into them when my part in your own story has been played. Some of you stay in touch but most don't. Even in the local community, I'm that eccentric old fart, living in that ramshackle house at the end of the street, where I mess with paints, woodcarving and typing away on a keyboard without so much as a single thought to the welfare of the village community outside. A mountain man – I can live with that a lot more comfortably than those disappearing years.

Then equally suddenly, I realised that I was writing my own epitaph so that when I'm gone there could be no misunderstandings. I live this way by choice. What a depressing thought that could be for those that write diaries but can't handle the downsides of life.

At least it gave me more to think about on those empty paths. At which point, I hastily add this reminder to shoot down some of the glittery notions that you may have attached to my status. As a loner, you do get an awful lot of time to think about such dismal prospects as that inevitable ending. Particularly when nobody has any idea where you actually are because a whim demanded a route change. After a while, you get used to it and develop a sort of resigned attitude and find yourself humming *Que sera, sera* (whatever will be, will be) written by Livingston & Ray and a hit for Doris Day in 1956. One of the first songs that I clearly remember.

Then indignation sets in at the prospect of others taking my epitaph-writing as morbid and far too sombre for one so active and alive to laughter as I. Which in turn causes me to react with my customary indifference. I will flippantly shrug off their distaste as just ill-thought-out empty words trying to fill a conversation void. Why shouldn't I write it? Isn't that what every diary writer is doing? Over two-hundred years ago, Samuel Taylor Coleridge did exactly the same sort of thing for his gravestone.

> Stop, Christian passer by, stop child of God,
> And read with sombre breast, Beneath this sod,
> A poet lies, or that which one seems to be.
> Oh, lift a thought or prayer for STC.

I was so impressed by this when I discovered it that, just like Gustave Doré, I illustrated it with a cartoon. (There are four more lines but these are enough for us ordinary folk. Make it too long and we're looking for the TV remote.)

There are no rules in my lifestyle that can't be bent and broken by me to suit the mood of the day. I'm the loner. It's my world. My choices. If nobody ever wants to read it…well, that's no big deal either because it keeps me amused writing it. Here in my shabby old home while trying to weigh up whether I should continue to do so, open a new bottle of indifferent Rioja or go out into the hills where it's so much easier to just think, walk and do nothing practical at all. (I have to buy cheap wine because if I buy the good stuff I have to drink it. Whereas the cheaper stuff has a built-in deterrent in its taste.)

So having got this far you are now actually on *The Trail of The Aimless Rambler* but by just another name. Although I constantly claim that I keep it simple, with this as an example, that is not the case at all. I try to. Yes, I sincerely try, but I also have a grasshopper mind that denies such simplicity. Everything is simple. But things are just mixed up a bit in their entirety.

Is it any wonder that I never finish anything? Mind you, an epitaph would have an end date. If only we knew when that was to be, as it would make things so much easier to work to. Like everything else, the odds against me finishing it on time, to my own satisfaction, would still be stacked enormously high. On the other hand, not finishing could be seen as equally good as it meant I never saw the end coming. I kind of like that: The Unfinished Epitaph. It could suggest that my life was too full to get around to completing it. There was always just another hill…or that I was indeed a lousy writer of course.

Anyway, what would a self-written epitaph be called? An autotaph is a nice word. I think I may run with that. It's better than autobiography because that smacks of thinking that you're something special which, even if I was, I don't want to be. And now we drop that subject, as further speculation is totally pointless since I won't be around to witness any reaction.

> Why do people say 'Words cannot describe it' then insist in going on trying to do so? – The Aimless Rambler

Back to my background. I crossed the north/south divide in 1975. Many people, notably those living on the south side of it, will claim that this line doesn't exist. But they will also be quick to point out that this lifelong failure of mine is all my fault because I crossed it the wrong way. I moved south to north. Which, despite my protests to the contrary, may imply a hint of stupidity in poverty after all.

There's a lot more to this than just telling you about where I am from and how I come to be living in the south Pennines. This is because I have been crossing invisible lines ever since. So many in fact that the novel that I am never going to write will be called *Across the Divide*. This, if by some miracle it did ever get written, it would be thanks to Joseph Heller (deceased) because *Catch 22* is my favourite book of all time. *Across the Divide* would be my peacetime version of it, loosely based upon my job in the civil service that clashed with my outdoor lifestyle. And please note the deliberate use of the word 'job' rather than the socially more acceptable 'career'.

A divide is the area where there are clearly two sides but it's impossible to determine where the line that separates them is drawn. I love this stuff. How on earth can you live in the west? The planet is a sphere. So when the Americans get rattled by things happening in the Far East, that would be us. Sneaky buggers. I knew we shouldn't trust them. Then there's the whole business of left and right. The division is infinite. No matter how thin you make that line between the two, you can halve it again so ne'er the twain shall meet. Yet if it doesn't exist, then how can it be crossed? Clearly I spend too much time on my own.

In the context of this work then, walk and climb would be one such divide. I walk but I will scramble, which is crudely still walking but will demand the use of hands, a head for heights and a fair amount of bravery. We normally associate climbing with the use of ropes for safety reasons but nowadays there is more and more free climbing – or in other words a walk up a vertical wall. With a touch more frivolity, and to cloud the issue, it's worth mentioning that on some accepted scrambles for walkers, a rope is recommended. The division is blurred. Thus a divide exists. In this particular scenario, I actually would describe myself as a mountaineer and let everybody else sort it out.

And of course within that divide another divide exists. There are those who walk and there are walkers. To confuse it further, let's put it into a hill-walking context where the walkers go. There you will find there are walkers and there are other walkers. I am one of the former, if that makes it any clearer. Although it could be the other way round, so to make it easier still, I'm going to add a capital W. There are now Walkers and walkers. It is the ones with a big W who are dangerous. Got that? Good, because I have a big W.

The biggest clue to this is in the solo status. While the walkers are still talking, the Walkers are already walking. There is not a lot else you can say but I'll try.

In terms of w or W, the use of the word Rambler in my pseudonym could well lull you into a false sense of security because we all know that ramblers are a jolly group of people wearing gear fit for the Himalayas to cross an apple orchard in Kent. Walking for such folk is no less vital to them than it is to me but the significant difference remains, walking rather than talking. While they fret over whether or not the gate is the correct right of way or is there a stile somewhere that they missed, I'm already halfway across the field. My use of the word Rambler was because it was closer to STC's mariner and that's all.

Nor do I have any interest in that gate/stile scenario. That's why I moved to the north in the first place. My heart lay in the rough country which for the most part is open. As a kid, it was great growing up on the Buckinghamshire farm but as a bigger kid at twenty-seven I needed something a whole lot more demanding. I wanted Scotland but compromised with the north of England for the sake of that career and not isolating ourselves from the rest of the family remaining in the south. Neither of which turned out as hoped. The career became a job and moving out of the Home Counties was nothing short of an unforgivable sin to those we left behind. Forty-odd years later and I still live in voluntary exile. Up north.

And to some degree I have become more Northern than many of the current natives. Those days of hardy mill workers taking to the hills for a spell of walking on a Saturday afternoon or Sundays, wearing cloth caps and hobnail boots, died with the cotton industry and mining. I'll not go into the politics of it all but a lot of the Northern pride and self-assurance seems to have gone with it. It was if they rolled over and said, 'Okay, the divide doesn't exist and we're just the same as you lot down there but poorer.' That image of the hardy, straight-talking Northerner seems no more, except in old photographs and a few fading memories of the older folk.

I could well have gone into the same bland obscurity but for that severe lack of money to spend on anything other than household bills that kept me true to those new Northern roots while looking for free recreation in the neighbouring hills. I might have difficulty sussing out the subtle differences between the red and white roses but I still walked those hills between them no matter what – and wearing whatever I could. It never occurred to me that I should join a walking club or group. I didn't need one and couldn't have afforded it even if I did.

Why do I want to write it again? I'm old and I can still do this stuff with very little evidence of slowing down so surely there must be other like-minded people out there somewhere who wouldn't mind sharing my take on the world of walking for a while. Even if it's just something else to moan about between trips or to pass the time in a long overnight bivouac. I am no different from them after all.

When it comes to achievement, I'm a time-served veteran, but until now I hadn't actually achieved anything that I could hang it all on. I really was an aimless rambler who never tired of venturing out but I had no particular goal. In addition to my UK wanderings, I had also walked some classic long-distance trails in Europe, including the original GR20 that, before its re-routing to avoid the Cirque de Solitude, was generally claimed to be the toughest Grande Randonnée in Europe, the Tour of Mont Blanc (much of it repeated several times and alone) and the walker's haute route from Chamonix to Zermatt, along with the GR221 across the granite mountains of Mallorca – some of it deliberately done in the dark.

None of which singled out my walking as anything beyond the normal. There was no Everest. It had no continuous thread towards a specific goal that captured the enormity of what I was doing without specific purpose. I rambled aimlessly. My decision to go for a thousand UK summits was not made with a view to relaunching my attempts to write a book. It was nothing more than a vague joke that grew alarming quickly once the decision had been made.

It started in the Lake District, where I had been on a walking holiday with a friend, Owen Bryant, who was my senior by ten years or more. During our week of walking, we met a guy who was just finishing his Wainwright tops, and, at the end of our week, Owen gave me a present of a Wainwright summit map and said, 'I bet you've done most of them already.' I glanced at it and realised that he was right. I had.

Like many walkers, I suppose I was vaguely attempting to do the Munros, even if it was only being used as a reason to go out to different mountain ranges in the Highlands, but I had no other objective. Getting all the Wainwrights was a bit of a soft option, but closer to home, so, like the Munros would give me a reason to visit some of the more obscure ranges that I might previously have skirted, I set out to finish the list off.

Then, shortly afterwards, I met a guy who told me he was doing the Nuttals. I didn't know what he was talking about, so, having bluffed my way past the conversation with some knowing nods and a grunt or two, when I got home I checked it out. They were every mountain over 2,000 feet in England and Wales and that had a bigger appeal than the Wainwrights. I might as well do them as well. Hang on, I'm not giving up on my Munros just to get this lot done. Sod it, I can't be bound by the rigidity of being defined by the targets of others, I'll climb everything. I know what, I'll go for a thousand and take it from there.

At around ninety per cent done, I was going through a minor crisis of a general direction loss through life when the book idea poked its head back up over a peak. A thousand mountains. That had a nice ring to it. A book could work this time. The crisis briefly mentioned there brought about some challenges that subsequently developed into epic adventures that provide the conflict that I felt such a book needed to make it just a little more interesting. With 992 peaks done, I took a more positive action to start it. I bought a notebook to try and formulate the layout. At 998 I gave that up and asked my sister, Brenda, if she would help me. She agreed. The rest, as they say, is not so much history but what you are reading.

After all that I've done, I'm still here – so it would seem that I actually do know what I'm doing and this flies in the face of other popular books on hiking where the authors seem to feel the need to make lame excuses for what they see as a poor performance on their part. When you add to that a never-ending list of celebrities making such a big deal out of what so many of us do with ease, it starts to ruffle the feathers. Bugger that. My own walks on a daily basis would surpass many of their greatest efforts and I too would normally play this down as each to their own, but surely there has to be room for some gritty humour at success to balance out the rather desperate soul searching of those that feel out of their depth in the outdoor world of my hills and mountains. I believe it's time for the rough voice of the rough folk from the rough country. When it came down to my approach to the mountains, and how to tell it, I could see myself as the walker's version of the climber Don Whillans in his wonderful book *The Villain*, which balances out the articulate Chris Bonnington in his.

I tell it how I talk it. By saving the intricate detail for my art, I keep my writing plain and simple.

If I'm wrong, then so be it and you may have picked up this copy of my autotaph at the one funeral I was kind of hoping to avoid. Either way, if you do take time to finish reading the rest, then maybe, like the wedding guest in 'The Rime Of the Ancient Mariner', you may wake the morrow morn a wiser man… Oh, bugger.

Look, you sort out what gender you want in there. I have enough to do with mountains to climb and pictures to paint. Meanwhile, I have another connection with Samuel Taylor Coleridge that adds a nice twist to this. He's believed to be the first person to write about a mountaineering experience as a pleasurable recreation. In a letter to some woman I've forgotten already, he described his descent of Broad Stand, between Scafel and Scafel Pike, while out walking. Broad Stand, if you want to give it a whirl, is just a short but difficult scramble that will hopefully kill you if you get it wrong. You will most certainly need a very big W. I looked at it and said, 'No, I'll find a different way.'

Summit Talks 3

> Most of what you read about gear and hardships that has been written about walking is waffle and bullshit...including this. –
> The Aimless Rambler

Dark days in the Dark Peak (somewhere north of Watford Gap)

I said at the beginning that this is not a chronological diary of my mountains climbed but, like sex, we all remember the first time.

I was living in London at the time that my apprenticeship to becoming an ardent adventure seeker began. That'll be at walking – not sex! It was during the early seventies when the offer came from my colleagues to go walking. The objective was to 'Knock off Kinder' and 'Do the Downfall'. It was a lads-only trip planned for the second weekend in February because, as I was being told, it was usually a good month for the bonus of snow on high ground. I knew immediately that I wanted to go and accepted without a moment's hesitation... before I had even asked my new wife for permission.

As geography had been one of my better subjects at school and having established where it was and that Kinder Scout was a plateau, which was a 'flat-topped mountain', I couldn't see it presenting any difficulties. It was surrounded by towns more densely populated than those around the farm I had just left, following our wedding six months earlier. Nevertheless, with my experience of walking on hills being limited to about three trips, by bus, over ten years, to Devils Dyke on the South Downs above Brighton, where we went for our summer holidays between haymaking and harvest, I kitted myself as advised by the others – but I'll get to that after I have set the correct levels of misery.

We had finished work in London and driven up to Derbyshire, in the dark and rain, on the Friday night and arrived in Edale quite late. Too late to see anything outside the beam of the headlights which revealed that the rain had turned to sleet. We were among a scattering of small tents on a squelchy, sloping field where a few people, hunched against the wind and wet stuff, scurried about fetching things between cars and their minuscule canvas refuges for the night. Nylon tents had yet to make their appearance as an affordable option to the people who needed them most. That was those that had been reduced to camping, whether they liked it or not, because they couldn't afford the alternatives when visiting the area in question. It was too late to try out the pub as planned so we put our tents up and got through the night as best we could.

It was my first experience of winter camping and, with all these years and experiences to look back on, I would rate it now as about average for the location and time of year. At the time, it felt squalid but wonderful. I took to it immediately, like a duckling to water. Three of us shared a two-man tent, while the fourth member of the party, who was more local and had arrived there long before us, had an identical tent to himself (Vango Force 10). I never found out why that was but it turned out that we got the better deal because there were three of us warming a small area as opposed to just him trying to heat more space with only his escaping body heat. Those were the days before sleeping mats had caught on and we used newspapers as insulation between us and the groundsheet.

I, being the shortest by an inch, slept in the middle between the poles at each end, while the fidgeting farters on either side fought their own battles for sleep as the flapping canvas pressed upon them. It was cold, wet and smelly and that is about all I remember of that night. That's most likely because, in the morning, it was to be surpassed by an even greater and prolonged hardship – beyond my wildest imagination until then!

I was to learn from that first experience that, no matter what the weather forecast promised, every weekend there are people prepared to give Kinder Scout a go, so the campsite was quite busy in the morning. Because we hadn't slept much, we were away first and soon following the path up Grindsbrook Booth towards our goal.

Today, the vast majority would follow the Pennine Way to it. I would find out why many years later, but even after all of what's being told here, I think that way misses something vitally important. Unaware of what that was to be and coming to terms with the word 'hostile' rearranging itself in my head from an immediate association with people to one with the environment, I was getting that first inkling as to why I had bought or borrowed all that gear just to go for a walk. I still think my father would have gone up there in his boiler suit, gaberdine mack and gumboots, or sat in the pub, 'While other silly buggers did.'

I had a 'fit bit' once, so I married her. – The Aimless Rambler

Even in those early dark days of Pennine exploration, a long way from the West End where Diane worked as a model, fashion still played an important part in the selection of my correct kit. In those days, walkers wore a pair of hairy knee-breeches, three pairs of socks, a bobble hat that could be converted into a balaclava, an anorak and a cagoule. Finished off with a rucksack packed with enough emergency equipment, including the obligatory Kendal mint cake, to support an Everest summit bid.

Most importantly, I had to have a huge pair of walking boots with screw-on Vibram soles sporting the tread of an off-road 4X4 tyre. For anybody who wanted to be a somebody, those boots should come from a recognised trade name but mine weren't…which perhaps started to single me out as an oddity from that first day. (Although I have since learnt that there is a higher ratio of 'oddities' per norm in the mountaineering community than in any other walk of life… with perhaps the exception of a Social Security office customer waiting room.) My pair of second-hand anonymous boots lasted me ten years before some undesirable lowlife stole them, otherwise I would more than likely be still wearing them now. It's the poor farmer in me that has to use something through to destruction – and then keep the laces as a spare pair for the replacements. Until Gore-tex found its way into footwear, a man could be seen spending more time caring for his boots with Mars oil and dubbin than his wife would spend doing the ironing for the entire family – and his elderly mother.

The wearing of three pairs of thick woollen socks from Norway was also deemed essential. It would seem that the advertising industry had found enough gullible walkers to believe that Scandinavian sheep knew more about keeping warm than the UK breeds to make this line worth pursuing. The idea was that you wore one short pair as liner socks, and then a longer pair to cover the gap between the top of your boot and the bottom of your knee-breeches. These were followed by another short pair that were then folded over the top of your boot to cover the lace bow to prevent those clever twigs and stiff blades of grass from untying them. This was also thought to stop small stones from getting into your boots but I found the artful blighters went down between the socks instead. You also had another three pairs of socks in your emergency kit in case you got your feet wet. Gaiters were for those with money to burn.

The knee-breeches were horrific, even by our hardy standards. These great big hairy kecks were as stiff as boards and mercilessly chafed any unprotected flesh they came in contact with. Thus making the wearing of long johns mandatory – even in summer – with the thick socks to hide those unmanly bits that stuck out! Mine had a double layer on the arse so that you could sit down on damp ground without getting piles. The trouble was that sitting down in them was mission impossible so the benefits of their medical attributes never got tested. Mind you, I never suffered from piles either, so perhaps it was the method of prevention that I was confused about. Despite all this negativity, if they were good enough for Mallory and Irvine on Everest in the 1920s, then it was a small price to pay for the would-be hard man of Kinder Scout in 1972.

Thick, checked shirts were also part of the standard kit, with something like an Aran sweater to finish it off as another layer if the weather was cold. An Aran sweater! Whoever came up with us needing a white woolly jumper in a land of sheep shit and mud was a marketing genius. These were the days long before any breathable materials like Gore-tex, so many a walk finished with a soggy wet Aran hanging down to the knees like a shapeless bloody dress. One of my shirts was stolen with my boots and after thirty years the other saw its demise when I used it as a decorating overall and the paint wouldn't wash out. (I used it as rags and kept the buttons, though.)

I think the Blacks bobble-hat/balaclava has been the greatest loss to the world of outdoor pursuits. Straight away, everyone from all walks of life saw a rambler they knew if the characters in my cartoons were wearing them. Now the headgear is far too diverse for immediate association – especially with those damn baseball caps. As for those Peruvian hill shepherd's hats…can it get any worse?

Nowadays, it doesn't matter so much what you wear but whether or not it has a huge manufacturer's logo in full view of everyone within a two-hundred-metre radius. If it doesn't, then you would be looked down upon as some wet behind the ears novice that shouldn't be allowed out on their own. Dead but wearing big labels is okay. Yet many amongst them could well deny that they followed such fashions and would run off to the hills to escape such foolishness. At least they might if that was seen as trendy.

Only that youngster of today, doing his Duke of Edinburgh Award expedition, trudging over that same terrain in his brother's old boots, wearing that high-vis fluorescent yellow roadworker's jacket that his dad got for him on the cheap, while his other five companions have the absolute latest in fashion and quality, can begin to understand what I had to go through to reach this level of complete indifference to what others may think. The skin has to get thicker or you will go under.

Back to my induction on Kinder Scout. I was the only novice in the party but found no hardship in walking for pleasure. Life on the farm had never brought me into contact with walkers and I was already in my twenties before I found that people did that sort of thing as a hobby. Walking for pleasure, now that was novel. We walked because we had to. More or less everybody in the village did, except my father, who had a tractor.

In those days, there were also a lot less walkers to be seen in the south of England. By all accounts, it was a peculiarity of the northern folk that found favour in the south as these refugees started to trickle over the Divide. With hindsight, I can see an accumulation of the little niggles that accompany winter camping closely followed by walking the rough paths becoming a major obstacle for a person brought up with the comforts of modern living, but for me it was not much different from my childhood upbringing. It was basic and you got by with what you had.

So I should go back and revise my second paragraph to this chapter because my apprenticeship to adventure had begun from the moment that I was born in that ancient farmhouse. To endorse that, I was about to insert my capital W on walker already and we were still only an hour into my first proper walk.

It was cold and bleak, with snow, as predicted, on the higher ground. In the valley, the muddy path twisted and turned its way around boulders and over streams. We all chatted excitedly and picked papier mâché from our clothes as we walked, because the tent had leaked. In the upper reaches of Grindsbrook Booth, around the last Y junction of the descending streams, there was a film of frost underfoot and the mud had got harder as we climbed higher. The last steep ascent to the plateau edge was covered in a thin coating of ice and dusted with snow.

The ice got worse. Right under the very rim of the plateau it covered everything both level and vertical. Progress was desperately precarious as we made our way from one drift of soft snow to another by the shortest way across the sheets of ice. The French call it *verglas*. I called it exciting. Once over that rim, it wasn't long before the ice gave way to snow. Deep and drifted snow everywhere. It was a rolling blanket of continuous white, broken by the occasional stand of dark boulders. I stared in absolute wonder. Almost mesmerised. I was mountaineering and I had never expected that when I was asked if I wanted to go walking.

I recently read a book about a guy who walked the Pennine Way from north to south, during the summer, which meant that he had to deal with Kinder Scout to finish. His bottle went at the prospect and he gave up without even trying. He could not bring himself to even attempt it. Seven miles from the finish, he quit because of that mountain's reputation. I find that a bit lame. The Pennine Way doesn't even go over Kinder Scout. It goes along the edge where there are no bogs and no navigation problems, and hundreds of people use it, so you're rarely alone. However, it's the making of such drama out of trivia that keeps these folk happy.

Kinder Scout's sombre reputation hasn't been earned from that stretch of the Pennine Way that skirts it. Its menace is in its heart and very few of its visitors ever go that way to find out why.

Kinder Scout may be a plateau, that flat-topped mountain as the description suggests, and the absence of map contour lines depicting slopes would confirm this but what all that fails to tell you is that it is wrinkled. Very badly wrinkled! Those contour lines only appear where there is a height difference of more than ten metres. For those who struggle with map reading or metric measurements, that means the maps, exquisitely drawn with remarkably accurate graphics, need not show undulations the height of a house. Kinder Scout's entire summit is a maze of twisting peat groughs. (I have always called them this – pronounced 'gruffs'.) While they're not the height of houses, you may have to climb over as many as four or five garden sheds and the garage just to travel a hundred yards in a straight line!

The vegetation, when you can see it, is mostly knee-deep heather clinging to the tops of these groughs, complimented with sphagnum moss, cotton grass, reed grass and other water-loving plants that I have no botanical knowledge of. The bottom of each steep-sided wall of black peat is the bog. The ankle-to-crutch-deep ooze waiting to suck in your boot and fill it. They may be deeper but because they're narrow you usually have one foot on firmer ground and further immersion tends to stop once you have sunk a foot in deep enough to chill your tackle.

On a snowy day, such as that of my initiation, the blown snow collects in these troughs in huge drifts and gives the appearance of levelling them off. To make it worse, on that day the snow was so deep that it had acted as insulation so unlike that exposed edge, with its layer of *verglas* to entertain us on arrival, the bogs below them were unfrozen…lying in silent menace, waiting with a completely different form of entertainment.

When looking across those groughs, even in the best of conditions, there are three noticeable absences. They are recognisable landmarks; paths; and any chance of walking in a straight line. Crossing Kinder Scout has a tendency to probe one's fortitude under duress and test navigational skills to the limit on all but the rarest of occasions. (Frozen rock-hard is the only time I have encountered any easing of such labours.) That's what earns its reputation. Not the squeals of some bunny skipping around the edges, admiring the wonderful waterfall and surrounding boulder collections, but afraid to take on the big bad wolf in case they get dirty.

And we were about to cross Kinder Scout. To get to the iconic Downfall, which has a habit of becoming an upfall if the wind is in the right direction and gets under its skirt, we had to be on the other side. That was just over two kilometres as the crow flies. Which is in straight lines – allegedly. But there are no straight lines. Hence no crows. Instead of crows, there were other birds that were proving more poignant to this setting of Christmas card wonderland. Nope, not robins either. They were grouse.

Another trait of mine is that I sometimes 'twitch' a bit when it comes to wild birds. Good, but not brilliant, I knew enough to identify them without a field guide as red grouse. The first I had ever seen. There were several of them flitting noisily about, presumably calling to each other. I say 'each other' because all the books of bird identification that I had, and there were several because I was also learning that you can't have too many books about the subject at hand if it's a passion as strong as those that I hold, stated that call of the red grouse can be likened to 'go bak, go bak'.

That should have served as a warning when you are a fledgling adventure-seeker, standing there beside the rock called the Anvil at the top of Grindsbrook Booth. Looking upon all that drama for the first time, it is pure magic. When our democratic leadership had finished checking the map, someone pointed across to nothing and said, 'It's that way,' it was as good as getting married again. Well, certainly more exciting and untried. And like most modern marriages of today, it didn't last long!

The seven-year itch began after about an hour of hapless floundering through snowdrifts from one bog to another and seeming to take us nowhere very slowly. Distant horizons had disappeared and replaced by the sea of groughs that had to be crossed to maintain direction. We waded up the snow-covered banks on one side to then slide crazily down the other to end up in the muck at the bottom. Only to repeat it over and over again as we toiled across. My boots were full of water, and snow had got in through every chink of my clothing. Jokes had become few and far between. The honeymoon was over and divorce proceedings started.

Some two hours later, when murder seemed the only logical way forward, almost suddenly it came to an abrupt end. We were back to standing on the edge of the plateau, with the ground now dropping steeply away, as it was upon our ascent. Safely across, the relief was enormous and those fickle spirits of reward for effort rose once more.

The snag was that it all still looked exactly the same. That was snow, boulders and edge. With a complete lack of waterfall. Looking down over the valley bottoms, snow was almost non-existent, along with much sign of human activity.

After some debate, we weren't sure whether the waterfall was to our right or left. Which I was to learn later, before the advent of a GPS that told you exactly where you didn't think you were, was why we sometimes indulged in a little aiming off. This meant instead of aiming directly for your target you deliberately head to the right or left of it so that when you reached something obvious, like a river or in this case the edge, you knew which way to turn to reach it. On that day of learning, it meant nothing more than hitting the right spot first time when trying to piss your name in the snow.

Until that point in my life, I had never done any kind of serious navigation, although I had mucked about at some basic map reading while in the scouts some ten years earlier. It turned out that, like my art, it was going to be something else that I was pretty good at. And believe me, when I tell you that's a real bugger. You could be forgiven for thinking it is a wonderful gift but I can assure that in the company of others it's a curse. It's the cause of so many heated arguments on cloudy mountain slopes. A ruthless destroyer of both short and long-term friendships. It started for me on that day.

The instinctive navigator within me, on any trip, never trusts what anyone else says. I have since discovered that I always have to know where I am and that's why I could well be seen religiously watching the little aeroplane crossing the personal TV screen map on a transatlantic flight instead of the in-flight movie. As soon as someone else makes a directional decision that flies in the face of my own logic, or even plain old gut feelings, my defence mechanism kicks in.

Attack being the best form of defence, the decision gets challenged and disaster strikes. Navigation by committee begins. A fiasco is awaiting in the wings. Committees never agree. To admit I'm wrong in front of others is impossible. And make no mistakes on this, I could be. Remember I'm self-taught on everything not found in the basic school curriculum. I left school without a single qualification. I hasten to add that I didn't fail any exams either. I didn't bother taking them.

Even when faced with overwhelming evidence that opposes my

views, excuses will be sought. I'm one of those really annoying people who believe they have a natural sense of direction and, like migrating birds and animals, I move ever onwards with unerring confidence.

Going back to birdwatching, it's worth noting that when you see stories of twitchers swarming to a back garden in Swindon's suburbia to view a scarlet tanager from America, it's lost. Even the experts can get it wrong.

Like I said, this skill is a curse because while I may doubt others and am usually proved right(ish), I'm also too scared of the consequences of error to trust myself purely on instinct and thus spend hours upon hours ignoring the telly and poring over maps. I may still try to kid myself that this shouldn't be necessary because of man's superiority to the less complex animal species but after all these years there is always a map in the pack. Along with the latest in top-range satellite navigation systems because, hardy as I may appear, I too like my comforts and will make things a little easier where I can without compromising the objective.

Whales will navigate thousand of miles of ocean during their breeding season migration and all they can see is sea; so surely there has to be something else there? Or can the promise of sex really be that strong that it acts as a magnet to draw them in? There is no chance of sex on Kinder Scout in winter so we had to get back to the map and the pressing dilemma.

On that occasion, I thought that the road I could vaguely make out in the valley bottom might have given us a clue to establishing our position, so pointed it out and added fuel to the deepening crisis. You can't see any roads from Kinder Downfall or from anywhere near it, for what it matters. And it did matter! By process of elimination, we established, mostly by counting the amount of traffic on it, that this road was the A57, the Snake Pass, and although we had not deliberately aimed wide of our target with intent, we had still missed it by ninety degrees and at least three kilometres.

We discussed it for a while, ate some early lunch and discussed the options some more. Those options, as the consensus of the committee saw them, were

– follow our tracks back to the start and call it a day

– follow a compass bearing to the Downfall and cut a new line across the top

– follow the edge anticlockwise all the way round and therefore keeping the steep drop off to our right as a perpetual marker.

The first was dumped immediately as the wimpish way out. Option two involved a few technicalities such as knowing exactly where you were to take the bearing from – if you had the necessary compass – and knew how to use it. The third choice was probably the worst one that we could make, so it was inevitably taken.

While it was about three kilometres across the plateau, to go around proved to be closer to ten and that only got us as far as the Downfall.

I have since crossed that plateau quite a few times, usually alone, because it is now not far from where I live. I have also walked right around it along that rim and that's further than you may think glancing at the map. What I have also discovered during my wandering about up there is that if you know where to start from, there is a fairly easy, straight and level, natural route to the Downfall from that northern rim – not too far from where we must have been. Although I seriously doubt that we would have had the skills to find it even if we had known of its existence. Would I be the same person now if we had?

I don't remember very much about that next part of the journey, which suggests that it was dull compared with what we had done and what was still to come. At some time during the late afternoon, as what little daylight was left threatened to cloud over, we arrived somewhat wearily at Kinder Downfall, where we were greeted by a wondrous sight. Tracks! Footprints in the snow made by other people rather than ourselves going in circles. We relaxed again. I vaguely recall huge icicles where the waterfall had frozen but that may have been from later trips. At the time, after the initial relief upon arrival, I think we were getting just a little more concerned about the absence of any people who made the tracks and about darkening skies.

A couple of decades later, my sons and I, having taken another snowy, direct line over the plateau, came upon a scene, not far from the Downfall, that I can use here to illustrate the unexpected dangers that await the unwary and have to be dealt with or people will die.

We were following the stream towards the Downfall from the heart of the plateau. It was flowing but there were drifts of snow and ice bridging it in places. A couple of hundred metres short of the waterfall, and just out of sight of anyone there on the main route, two guys were using one of the ice bridges to cross over and join a companion on the other side. It's not too deep but you do try to keep dry if you can. Almost across, the ice gave way and both went through to end up standing almost waist-deep in it.

It became apparent very quickly, for reasons that we couldn't understand from where we were, that they couldn't get out. We went to their aid and discovered that their feet were pinned down by huge sheets of ice that were weighted down by the water flowing over them. I had a rope and we used it to try and pull them free but so firmly were they pinned to the river bed they couldn't stand the bite of the rope and we couldn't shift them anyway. In a fairly desperate last-ditch effort, we frantically tried to break up the ice sheets with walking sticks and my ice axe. As fast as we broke lumps off, other sheets would move in and cover the ones that we couldn't seem to reach further down. We carried on regardless. There was nothing else we could do and the Grim Reaper was not going to wait long in those bitter conditions.

Suddenly they were free. Our continued efforts and a long wooden walking stick that my son was carrying had finally broken the grip of that deepest sheet. We pulled them out of the water and had to figure out what to do next. Seriously wet and severely cold, up on a mountain, is enough in itself to finish the job that the river had started.

However, news of commotion and disaster travels fast even in the wilderness. Other people from the Downfall had arrived by then so, job done, we left the victims in their hopefully capable hands. This was a bit of a selfish move on our part because they were still not out of danger. They were at least two hours away from warmth and safety with their transport being down in Hayfield, but our car was in exactly the opposite direction. Down at the Snake Inn. We hadn't left them alone and we had become quite wet ourselves in getting them out, so hanging about wouldn't have been good for us either. My conscience was clear. We had done all that we realistically could have done but would I have acted the same way if others had not been there is the real question not answered.

As it was, the wake-up call is that they would probably have died if there had been no one to get them out. Whether the third member of their party would have been able to do what the four of us did on his own, and in time, is purely speculative. However, call it irresponsibly flippant on my part if that pleases you, but the way I see it is that that's the nature of the game. If you don't like it, then don't play.

With the Downfall duly done and Kinder sort of knocked off, we set off again after a short rest to eat what was left of our lunch. We still had the edge to navigate by but now we had other tracks to follow as a morale booster. Spirits rose again.

An hour later, we were laughing our way back downhill on a good walled track and looking for a well earned pint or four in the Old Nag's Head back in Edale.

Light was fading alarmingly fast but the track was easy enough to follow. It might have been totally dark had it not been for the white of the snow but there were no alarm bells ringing. Just the whispering nag that there had been no walls on our way up. But I was assured we were okay and on our way down to Jacob's Ladder and a different way back.

The torches were safely tucked away in the tent at the campsite so that we didn't waste valuable battery life playing about with them when they might be needed during the night for something vital like finding the bottle opener. Besides, walking from daylight into dark, the marvel of night vision had kicked in. We were the intrepid explorers and there was no hardship that this bold quartet could not endure and overcome. We felt good. Elated at besting Kinder.

Then a guy came walking out of the gloom, going the other way.

'How far to Edale?' one of us cheerfully asked.

He looked around the group and then back in the direction from which he'd had come. 'About twenty-six thousand miles if you reckon to go that way to it,' he replied, and then walked off into the night without another word.

Our euphoria slowly melted when the meaning of what he had said penetrated our stupefied brains. We were going the wrong way. That was one hundred and eighty degrees the wrong way. An increase of a further ninety from on our previous digression and we were literally beginning to go around in circles. Worldly sized circles. I can't say for certain because memories of adventure become blurred with time, just as the visions of artists differ from what may actually be there, but I think that I knew we had been going wrong for some time, which was why I had mentioned the walls but had followed the others with novice naivety.

Choice was no longer an option. Nothing was discussed. We turned round and retraced our lost height back up that hill. By then, that cloud had moved in and it was snowing harder then at any other time during the day and any semblance of footprints, be they our own or others', were gone. Our error was realised when we came upon the monument of Edale Cross. We had missed it earlier by veering too far west and picking up the packhorse road leading to Hayfield. Those reassuring footprints had not been going our way. With another lesson learnt, the final descent began again.

That same route is unrecognisable nowadays. Today it's flag-paved and the Jacob's Ladder footpath that we had to find in Barber Booth is now stepped and fenced. The latter can be used in any conditions as a handrail and navigation aid. There is an alternative to that staircase if you follow the packhorse track/bridleway to the other side of the steep ground ahead, where, because of the longer route, the angle of incline is a little easier. (If you'are very fit and able, it is just possible to ride a bike up it.)

We had nothing to help us. The packhorse track, now in the lee of the prevailing winds, had drifted over. All we had was the right direction taken from the cross to start from. Things were getting desperate. Even I, the novice, had worked that out. Unbeknown to at least two of us, as we continued down steepening ground in that swirling snow and dark, we managed to take the direct route between the two safer paths. The bit the paths are taking you safely around.

My own uncontrolled descent was a combination of slides and somersaults that brought me to rest, miraculously uninjured, wrapped around a post at the bottom of that steep ground. What made it so crazy was that I didn't give a damn. All I remember clearly to this day was standing up and seeing the distant lights of a farm or other buildings. On the same level as me. I was down and that was all that mattered. I was joined shortly afterwards by the others who, like me, were all uninjured and with eager tales of their own scary ways of descent.

With four decades of experience between then and now to influence the speculation, I think it was the cushioning of snow that saved me from any superficial injuries and the rest was down to pure luck.

A couple of hours later, we were in the Old Nag's Head and eagerly catching up on those pints of anticipated ale as we laughed with strangers about our misfortunes. Later that night, as we slept in a fuggy haze of too much ale and well-being, hungry rats got into the tent and ate the breakfast.

When Sunday arrived, we went home.

I doubt that we actually summited Kinder Scout on that occasion. It sits on that western edge between Edale Cross and the Downfall, beside the Pennine Way. We probably walked within a few metres of it and that is also likely to be where our second navigational bloomer may have had its roots, but I have been there many times since so have no qualms about counting it as my first mountain.

The four of us gradually went our separate ways with no animosity but I think it was safe to say that I was the only one to come out of that experience with a hill-walking habit.

In Cheryl Strayed's book *Wild*, she tells us of her attempt at some of the Pacific Coast Trail to help sort out her troubled life that included a drug problem, whereas I had just taken her cure as my first fix on what could be my hill problem! My two fondest memories of that walk was the guy we met on the track to Hayfield. I so very much wanted to be that guy. So confident and sharp enough to come up with a cryptic reply to a stupid question. He then went on to cross that very same route that we had to take – alone and in the dark. We never saw him again. He could have died up there that night for all I know, but was he cool or what?

The second were the red grouse. I can't cross Kinder Scout without the sound of its very own subspecies with their unique call to accompany me. Even if they're silent, the very air will echo with their call! 'Go back, Shit for Brains. Go back.'

As a footnote, I think it's rather ironic that the only real dangers that the author of that Pennine Way book could have encountered on that summer's day have been all but nullified by the established, well marked, circuitous route around it – along with Jacob's Ladder being made idiot-proof! I have experienced and survived them at their worst, on the same day that I took on the very real challenge of crossing Kinder Scout. On my first day in the mountains. Yep, Walker will do me nicely.

Those are the foundation stones on which I have built my skills and went on to earn a reputation that I am seriously fond of.

Summit Talks 4

Are peak-baggers just lonely souls with no one to share their time with? Or are they lonely souls because they are peak-baggers? – The Aimless Rambler

Becoming a peak-bagger – with hiccups

Robin Hood's Picking Rods will remain a dilemma with me for quite some time. Probably until I've climbed about another hundred mountains and have forgotten it. You can log onto the internet and find all sorts of speculation about the origins of this landmark if you want to, but none of it is very sound and has nothing to do with me or my goal.

Robin Hood is a fictitious character, which throws a doubt over any of its authenticity before going any further. It would seem that somebody somewhere has grown a little fanciful in their history making, and it's become more of an ideal rather than reality, which just happens to take this ancient monument across into my own troubled world.

Clearly, the monument has been shaped by man and those that believe in fairies would have it that Robin Hood used it to bend his bows. While I do have this thing about fairies, I'm fairly confident that an outlaw would not risk traveling all the way from the forests of Nottingham to Cheshire just to string a bow. However, my concern isn't what it is but where it sits. There is clearly no downhill between this rocky lump, standing beside the path, and the top of Cown Edge, which rises several hundred feet above it about a kilometre or so behind. So can I legitimately claim it as a peak attained?

As a matter of fact, I could if I so chose because, according to my source, it is the highest point in the County of Cheshire and thus a listed summit. That places it within the rules I set. Kinder Scout is the highest point in Derbyshire, as Scafel Pike is to Cumbria and somewhere in Essex will have its highest point and it all gets silly again. They are our county tops. Whether I do count it or not is a predicament that I often find myself in. After my confused start with the peak-bagging, I clearly told myself and anyone who was listening that I was going for all listed peaks. Yet its inclusion in my list diminishes the quality of my achievement.

Now, the Great Hill that I referred to in the mountain definition right back at the start of this book I have probably gone up around ten or fifteen times a year. It isn't an easy hill as it has no paths. The approach from most sides is knee-deep, ankle-twisting tussock grass that none but the foolish would relish. We used to call this tussock grass 'Turks heads' because it was like walking through a crowd of turban heads. A bit like the end of the film *Crocodile Dundee* when, in the New York subway, Paul Hogan walks over the top of the crowded commuters to get back to his lady love. (I'm not the only one who believes in fairies if you can imagine that someone could actually get away with doing that without being well and truly sorted by disgruntled passengers.) I expect we would be accused of all sorts of raciest accusations if we used such a metaphor nowadays but I still think of them as that, but not out loud, because it's such an apt description and has been with me all these years.

The other approach to Great Hill is from the well trodden Pennine Way, but that involves about a kilometre of bog avoidance. Not the deep groughs, like those found on Kinder Scout, but large areas of surface water hidden, until you're right on top of them, by a mixture of low moorland vegetation. There's no sure way of knowing how deep they are until you put your foot in them, because that water is peaty black. Probing with a stick or trekking pole is the quickest guide but can be misleading because of the soft ground beneath the water.

However, they are fairly easy to negotiate once you have learnt how to read that vegetation. You don't need to know the assortment of botanical names, only get used to what the different plants like to have their roots in, because that can give an instant guide as to whether it will bear your weight for the brief moment that you pass. Most of us call this soggy terrain variations of bog country, but it's more of an inconvenience than a dangerous hindrance and sooner or later you will miss a footing or read it wrong to end up with a boot full of water. (Unlike TV survival gurus, I've been out there all these years but have yet to find one armpit deep.) There is an uphill out of this large boggy area to the summit of Great Hill, but not enough for it to qualify as any kind of listed summit.

Great Hill doesn't count but it's far more worthy than Robin Hood's Picking Rods so I could include the latter by offsetting one against the other. That makes it a little more creditable. But neither is very high. Higher than some of Wainwrights, though, say I carefully, because an awful lot of his guidebook followers and summit-baggers will be very put out by the devaluing of their noble hero's fells. Wainwright (deceased) and I have a lot in common. We both walk, both draw, both write and were both old before trying to do something with those skills, but that's where it ends. He was considered a gentleman, whereas I am a dishevelled slob – even when dressed up. To help ease his fans' anguish, if I count the ascent to the summit of Great Hill from my front door, then I've got Munros ticked off with less of a height gain from where I'd parked.

Then there are Marilyns to contend with. Because Munros are all a long way from the majority of the UK population, many people go for Marilyns as it provides summits that are nearer to home between the long trips to Scotland. A Marilyn can be any height providing it has a cleavage of at least 500 feet between it and the next peak, and I sincerely hope that was what Alan Dawson was thinking when he drew up the list because, if you haven't worked it out yet, all Munros are Marilyns. With 1,556 of them in Britain, that is considered a very worthy target and it's unlikely that it would attract any criticism.

Except that Ditchling Beacon, in the South Downs, is about a five-minute walk from the road and the notorious cycling hill climb of the same name. You can walk to it while waiting for the bike races with hundreds of other tourists on a sunny day, without really knowing that you've done so.

Not to be outdone by a bunch of Southerners, this is surpassed by those hardy Northerners who virtually drive over Bishop Wilton Wood on their way to the seaside at Scarborough (the A166 out of York). I've done so several times, once on a bike, but it's not on my list. Yet. It has nothing to attract the passing traffic whatsoever, because it's just a field surrounded by other fields.

The road narrowly bypasses that Marilyn summit by a couple of hundred metres but the height difference is minimal. Could it be counted from the road or should the exact summit be stood upon before it gets added to the list? This, believe it or not, isn't as straightforward as it may seem.

If a summit has a rocky top, everything is fine and could well have a few stones piled on it to single it out, but many of the lower peaks don't. There may be no stones! Instead, the top could be any number of humps and bumps of turf or heather-topped peat that all look higher than each other. And they move. You stand on what you feel is the highest, and you'll look around triumphantly only to find the previous one you were on is in fact higher. But that isn't as high as the one off to its right. Which, when you get there, is lower than the one just beyond it. Looking back, that first one was definitely higher. 'Near enough,' goes the cry, and on to the next peak.

Bearing that in mind, on another trip you may find yourself separated from your summit by a six-foot-high stone wall topped with barbed wire. It's only twenty metres away and a mere foot or two higher than where you stand. There's never a gate when you need one. If you break the Country Code and climb the wall, you'll have to climb back again after the thirty-second excursion because your chosen route demands it. Nobody will know but you. Do you count it? Now hold that thought.

Finally you take that same dilemma to the Inaccessible Pinnacle on the Isle of Skye. The name is the clue. This infamous shark's-fin is a Munro and you can't walk up it. It's a climb. You stand with your hand on the first holds and it soars twenty-five metres or so above you. A menacing, sheer and narrow blade that will test the nerve of all walkers. While not exceedingly difficult in terms of technicalities, the exposure is extreme and you wouldn't want to survive a fall. There are also likely to be a few parties of mountain guides and their clients all roped up ready for their ascent to watch your progress while waiting.

Very close by, the next highest piece of that mountain is eighteen metres lower. If you counted the one over the wall because you deemed it near enough, can you count this one as well? I haven't. I may be a touch cavalier at times with some of the lesser peaks, but I don't mess with Munros and the InPin which, while not the highest, is the Big Daddy of them all. It's the one that every Munro-bagger really wants but may have to go without. (I do wonder how many times it has been claimed by those less scrupulous of the Munro-baggers who like me have touched its base.)

Then come the amendments as surveying techniques become more refined. I know for a fact that at least one of my summits has been demoted and struck off as a qualifier since I have climbed it. Should I be taking it off my list as well? It's still listed but now as an ex-Nuttal.

And so these anomalies keep me thinking and rethinking, but at the end of it all I make and break my own rules as I go along. Its worth has to be rated on more than just height, because I am a Walker. What others may deem an innocuous-looking hill that I have claimed could be just one I crossed on an eight-hour slog through bogs in my bid for five or six other more worthy tops. When you work that hard, it seems almost disrespectful to the hills themselves not to include it. I have friends who are appalled at what I've taken them through to get to some of these lumps, bumps and humps that get so very few other visitors. Only the grand or highest peaks have paths that are easy to follow.

Critics will always have their say but the one positive thing this project has taught me is that I no longer have the slightest interest in any input that they may wish to make. Be it either good or bad. Unless you have walked as far as I have, along with climbing every piece of high ground you can find on the way, be it a listed summit or not, and done most of that alone, then you are not even part of my world. You are an alien with very little first-hand experience on which to base any observation. If you have done similar to me, then you will understand my indifference to the opinions of others because you too will have to have made your own difficult decisions in all these shades of grey. We answer only to ourselves. Robin Hood's Picking Rods epitomises that.

When I discovered the hill-bagging website that I refer to as my base from which to work, it wasn't difficult to count my peaks at all. I'm not geeky enough to start my one thousand bid from the date that I made the choice to go for them but I'm enough of one to remember every hill that I have ever been up. Not only that, but by which route and who was with me at the time. I can't remember all summit names, though, nor the exact dates that I did them, but I can look at a map and pick them all out, so it was just a question of identifying them on the website, tick the box by entering an estimated date and IT does the rest. I became a peak-bagger.

Sadly, for accuracy purposes, that's about as far as I go on the geek front. That wasn't even enough to note the date that I started this nonsense on but I would think it was around 2012 because that was when, on looking back at the figures the website produced, my yearly numbers started to significantly increase. I found it interesting that before Diane passed out of our lives in 2005, it turned out that I had already done 128 listed summits simply because they were there as part of something I was doing. There were some very significant challenges met during those preceding years that did involve peak-bagging but more for the demands made than being able to say I had climbed that mountain. If peaks were bagged, it was because they were among the nation's classics or in the right place at the right time as I chased other dreams.

For a good example of this, I had already done the Welsh Three Thousands and that gets fifteen in one day.

The Welsh Three Thousands were for many years traditionally referred to as the poor man's Everest. There are fourteen mountains in the world that top eight thousand metres high and before they started messing about with them to satisfy some pressure group or another, there were fourteen mountains in Wales that were over three thousand feet as well. There are now fifteen and it is worth a little side track to find out why, but I'll just finish the poor man's Everest bit first.

Beside the number match, to complete the Welsh Three Thousands in a single through hike involves ten thousand feet of climbing, which just happens to match the height difference between Everest Base Camp and its summit – or so I was told but I haven't checked. It sounds about right and is near enough for me to be happy with the similarity. To which, similar people to those who messed about with our numbers game will probably say that I'm too easily satisfied for my own good.

The first recorded time for this challenge was in 1919, with around twenty-two and a half hours. That's probably the target that most folk of today will try to get under. Joss Naylor, the hill farmer and runner from the Lake District, was the first person to take it under the five-hour barrier and in 1978 John Wagstaff did a triple crossing inside that 1919 target. It isn't any less than twenty-four miles but the actual start and finishing places, along with the route, tends to be optional. I actually think that the timing may only count from the first summit to the last and not the getting to and from those two, but that's for the purest to bicker about. The rest of us just do them from car park to car park.

Now to that extra one. The mountains in the northern range are called the Carneddau, usually referred to as the Carnedds by the non-Welsh. Among them are Carnedd Llewelyn and Carnedd Dafydd, named after two Welsh princes who gave the English a bit of a hard time a while back. I believe they didn't fight fairly either, preferring to have their soldiers sneaking about the invading English and attacking them when they weren't ready, and then scarpering before the disgruntled knights could get their kit on. I hope that bit of this tale is true even if the rest isn't.

For quite a few centuries, about eight I believe, this happy affair sat well with the people. Until someone felt that the lack of female representation in these peaks, despite the cleavage aspect, was unfair and rattled their cage loud enough until a rather insignificant gender-neutral spot height, named Garnedd Uchaf, became Camedd Gwenllian, who was some princess or other.

Before this, our Gwen's hump was deemed nothing of note and not big enough for inclusion in the three thousand count. True, we generally included it anyway because it was on a direct line between two others that did, but until the Nuttal's mountain criteria also included it as one of theirs, I would have said there was virtually no height difference between it and the lowest point northwards to Foel Fras.

For the average walker, with a time of around thirteen or fourteen hours at that point and thirteen mountains behind them done, it wouldn't even have been noticed if you weren't looking for it as you trudged wearily on. Going the other way, there is so much left to do that speed is the essence and the eyes are already on the bigger ones beyond. It looks like a rocky pimple on the ridge and nothing more. For the purpose of this book, I looked it up and discovered that the cleavage for Gwen is thirty-two metres – whatever that is in feet and inches.

You may have noticed that I do jump about between imperial and metric measurement but that's largely to keep with tradition in some of the history that I wish to relate. At heart, I have travelled metric for the last thirty years at least. It's so much quicker but when it comes to relating it to another a 'couple of feet' is so much easier to say, and be understood, than saying…er…where's that ruler? Right, got it. Sixty centimetres.

We need to continue this little deviation to sort out some other nonsense. I may refer to a kilometre as K (kay) in speech sometimes but never with the forces jargon of a 'click' or should that be 'Klick'. The other one that will raise my eyebrow is the use of imperial and metric together. 'It's half a Klick.' Do we say, 'It's point five of a mile?' I don't think so but the car's sat nav will tell you that it's 'Seven-tenths of a mile' if you stay on miles as your default settings. I think we may be talking 'Imperialism' here. Or is that measurementism?

Here's another piece of military jargon that makes no sense whatsoever. We all know that the SAS are our secret black ops forces. Covert missions behind enemy lines and all that stuff. So how do you spot them? Simple: look for any civilian who calls a rucksack a 'bergan'. (Then check the biceps for a tattoo of the regimental insignia.)

The first time I did the Welsh Three Thousands it was south to north with a mate, Pat Murphy, and one of his colleagues whose name escapes me. We learnt a lot. It was bloody hard! Wearily we had sat at the Llyn Ogwen café looking up at the mountains towering over us to the north. It was late enough in the day to see that all other walkers were coming down and, with two ranges already done, we were about to go up. We had yet to finish our walk with more mountains to climb and distance to cover than the average walker would do in a day. Indeed, the Welsh Three Thousands would make three good day walks for anyone. We succeeded and our bar was set. I think it was safe to say that our big Ws could now be printed bold.

The next time, we did it north to south. The group were policeman and after our success the previous year, their area sports and social club were doing it as a weekend outing. I was invited along because of my knowledge of the route and what it takes to complete such a huge undertaking. My son James, twelve at the time, was also invited. There were about two dozen of them and unlike the first trip we had vehicle support at the two road crossings.

By the first road crossing, with the northern Carneddau range completed, a select group of five were so far ahead that the others weren't even in sight behind. That group was made up of three policeman, James and myself, the leader by default as no one else knew where we were going. We swigged our drinks and scoffed our bacon butties hurriedly so that we could dash off before others caught up and tried to get us to slow down. Any slower and success would have been in doubt.

The Glyder Range (Glidders in English) were next. I don't even recall stopping at a support vehicle at the second road crossing in Nant Peris with just the Snowdon group left to do, but that could be down to fading memory. What I do know is that only seven people finished it. Us five and Pat, with the other guy from out first time. These two passed us going the opposite way on the penultimate mountain, Crib Ddysgl (Crib de Seagull) which underlines the differences of the route choice available. They had Yr Wyddfa (Snowdon) left to do and we had been going for the notorious Crib Goch. Those two Welsh words translate to a number of things but are all variations of 'What? You went over that in the dark! Are you out of your tiny little minds! I wouldn't go over that in daylight.'

James and I had led the way over Crib Goch in the gathering dark. It's not that bad. You can only go forwards or backwards or down very quickly. When across, we had to wait about twenty minutes for the other three to catch up because they couldn't believe we had deliberately gone across that final knife edge. In the gloom, they thought they had missed us turning off somewhere. Both James and I had been over it before and knew what to expect but it was hats off to those guys who followed when they realised there were no turnings off and they had never even heard of it or its reputation. A fall off Crib Goch has a similar prospect of survival as that from the Inaccessible Pinnacle but it is a walk. Sort of. Dependent upon your nerve.

With the Welsh Three Thousands completed again, I remember the seven of us sleeping in the minibuses while the rest of them finished the outing in the pub.

I joined them again the next year for a third attempt but that time we went so fast that both Pat and I burnt ourselves out on the Glyders range. James completed it again with the same three as before.

The next year, the National Three Peaks was their target. Those are the three countries of mainland UK's highest mountains. Ben Nevis (Scotland), Scafel Pike (England) and Snowdon (Wales) in any order that suits but with a target time of under twenty-four hours including the driving. Over recent years, this has become a huge charity challenge for thousands of people every summer and things have changed. That twenty-four-hour target has been reduced to walking time only and leaving your litter and half your clothing behind seems to be the accepted norm.

On our trip, I ended up as a minibus driver instead of a walker because of a last-minute drop-out. My other son, Simon, was injured on Ben Nevis and had to pull out, while James completed the challenge, well inside the twenty-four-hour deadline, with what had now become a very elite group of those same three and Pat. (The following year, one of them was almost killed when trying to stop car thieves. They drove off at high speed with his arm trapped in the door window. Which is a good reason for not putting off what you can do until later, because anything could happen tomorrow.)

I couldn't let that National Three Peak challenge go that easily. I wanted to give it a try myself but somewhat less conventionally. I decided to scrap the hours of sitting in the car by linking them by bike so that it would all be done by manpower. Until I discovered that it had already been done in a time I couldn't hope to even get close to, so I dropped it for a minute or two. Until I had a brainwave. I was approaching my fiftieth birthday so decided to still keep it different and make it a little more worthwhile by adding a bigger challenge to it. The National Big Buggers by manpower alone.

James and I, with support from Diane and Claire in the car, would cycle from home to Fort William. From there we would walk to do all the 4,000-foot mountains around and including Ben Nevis (4). Then we would cycle to the Cairngorms, where we would knock off the remainder of Scotland's 4,000-footers (8). In those days, I had no concept of what counted as a mountain, so we would top everything with a spot height on the Ordnance Survey map of 4,000 feet and above. That done, we would bike back to the Lake District and do all four of England's 3,000-footers (4) and then, as you have guessed, cycle around to Wales and do that lot again before cycling home (14 or 15). It took us just under three weeks and we got home for my birthday with two days in hand before returning to work.

On perhaps a sadder note, but one that both Diane, along with friends and family, often joked about, and still do, was her complete and utter failure to grasp the enormity of endurance sports and what it takes out of the participants. She hadn't the slightest idea of the detrimental effects that poor support has on both the participant's mental process and their physical recovery. Especially if that support team are not where they are supposed to be at the right time, with the food, drink and perhaps dry clothes, because they were looking for souvenir tat to take home in a shop twenty bloody miles away! For her, it was as much her day out as ours. My two favourite examples of this will have to follow now to get these differing attitudes to the task in context.

Quite a few years before the National Big Buggers trip, we were camping near Ingleton and it was decided to do the Yorkshire Three Peaks. These were Whernside, Pen-y-ghent and Ingleborough, which formed a classic walker's challenge, long before the National Three Peaks stole much of its thunder.

This was to be by bike where we could, because the three lads coming with me were a bit too young to walk it all. That was Simon at about ten, James three years younger and a friend, Ewan, and his son Allan, who was another year younger than that. We cycled to the bottom of Wernside, locked the bikes up and then went up and back down as quick as we could. Then we cycled around to Ribblehead Viaduct – where our vehicle support and breakfast was fifteen minutes late because they had stopped to have theirs at the campsite first! We went on.

After Pen-y-ghent had been ticked off, wet and cold with no money whatsoever because of the support vehicle, we sat on the pavement outside the café in Horton-in-Ribblesdale for an hour and a half because they hadn't expected us to get there so quick and there were some lovely shops in Hawes! Allan was too cold by then to continue but my lads and I, probably fired up to exploding point with frustrated anger, did go on to finish.

On the Cairngorms element of the National Big Buggers, James and I arrived back at the campsite in the dark and pouring rain. We had been walking for something like sixteen hours, done all the 4,000-footers and a few other mountains that sat between them in a distance of around thirty miles. We were wet, cold and totally spent. The next day we had to be up early and cycle to Pitlochry on our way back to England. Diane was glad we were back safely because, sick of the notorious Scottish midges that I just failed to mention, she wanted to go to bed – and did without so much as making a brew.

Strange as it may seem, I did understand what it was like for her. When I drove the minibus for the National Three Thousand, it was horrible. I drove to Glen Nevis while they all laughed, ate snacks and drank beer or brews in the back. When we got there and it was my turn to relax, I couldn't. It was in the middle of the night and everywhere was shut. I couldn't go anywhere, even if I wanted to, in case of dropouts needing a refuge. It was too cold to sleep without the sleeping bag that I hadn't expected to need and therefore didn't take. Then when the walker contingent did get back, I drove all the way down to the Lake District while, after half an hour of a chatty breakfast in the back, they slept to recuperate.

It took them forever to do Scafel Pike but where I waited it was too noisy with traffic and other walkers to sleep. There was nothing to do but wait while the others were all enjoying themselves. At the time, I figured even those who weren't actually enjoying it still had things better than me. Upon return, they slept again while I drove to Wales. After finding somewhere to eat, I got about an hour's sleep but when they returned from their third peak, well inside the twenty-four-hour deadline, I couldn't relax while they exhaustedly slept again, because I had just found out that one of them had to get back to Manchester to start his shift in two hours' time.

Support is a thankless task. Bad support is worse. I have found it so much easier to be self-reliant from the outset. By removing the need for others, the downside, for some, is that it's taking the first step towards becoming a loner. Perhaps not a welcome prospect. The upside, for me, is the contents of this book.

It's safe to say that all through my childhood, adolescence and the first twenty-odd years of my married life, I had no idea what I really wanted to do. I still don't, but it was during this period, from my mid-forties onwards, that I discovered, with the likes of these tough challenges as a yardstick, that I was indeed different from what was generally considered as normal.

Where others suffered, I was in my element. I loved the demand on one's gritty resolve and the glow of inner satisfaction when all the hardships and efforts have paid off with a rewarding finish. 'I've done that' is all I need for a trophy. I wasn't as good as those at the top of this game but I was way above the average.

To make it better, my kids were coming with me. This was unfortunate for Diane because her continuing poor health meant she was getting left behind more often as the kids grew up and got better. I went with them and I too then got fitter and bolder. Instead of growing old with grace and dignity, this kept me young, both in heart and body. Low-budget adventures became the focus of my life. It was also harder for Diane because the cost in time, if not the money, meant that the DIY improvements at home and progression up the homeowner ladders took the same course as my work. To nowhere. Work was the funding, while home was the base camp. I was a big kid and could see no further than the next playtime. That is best shown with the following anecdote.

On the hills around Moel Siabod, in Snowdonia, one winter's day a group made up of half a dozen of our friends and families, numbering around twenty individuals, were walking. It was intended to pass beneath this mountain but if some of the fitter ones wanted to go for its summit, I would take them.

There was a fair bit of snow, and group dynamics are both slow and difficult to manage in such rough country in those conditions. The older kids, my lads in particular, tired of waiting, kept going off ahead. This was deemed dangerous by some and tempers began to rise. After one such outburst and consequent regrouping, one parent chastised their son and stated that since they wouldn't do as they were told none of them were going up the mountain.

My sons looked at me in absolute disbelief. I had to make a decision. Did I support the other parents or follow my heart? As that big kid myself, I knew exactly how they felt. I was feeling it too, but unlike them I was an adult and could make my own decisions. Half an hour later, the three of us were wading happily through three feet of dry powder snow across the summit of Moel Siabod.

Boys will be boys. Girls as well if they want to but the trappings that go with fashion and glamour have to be left behind. This doesn't mean that as a parent I don't care about the safety of my offspring. Nor does it make me immune to fear for them, even after they became working adults. The Leap of Faith brought that home to me.

This can be found on Stac Pollaidh (Stack Polly) in the Highlands. The Leap of Faith is a notch in the summit ridge of that mountain and the challenge is to jump across rather than descend one side, cross the bottom and then climb up the other. It's a dare that has been around since man first began climbing mountains for fun but something I can't bring myself to do.

There's another similar challenge on the summit of Tryfan, in Wales, where the objective again is to step from one upright boulder to another to earn the freedom of the mountain. Adam and Eve they are called. It's an easy step but could be extremely painful if you get it wrong and was just far enough apart to raise doubts.

The lads and their mates found the Leap of Faith easy and then searched the entire summit jumping from one high boulder to another and getting progressively harder as they went on. In the end, I could no longer watch, so took myself off. They were adults and, just as I had to, they needed to find their own levels. I just didn't want to watch them doing it.

That's also why the Inaccessible Pinnacle remains outstanding on my list. I was there with James and two others, all adult and working, but when it came to it, I didn't want to tie on to the same rope. If there was an accident, I didn't want to be the cause of it. My imagination ran riot with horrific permutations of fatalities and survivors. I could watch and photograph them climb with no apprehension whatsoever and if James hadn't been there, I'm confident that I would have ticked the box and added one more Munro to my achievements.

> I am an amateur, therefore everything I do well is going to gall the professional, so it could well piss them off wholesale when they find out that I am also self-taught. – The Aimless Rambler

Diane had tried to keep up with us on these adventures but did struggle as she was never quite as committed to it as me and the kids. She was proud of us but uncertain of what we were doing and perhaps where it was going when compared to what she thought of as family life.

I don't want this to sound critical of her because she enjoyed many great adventures with us. However, it was perhaps my late development that widened the differences between us, and they had been huge from day one. That good old 'different sides of the tracks' upbringing that creates the theme for so many romantic love stories, with no prizes for guessing which side each was from. The Lady and the Tramp being a very apt description. Diane would have colour-coordinated Tupperware sandwich boxes, whereas I would be seen stuffing lunch in the bag that the bread had come in.

What I'm also pleased to be able to say is that throughout the hardships endured by my calling to gruelling endurance sports and the trauma, along with Diane's ill health that this created in our home, we saw it through. For richer for poorer, for better for worse, in the sickness that Diane had more than her fair share of, and in health that I enjoyed, we made good on our promises. Make no mistake, we were constantly tested. Now when I look back, I do sometimes ponder over whether the qualities required for success in a difficult marriage of opposites are not the same as those needed for taking on the demands of the rough country adventures alone. Or vice versa.

My favourite anecdote to capture those differences and the humour needed to work them through was the shopping trip in Plumet, a small town in north-west France. I have chosen that town by process of elimination to give a rough idea of where we were but I could be wrong. It was almost thirty years ago and changes take place when we aren't looking. New roads are added and towns grow, and my memory twists and turns between what there is and what there was…with the added slant of what my cartoon mind wanted there to be. Where is not as important as what happens in this town that makes this so memorable. I do need a somewhat lengthy preamble to fully set the scene or the enormity of it will be lost.

We were in Scotland when the roots of our rather epic cycling holiday in France began. 'There are too many hills for cycling,' was the complaint from Diane. This was joked about with our friends Wendy and Ewan who we were camping with and exploring the kind of adventures ordinarily associated with adults and not families with young children.

Holland was Diane and Wendy's suggestion for a cycle/camping holiday for the following year. Nice flat roads, canals and fields of tulips with windmills far removed from the squalors of my kind of adventure.

The type of holiday sounded promising but not the destination, because I knew about the reputation for wind in that area. I've since ridden there and can confirm that, once on a bike, whichever way you go, that fickle wind always blows in your face. Hard. We compromised on France.

The following summer saw three families disembark from the ferry from Portsmouth and cycle out of St Malo carrying everything we needed, except food, for a three-week holiday on our bikes. Six adults and seven kids with no actual route plan as we were going to make it up as we went along.

About a week later, we were leaving a campsite near Jugon-les-Lacs and heading kind of south and west. After several hours, we arrived in a town, which could have been Plumet which, like most French towns at any time of day, was asleep – including the shops we needed for resupply. Our modus operandi was that Ewen or I, the two fittest, would cycle on ahead to look for campsites, so on this occasion he went off to check out a site listed in a book we carried for that purpose.

Meanwhile, the rest of us had a picnic lunch outside a small supermarket while we waited for it to open, which turned out to be long enough for Ewen to cycle thirty-two miles. Sixteen miles there and back to a campsite that was now reserving a big space for us. By sheer coincidence, the shop opened at the same time. Diane went shopping while I waited outside to look after the bikes.

The others had gone on because we thought the kids had hung around for too long already and were getting tetchy. Diane and I would endeavour to catch up or meet them at the campsite. That is, two bikes with panniers filled with essential camping equipment, clothing and accessories like first aid, tools et cetera, and a small rucksack for those shopping trips that I would carry on my back.

Tired of pasta dishes that had been our lot so far on the holiday, Diane, at her turn to do the shopping, had decided to stock up on some 'decent food for a change' and came out of the shop pushing a trolley full of it.

That sleepy town suddenly woke up to watch.

Rising to the challenge with a trolley load of food stashed and tied to everywhere I could find on bike or person, much to the amusement of everyone who saw us, I cycled, beneath a hot sun, sixteen miles to the campsite with it all in one go. The irony being that at exactly the same time there was unrest in the Tour de France because there were a few riders complaining about being treated as nothing more than donkeys by some of the team managers. They had no idea of what they spoke!

It was a great holiday and to keep my hardy family in its correct perspective, a few days later we lied, upwards by two years, about how old Simon was so that he could enter a kayak, bike and running triathlon. Out of a hundred and fifty starters, he finished eighteenth overall and aged eleven (thirteen in French) he won the under twenty-one class. That got him five hundred francs in prize money and a large granite trophy to add to our heavy loads!

I lied too, so that I could enter. I told them that I could swim and it turned out that I can't kayak either. I did finish. Eventually. Perhaps the hardest bit for Simon was me trying to explain to him that at the prize-giving the mayor might try to kiss him, and that it was okay, because they do that sort of thing in France.

On that holiday, Claire, the youngest, rode around two hundred and fifty miles on a beat-up BMX that had been second-hand even before getting passed down from her two brothers before her. She was also carrying her own sleeping bag on a rear carrier that I had somehow fashioned to it with a collection of bent metal because a BMX is not designed to have such a contraption. Claire was six years old.

Peak-bagging was probably always in my heart but I hadn't recognised it as such. The record shows that it was not until 2010 that my peak-bagging, as an objective, began to take a more committed approach, as around then there is a steady increase in activity. Possibly because I was definitely Munro-bagging at that time. However, between 2005 and

2012, I was fairly busy trying to find what I could do with this carefree life that was now mine. I was absolutely free, within my financial means, to do whatever I chose but didn't know for sure what it was. Please be patient with me on this because that condition continues to plague me even now. For a loner, that grasshopper mind and too many strong callings has a distinct disadvantage. There is no one to keep you on track!

The mountain-biking that I was so good at had drifted away to nothing. While at work, my commuting had a hidden agenda. I wanted to do five thousand miles a year solely on going to work and back without including any of my other leisure cycling. This isn't as difficult as it may seem once you start to break it down. A hundred miles per week will do it. Twenty a day plus another five or so to make up for holidays and any sickness. Since that is commuting, that splits it down to two separate journeys a day and it all becomes easier still.

To do this, even if I didn't go off-road, I just went the longer ways round. When I retired, the overriding factor to make such journeys each day was removed and I gradually lost interest. Accidents while cycling over rough country are more common than when walking, and by the very nature of the sport the chances of serious injury were that much greater. Along with being safer, walking on my own had a much stronger appeal because it lends itself better to looking at what surrounded me. This doesn't mean that I wasn't seeing the country as I rode through it but there was a bias towards scanning for the bits that would hurt when we collided rather than the wondrous nature of the whole.

For a short while, I messed about with solo road-riding but couldn't find the enthusiasm that I harboured for the long-distance mountain-biking. I suspect it was too far removed from the natural world and without companions I know that I would give up on a whim to follow a different thread of interest. I found that out through a practical exam.

As part of my quest to find new interests, I used to read the occasional adventure-orientated magazine for ideas. In one such magazine, *AT Travel* or something like it, I chanced upon the Spam Challenge. Readers had to find an adventure holiday abroad for no more than seventy quid per person and then write about it for the magazine for a refund of the seventy pounds. The only compulsory requirement was that a tin of Spam went with you. Most of those I read about were variations of taking a cheap flight somewhere for a city break to spend a couple of days drinking. My friend Simon Taylor and I took on the challenge and gave adventure back to it.

Five Countries in Five Days. With cycles and camping equipment, we took the ferry from Dover to Calais, which also took the lion's share of our budget. France was the first of our five countries. We then rode to Belgium before turning south to skirt Brussels and onto Maastricht, Holland. Three done in two days. On the third day, we crossed the border near Aachan, Germany, for about ten metres before turning around and heading west for Luxembourg – our fifth country.

It then went wrong for me in Malmedy, Belgium (again), because instead of the constant bustle of busy traffic and people of big towns that were no different from those back home, we were suddenly on the continent for real.

Flower-bedecked Malmedy on that day was warm and sunny. People were sat outside bars and cafés, where they ate and drank in good humour. Solo, I would have quit there and then. Instead of our diet of camembert, baguette and beef tomato, washed down with water, I would have blown the budget and a lot more besides by joining them.

Simon talked me out of it and twenty kilometres later we were that desperate that we ate the tin of Spam before entering Luxembourg. We ate the Spam! All of it. Of such deeds heroes are made. Five countries done and all we had to do was get back to Calais. The Ardennes, noted for its hills, lay between us and that port. After the hills came the flats again and it was windy in our faces all the way back across them.

We achieved our goal with a couple of hours and euros to spare but that was purely down to Simon's drive. It was approximately nine hundred kilometres but the electronics that I was recording it on had given up at around six hundred so I don't know exactly how far it was. For once, perhaps the first time, I was the weakest link. In a civilised environment, I now know that I will give way to the soft options as quick as the next man if I'm starting to struggle. Out in the wilds that I normally roam, such social distractions thankfully cannot happen.

They printed our story in their magazine but we never got our money back.

The weakest link element was to start cropping up a bit more often as my sons and their friends had overtaken me in terms of fitness, speed and possibly endurance, but that was easy to live with. Rather than causing me to aim a little lower with my ambitions, I was using it to drive even harder. After all, I was over twice their age and therefore always had a ready-made excuse for poor performance. When I get tired or weary out in the rough country, I also have my secret weapon to fall back on. (Secret until now, that is.) It's little used but hasn't failed me yet.

That is my 'walk or die' philosophy. Throughout history, there have been millions of people who have had no choice but to walk or they would die. Refugees perhaps or prisoners of war, be they soldiers or civilians, being relocated or taken to labour camps. Victims of famine or other natural disaster. They had no choice. If they stopped walking, they died. I do have a choice and I'm only playing.

So when the self-pity starts to emerge, images of those people, or primitive man scratching a living on those very same hills that I may be walking, without all the latest high-tech equipment and clothing at my disposal, will kick in. I will walk. I should be ashamed not to. I may still feel sorry for my plight because I'm certainly no superman but I will walk until the safety of civilisation is reached. I haven't any choice. If I don't, I might die.

When safely back, I'll then have a drink and thank those nameless souls I dared to compare myself to. Then have another because I had no right to make that comparison…and then another because those first two tasted so damn good after my labours.

I will finish this chapter here and take a look in the next at some of the other things I was doing during those intervening years mentioned above as they are a major contribution to how, if not exactly when, I became the totally committed peak-bagger who has so much trouble deciding what to count…or where to go for his next adventure.

But first, for someone who rarely finishes anything that he starts, I wonder how far I'm along this list which I hadn't the slightest intention of ever starting. I can tick the following as seen. For a figment of imagination, that outlaw certainly got about.

Robin Hood's Bay
Robin Hood's Stride
Robin Hood's Well (two)
Robin Hood's Bed
Robin Hood's Picking Rods
Robin Hood's Cave
Robin Hood's Cross

Robin Hood's Grave is on private property and very close to home, so maybe one day I'll get lost and inadvertently stumble upon it but I'd be unable to publicly include it without risk of unwanted confrontation. What am I saying? Going to visit the grave of a fictitious entity – where's the practical logic of a mountain man in that?

Summit Talks 5

All abroad and thrill-seekers explained…or exposed perhaps

I was venturing abroad more since becoming widowed because I had the time and I was financially viable for the first time in my life. There was no magic formula for such a happy state of affairs but, with no influence whatsoever from my MBE award, at work I was successful at my very next promotion board when I wasn't even trying.

I was going for it for no other reason than to see if I could set a record of failed attempts, and subsequently failed in that bid to add credence to my claim to be the champion of lost causes. Despite protests to the opposite, from a disorganised management chain set on trying to retain credibility with me, I am certain the MBE clinched it because once that hurdle was passed, I went no further in this comical farce until the fight got really dirty. I felt it had been nothing more than a token gesture. On paper, I now had the management grade to wipe out the anomaly of having a lowly clerk brandishing his MBE while in conflict with the new breed of management that had crept in with another minister-prompted department name change, but I had neither the actual job nor wage increase to go with it. Nothing for me had changed.

With regard to my working life, that was the beginning of the end for me. A complete change in the management ethos had brought about the demise of an era where people were treated as such and within a very short space of time had destroyed any misguided sense of loyalty that I had left for my employer. All those years of helping the less fortunate than me, be they customers or staff, came to a head with this conflict. I had to help myself. It wasn't until I registered with an industrial tribunal my case of discrimination against them, on the grounds of my trade union representation, that it was resolved.

After two years of watching them fill vacancies suitable for me from any which way they could rather than offer me the job in junior management, whether they liked it or not, they were guilty of discrimination. They had promoted me and any one of those jobs which had to be filled, with the increased income, was rightfully mine. Then, within about five minutes of someone realising that if the case was heard at an industrial tribunal, win or lose, and they surely would lose, it was going to make the press. Bad press loomed! Suddenly, by sheer coincidence of course, I was posted to a job with the new grade requirement. Not much of a pay rise but better than I would have got without it.

Governments, of both political persuasions, had been squeezing the pay for their lower-grade employers since Thatcher first put the noose around our necks, but promotion guaranteed me a minimum rise enough to offset a couple of years' inflation. It was still five grand a year less than some of the women who did exactly the same job, but that is another story that has no place here.

We had finished paying off the mortgage and all other debts around the same time. Due to being terminally ill, Diane was also on maximum benefits that, by this time, she was too ill to use. The truth is that we saved them up and between chemotherapy treatments we took holidays abroad while waiting for the results. We just spent it, enjoying the moments and be damned. When she had passed on, my wage was still a lot lower than people would believe for an 'overpaid civil servant' but when there was only me and my bike I had no overheads at all. I received a lump sum widower's payment and then bereavement benefits for a year as well. After all those years of struggling with the raising of kids, now, when it was too late, I had enough to remove the immediate worries of everyday living.

As for how I dealt with the loss itself, in the main that is my business, but generally it's my refusal to make a drama out of anything unless it's for laughs. Flatlining is the term often used to describe it: hide any outward feelings, bottle them up and get on with life because it ain't gonna wait for you. It was perhaps made a little easier for me because becoming a widower didn't come as any surprise since I had already been told that at best Diane only had about a one in four chance of surviving five years of the particular strain of cancer that had sneaked up unseen upon her. She didn't quite make two of them but when you're living every day with something like that, there are no miracle cures or sudden endings. Just a slow and unstoppable deterioration until from one sleep there is no waking up. It kind of prepares you, the survivor, for the inevitable.

My boss at the time thought I would benefit from counselling but he was being a twat because the good managers guide says he has to do that sort of thing instead of thinking it through for himself. It's shite. Management by numbers, with generous lashings of gobbledegook to justify it, in an environment where staff are valued as resources rather than people. I'm from the era, before the days of managing with such drivel, where a decent boss would have known his staff for what they were, read the signs and, in my case, kept his mouth shut.

Anyway, it prompted me to follow up on an impulse and spend those bereavement benefits on something useful to me. After many years of looking after Diane throughout her sicknesses, I did feel that something completely different and totally selfish would be better for me than any of the usual stuff on offer for the recently bereaved. It was now only me and something I had to get used to quickly. Summiting a 6,000-metre mountain seemed to fit the bill. To do something really big without having to worry too much about technicalities. Thousands of people walk up it every year. Yeah, *morceau de gateau* (piece of cake). I'd give Kilimanjaro a go.

It was also going start a new learning curve. One where I, just an ordinary bloke by my reckoning, was going to find out that while it was still too early to really be a loner, from the moment I tried the all-inclusive adventure holidays that can take you to such places as

Kilimanjaro, with the minimum of organisational effort, I was the odd one out. At the time, I couldn't see why but now it's so clear that I do sometimes wonder how my life would have turned out if I had realised it at the time.

I was to discover that there are two distinctively different groups of people who seek their pleasures in the rough country. They are the adventurers that the majority will proudly claim to be; and there are thrill-seekers, which is what the majority of those actually are. It's because I most definitely belong in that very small camp of real adventure-seekers that my loner status, without a like-minded companion, had no option but to develop into what I am now. Hopefully it will become clearer why that has to be as this chapter unfolds.

I think I can safely begin this with the following phrase and drive the wedge straight into the gap between the two groups.

You pays your money and make your choices.

Money is the key. I can't go to Kilimanjaro without spending a lot of money, so that when I do go I want to maximise my return for the investment. By buying into a holiday company that does everything for you in order to make it possible, except the actual walking, that would seem to be a sound call. I thought so at the time. Ask me now if I would agree and I might still say yes it is, but perhaps not quite so quickly. I would most certainly be asking a lot more questions from myself.

On the trip to Kilimanjaro, there were sixteen of us trekkers, as I recall, and around twenty-five porters and guides. Maybe more or less with the porters because they were all employed by the same company and contracted out to the various trekking companies taking their clients up the mountain. For all I know, they could have been moving from job to job amongst the groups of walkers wanting go up. It would make sense to maximise the efficiency of the workforce by ensuring they were where they were needed most, but who knows or cares. We were there to climb a mountain. There was an awful lot of such groups that were to all get intermingled as the ascents began each day.

The campsite that we would be heading for that day would have just been cleared by those people twenty-four hours in front of us going for the next one up. It's that busy and no place for me any longer since I have grown older and hopefully wiser. Snowdon, one Easter, is the busiest mountain I have ever been on. Without exaggeration, there were thousands. Long lines of ant-like walkers on every path and the summit was heaving like a London rush hour when the trains arrived. Kilimanjaro was the same but fortunately spread over a much bigger land mass.

At the time, it was all new and I took it for granted that this was the price you paid if you wanted a big peak in your *palmares*. Amongst the things I had difficulty with there are two that stick out more than most.

Porters. It went against the grain for me to expect anyone to be carrying my stuff for me. I had to accept that is was necessary because I was going four times higher than I had ever been before with absolutely no first-hand experience to relate to. I had no choice but listen to the advice given. We were limited to fifteen kilos in identical bags that we had to mark in such a way that we could recognise which was ours. The porters had to carry two of them. Mine weighed about eight kilos because I still couldn't part with my usual rucksack contents of essential kit and I travelled fairly light even in those days. A lot lighter now! When you are having to carry it yourself, you learn very quickly that all the 'just in case' stuff is dragging you down. All you need is enough to keep you alive. Appearances? Funny enough, that is for the thrill-seekers.

Such is this game that when the bags were being weighed before we left on the first day, my bag was the lightest. Immediately a woman in the group piped up with a request to put some of her stuff in with mine. She was having to leave these things behind at the base hotel because she had exceeded the allowance. Before I could even formulate a reply of any kind, the chief guide told her quite emphatically 'no' on my behalf because if anyone had to turn back, their bag went with them. I was relieved and wished I had thought of that. But I would remember it for the future.

I was pleased that for the remainder of the trip the porters were almost falling over themselves to get my bag as one of their two each morning.

The other thing that rankled was the tables and chairs. There were porters carrying tables, chairs and large mess tents, up and down that mountain, so that we could sit like Victorian gentry at mealtimes. That stinks. Until you realise that there's no other work and, by employing porters to do this, food is being put into the mouths of their children. I still didn't like it and when I could I would take my food outside to eat and answer any enquiries to the effect that I hadn't come all that way to sit in a tent. I wanted to see the mountain that I was climbing, and meant it too. The moon was approaching full and there was so much to see.

There was a stomach bug going through the group that was catching people out between the purpose-built long-drop loos and I was actually chuffed when the guide commandeered a shovel from the porters and asked me to carry it for those who needed to go for a walk in the bushes. This was because the porters didn't walk with us. As soon as they had their loads, they were gone like rats up a drainpipe.

I had the shovel and our group used it but the 'tissue trails' don't just apply to the Himalayas. Who do these people think they are that it's okay to be so arrogant as to leave this shitty litter for the rest of us to view? They aren't the poor people who usually get blamed for this sort of thing, because they couldn't afford the holiday in the first place. All you have to do is bury it. Possibly burn the paper at least if you don't have the means to dig the hole. The shit itself will break down like any animal's droppings or get spread far and wide over the mountain as people tread through it because you are too selfish to take your business a reasonable distance from the path. As for those bloody wet wipes…

We set off for the summit after four days slow ascent to acclimatise. It was to be by the light of the full moon so that we could see the sunrise from the top. We progressed slowly upwards by walking for half an hour and then resting for ten minutes. The guide put the faster ones, such as myself, at the front so that we strung out more rather than get bunched up by having the slower ones in front. Our route was a single track zigzagging up a huge slide of dusty gravel which, if such a policy is not adopted, does tend to create a line of people, all walking right behind each other, with nothing to look at but the back of the person in front or their own feet. I won't do the 'train' myself. I will be either off the front or somewhere way off the back. When I carried the shovel, the others knew where to find me because up until that final ascent I was always off the back birdwatching, so they only had to wait, perhaps a little anxiously, for a few minutes longer.

After about three hours of a steady ascent in this manner, I started to feel odd at just over five thousand metres, becoming detached and not hearing what was being said at the rest stops. Then I was startled when someone woke me up. I hadn't seen that coming.

The last time I fell asleep unintentionally I had ended up in hospital! I just don't do that sort of thing. For instance, the only time I can sleep in cars is when I'm driving. You know, that sickening feeling when it all becomes a continuous blur and you can feel yourself slipping into a drowsy sleep and come around with a frightening start. That's when, usually on a motorway where there's very little actual driving to do, it's time to turn the music up, wind down the windows and pray to a deity of choice that you can make it to the next service station for a quick nap followed by a large dose of caffeine. For some reason, this doesn't happen to me as a passenger so if you need company on a long drive to keep you awake, I do have my uses.

It was two winters after Kinder Scout when I first fell asleep on a mountain. We still lived in the south and had no children. A group of us were camping in the Lake District primarily to watch a stage of the RAC Rally, which has now been replaced by a somewhat tamer version in the shape of the UK round of the World Rally Championships – that seems to be stuck in Wales. As part of the week, we did some walking, a lot of drinking and that year some off-roading in 4X4 Land Rovers.

I was recovering from a near-death experience with man flu the week before which, as it turned out, all flippancy aside, threatened to become my nemesis. We were high up on the hills. It was snowing. One Land Rover was bogged down to its axles and there was doubt as to the feasibility of going any further once they had got it out. A return by the way we had come and to the nearest pub was beginning to look a much better prospect for continued entertainment, but the way forward could be faster if we were through the worst of it.

To that end, while the others dug, I went to scout the route forward on foot to see if it improved enough to continue as quickly as a return would take. After a while, I found my own progress was slow and laboured. I was feeling heavy-footed and drowsy. As the forward route showed no signs of improving, I turned around and made my way back. I wasn't well and knew it. That same feeling as the motorway driving when sleep is hanging over you.

I remember that the Land Rover was still stuck and someone telling me to sit down for a bit because I looked awful. They were going to tow it out backwards with the other one. I sat down by some rocks to wait.

I do remember waking up for a few seconds lying in the back of a Land Rover with the others piling coats on top of me. The next time I woke was with nurses taking off my wet clothes. Including the same shameful long johns! I woke up properly several hours later feeling absolutely fine. Just like any awakening after a sleep. I was told I had been hypothermic, probably caused by venturing out in bad weather before I was fully recovered from the previous week's virus. When it was found that I was camping if discharged from hospital, they kept me in another two days until the others had finished their holiday. The NHS isn't like it used to be. (My friends all came to visit me the next day but I said don't waste more time visiting me again when there's so much else to do. So they didn't. Hm.)

Another bubble just got burst there, I think, so before going any further, let's burst another. I was also hospitalised after a mountain-bike accident, which no one witnessed, leaving me with a broken collar bone and concussion so bad that to this day I don't remember anything from about fifteen minutes before the accident and until a week later. Which included a four-day stay in hospital. I went back to the spot where I'm told it happened but, unlike the movies, nothing came back.

There had been a group of us riding. Nothing technical or particularly fast. Just the vehicle tracks of Delamere forest in Cheshire. I had gone ahead for some reason that the others hadn't a clue about, and I have since lost because of it, but when my friends came round a corner I was found lying unconscious beside the track, in the bushes, covered in blood from head injuries.

Speculation has it that for reasons unknown I had gone over my handlebars and headbutted a tree with considerable force, because when they had taken my helmet off in A&E, it just crumbled to pieces, having only been held in place by the outer skin of the helmet and my skull inside it. Mercifully by this time long johns were no longer part of the wardrobe. Thanks to Ron Hill, the runner, I was wearing tights instead (Tracksters). Although it was only my friends and family who would have had to live with the shame of the old long johns because I was away in cloud cuckoo land.

On Kilimanjaro, somewhat shaken by the sleep, I also felt distinctly detached from the world as I stood up. Similar to that previous experience all those years ago, I fought it off as best I could and set off walking again, near the front, but no longer at the head of the line. My coordination was shot. I kept thinking that the feet of the person in front were mine and then couldn't understand why I was stumbling. Then I found myself waking with a shock from this drowsy state but not knowing if I had actually been asleep while walking. This sensation kept repeating for quite some time but I kept telling myself it was the high altitude and thus normal to feel groggy. The guides had repeatedly been telling us that we were all likely to struggle in one way or another and to just keep plodding slowly. 'Poly Poly' they would say to keep our spirits up.

Anyway, the next time I woke up, anxious guides were checking me for vital signs. Three days later, I was told by the person who had been behind me at the time that one of my stumbles turned me around completely. I then took about three steps downhill, muttered something and pitched over.

They say it was altitude sickness but I remain unconvinced. I had the shits. An assistant guide was assigned the job of taking me down because he was taller than me. He simply put his shoulder under my armpit, grabbed the waistband underneath my rucksack and ran like hell. When I couldn't keep up, my feet simply dragged through the dust and gravel until I did. I had a few minutes' rest at the last camp to clear the shit and then carried on down to a 3,200-metre camping ground, given some soup and a hot drink, and a bed in a shed. I woke up the next evening feeling fine.

I found out that night that the guide who had brought me down was an under two hour and twenty minutes marathon runner and wasn't good enough to qualify for the Tanzanian team. He practised by running up and down that mountain every day.

I wasn't put off by Kilimanjaro but I was very put out. I felt even more strongly that I was an ordinary guy and that trip seemed to confirm it. Not one of the Himalayan super-climbers or celebrity Antarctic explorers who can't fart without making the headlines. Just an ordinary guy with ordinary things happening. Altitude sickness? Hypothermia? Amnesia? That's not me. That stuff is of TV heroes and fictional drama and not the lot of an old fart of the South Pennines. There are now many new strains of man flu being discovered every day and don't I know it.

As soon as I got back, I sorted out a trip to Morocco to see if I would fair any better on Toubkal. At 4,167 metres, it is the highest mountain in North Africa and six whole weeks' wages cheaper than Kilimanjaro. But first I was going to school.

'But you're self-taught. You keep harping on about it enough,' I hear you protest.

And so I am. Well, mostly.

I knew that with my new-found total lack of responsibilities my mountaineering was going to get more serious, so I signed up to a winter skills and survival course in Scotland with an outdoor adventure school, just to make sure that what I had picked up over the years was good enough. I was pleased to find that for the most part it was. Indeed, I came away a little too cocky and within weeks I found myself on an unintended downhill slide on an ice sheet through lack of attention… and bravado instead of caution.

I had been solo skylining the valley of Greenburn, in the Tibberthwaite Fells, north of Coniston on a very cold day. It became increasingly icy as I climbed Wet Side Edge and I put on my crampons to follow the line over Great Cars, Swirl How and onto Wetherlam. As the snow and ice lessened on descent, I took them off again. With ice axe and spikes now back in the pack, I used trekking poles as my safety tool. A few minutes later, as I kicked steps down some softer snow between rocks and heather, one boot went through the snow to ice, where it failed to grip, but my second foot was already making for purchase one step lower down. That failed to grip too. That was all it took and I was going down.

It wasn't particularly far and I think there would have been a safe run out at the bottom had I not arrested my slide. Not with the ice axe as per the training, but by rolling over and with both hands jamming the point of one trekking pole into the ice. I came to a stop at the feet of two walkers gingerly picking their way up. They were staring at me with mouths open and all I could think to say was, 'I wish I'd planned to do that.'

I recovered the other pole that had been discarded and continued down, kicking myself, instead of the snow, for being so complacent. When I looked back up a few minutes later, to check on the scene and to try and work out if there had been any real danger, I saw that the couple hadn't moved. A row of some kind was taking place. We're just ordinary folk doing ordinary things.

This would be an appropriate juncture to tackle the subject of trekking poles. Very rarely will you see me out without trekking poles. I used to scoff at them as I walked by with my great big wooden staff so now we have to burst another of this hardy adventurer-seeker's bubbles.

I am scared of dogs. Quite justifiably so, if the evidence to date is anything to go by. I have watched my friends walk quietly past a compound with loose guard dogs inside. When I went past, they were almost hanging off the chain-link fence in their bid to get at me. Snarling and slavering brutes wanting to tear me limb from limb. Why me and not the others?

On another occasion there was a dog on a lead that would run down a fixed wire the length of the garden. It was secured but its owners clearly wanted it to have maximum exercise space while it was. So bent was this angry monster on getting to me as I cycled passed, on a legal right of way, that it hurled itself over the wall at the end of the run and was last seen hanging there by the neck. No, I didn't go back to help it. Come off it. Being eccentric doesn't make me a pillock. I've been bitten several times. An owner of one such culprit dog seemed quite worried for it because, as if it was so obviously my fault for being there, she said it didn't normally do that. Well, that was reassuring. For everyone else maybe.

Taking my young family into the rough country involved passing through a lot of farms where dogs run loose, I couldn't afford to show fear in front of them so I found I could be a lot braver with a bloody great stick. (The same one that Simon used to break the ice of the trapped walkers on Kinder Scout.) So, while I didn't use trekking poles for many years, I had always been walking with that stick. Thus getting other benefits from it without those being by deliberate intent.

I bought the first poles for Kilimanjaro because, while not compulsory, they were strongly recommend and since I wasn't going to get my staff through airport security I invested in a fairly standard pair of a popular make. They were cheap but with me they lasted for a lot less time than the manufacturer would have hoped for.

Before I left my failed Kilimanjaro bid for home, along with my trainers, I gave them to injured porters Mr Go-Lightly and his mate Mr Safari, who couldn't secure work any longer. For a very reasonable price, they offered an absolutely fantastic tour around the villages and rainforest from which treks to Kilimanjaro were based. About a fiver for the whole day it cost me. (The holiday representative based at the hotel was very unhappy about it. They were recommending that I went with a reputable company that they happened to know which had vacancies for a mere forty pounds…with a packed lunch included.) The poles? I loved them. They were so much better than the stick. The first thing I bought when I got back was the best pair on the market at that time. I still use them – one of them.

My super-duper pair didn't mess about with fancy bits of rubber. They were designed for cross-country skiing and sported titanium tips for use in ice conditions. Which accounts for why my slide on Whethlam was arrested instead of hammering away uselessly with a rubber end stop.

I use my poles but the vast majority don't. They are told they needed them, by the smart shop assistant, to safely walk along the canal but have no idea what to do with them. That is, carry them by the middle, parallel with the ground, until you get to the rough country. You don't, at any time, close them all up and stash them in the rucksack. There are a lot of dogs on the canals! You need to be able to swivel them deftly into club or lance depending upon your preferred option for defence – hence the need for holding them in the middle. Ever ready!

When you do get to the rough country, you use them to help power up the hills by taking some of your weight, and the rucksack's, in your arms, a third leg for balance when nipping down them a bit sharpish and for probing depths of bogs on the flats. They are a tool and not a friggin' wand to be waved around like the rest of the bloody fairies do when looking for magical assistance instead of the corkscrew. Don't be afraid of the damn thing! Dig it in and use it – which loosens the soil and speeds up erosion, the park ranger quickly points out. Not for me it doesn't, because I'm not on that path. I am that weird bugger way off piste trying to get away from the pole and phone wavers. I carry mine a lot, as described above, because on the 'improved paths' used by so many I don't find any benefits, but there are still those dogs. It's certainly too much hassle to keep opening them up and closing them when not in use.

Mine don't even match. They were so worn and bent that I no longer tried to close them together so when, up on a remote and pathless mountain, I found an even better one, made of carbon, probably dropped by someone like myself, I put aside the worst of my two and used it instead. The old one remains in my rack in the hall because it's still too good to throw away and has been up a lot of mountains with me. It may even have been the one of the two that I used on that slide.

(I do get sentimental about some things. Hence the house full of tatty rucksacks, worn-out boots, threadbare clothing and hundreds of maps. They are the faithful tools of my trade.)

How many people have you seen who can't even master the twist and lock systems of conventional trekking poles? Both of my odd pair have thumb leavers instead so that you can use them with thick gloves on but since I don't bother to lengthen or shorten them, a pair of non-adjustable ski poles, like continental ultra-marathon runners use, could be my next purchase if they ever become entirely unusable. So with a hundred quid's worth in each hand, I'm supposed to feel stupid when that guy proudly tells me that he just bought a pair round the corner for six quid – although, to be fair, they are probably good enough for that trip along the canal to the pub. They'll look pretty if nought else. I'll be long gone before he has worked out that twist and lock system and wondering how much his vet bill is going to be for fixing his dog's teeth. It was only playing. So was I or that titanium point on my bent pole could well have been sticking out of its arse.

The Moroccan trip was more rewarding than Kilimanjaro. On it, I was good and I knew it.

It was a smaller group, about ten of us with one guide, and instead of porters we had six pack mules and their handlers. From the start, it was very basic. Hot and dusty and not a lot of room for the trappings of modern living. It was also Ramadan which, with its fasting during the daylight hours, made it that much harder for our Muslim support crew. They had to make sure we ate and drank enough in the heat of the day while they couldn't touch it themselves.

That was another very valuable lesson for me to learn. They were just ordinary guys, doing their job, and they could add that hardship to it, on a voluntarily basis to support their spiritual beliefs, on the perimeter of the Sahara Desert. The bottled-water buyers, shopping down Oxford Street, now look even more foolish than they had done before.

Caution: don't ever tell me to drink more water. Like those guys, I know what I need.

> I have climbed over a thousand different mountains and have never bought a bottle of water in the UK. Will I live long enough to regret it? – The Aimless Rambler

After a dodgy start with a mild case of man flu again, that I think I picked up on the plane, I was back on top form after struggling for a couple of days. The Atlas Mountains were more my thing than the crowded Kilimanjaro.

Toubkal turned out to be no harder than going up Ben Nevis by the tourist route. However, it was still a thousand metres lower than when my problems started on Kilimanjaro, so the altitude question remains unanswered. It didn't matter much, because I wasn't going that high again. There seemed no point to it any longer because I had found that the actual height was not important. It was just a figure that people feel they need to add. The summits themselves were important to me but so were the journeys and I could get a lot more smaller ones for a lot less time and cost than those giants. Which, scaled down, is not unlike the argument for going after English and Welsh peaks instead of the Munros of Scotland when you live in the south of the UK. Nonetheless, a longing for those Highland summits will forever hang in the background of the big picture if your heart really does lie in the rough country.

The group on the Toubkal trip was quite a varied bunch with a wide range of age and ability. It was where I met Owen, who was travelling with another guy, Keith, who was slightly older than him. There was also a Russian lass that was a magnet for disaster and more lessons to be learned for everyone but herself. She was young, single, pretty, fit, confident and bloody dangerous in a Muslim country where she flaunted that combination of attributes with attitude. I actually found that I was indifferent to, or even possibly amused by, her plight when the women of a Berber village pelted her with stones for exposing her limbs when she had been specifically warned not to. When I say stones, what I'm talking about here is a quarter of a brick size. She came away in tears and bleeding but it never stopped her.

At one wild campsite between the fork of two mountain streams it was men to one side and women to the other for the ablutions. She sauntered over to our side in her underwear and towel draped over her shoulder. You can't make this stuff up. The muleteers were not impressed, though. They had her down for trouble that they could neither afford or even want. Such women were of no use for anything but a shiny ornament for causing trouble. Looking good didn't count for a lot with them in a land that was so unforgiving.

I got on really well with those guys. I also addressed the issue of not being waited on, as with the Kilimanjaro trip, by getting everybody to help out by erecting and taking down their own tents. I could tell there were some who weren't too happy with that arrangement but as they were in the minority they felt obliged to comply.

At every wilderness camp, I took it upon myself to dig the toilet hole and erect the latrine tent around it. In the mornings, I took it down again and filled in the hole, which again didn't sit well with one individual. I got the feeling that it offended their sense of dignity to have a fellow holidaymaker, who would have paid the same for the holiday as them, shovelling dirt to cover their shit. Me? I couldn't give a shit.

I was also quite forceful in any discussion on eating at night. The support crew had to go first, no matter what, as they had been without all day. There should be no them and us. We are all just ordinary people and the adventure-seeker in me wants to keep it that way.

At some time around then, I had made the conscious decision to stick with Europe for a few years and avoid the world hot spots like Machu Picchu until I knew better. Thanks to the financial restraints of family life, much of it on a single wage, I had seen very little of Europe, but enough to know, following my African trips, that I'd be happy with exploring what it had to offer for many years. Going further afield was still being looked at but I could take it or leave it and would make a decision as options, if any, arose. I wouldn't be going for the sole purpose of climbing one mountain, because failure, as on Kilimanjaro, leaves a very big hole.

Skiing would have been the next logical move, so I chose snowshoeing. Too many of my friends were blaming skiing for long-term injuries accompanying them into old age. I felt a bit too old to start. As it turned out, anyone can snowshoe without expert help. It's no different from walking. You strap them to your boots and go. Not knowing this, and with very little opportunity to find out in the UK, I went on another adventure holiday to learn and was rewarded with another excellent holiday in good company.

Apparently a couple of days before we had arrived they had experienced the biggest dump of snow all winter. Conditions were excellent as most of what was going to avalanche off had already done so. Today, assessing avalanche conditions is still my biggest worry. A fairly common apprehension, I would guess. So far, I have been exceedingly lucky; or I have been calling it right? I can't help believing it's the former.

A couple of winters later, I had used the snowshoes to climb a slope in the Alps and upon reaching a barn I sat on the steps in the sunshine for lunch. Shortly afterwards, I was joined by a French guy who looked ancient. He spoke even less English than I knew of French but we had a great chat made up with a lot of hand gestures, nods and guffaws. During which, with good nature, he pooh-poohed my *raquettes* as he had walked there in his boots from the opposite direction. He left the way I had ascended as I repacked my rucksack. I heard some yelling and then laughter. On moving to where I could see him, I saw that he was waist-deep in the snow, still laughing, and shouting, '*Raquettes bon.*' Snowshoes do work.

A final twist to that story is that people at home knew that I had lost my mobile phone before I realised it was missing. After I had gone, he had returned to the barn to follow his own ascent route back and there found my phone. He took it down with him and either he or a friend sent a text to everyone on my contact list telling them that he had found it. If one of them would provide him with my address, he would post it on. My phone arrived at my home just a couple of days after me. (This was the days before I was introduced to smart phones and passwords. In the UK, that phone would have been considered far too old to steal. And too cheap for a collector's item.)

The guide, for the want of a better word, who taught me snowshoeing, spent each summer guiding people around Mont Blanc so when I had put forward a tentative enquiry about the costs et cetera, he just laughed and told me straight, 'Don't be daft. You don't need a guide. Someone as good as you in the mountains should just go and bloody do it.'

'Shit or bust, do or die and spit the Devil in the eye.' Or words to that effect. I was going to give the Tour du Mont Blanc (TMB) a go. Owen and Keith had been talking about it in Morocco and I had stayed in touch with them. A couple of phone calls later and they were coming with me. It wasn't as simple as that in practice because of personality clashes but Owen and I finally met at Geneva airport with three weeks to walk from Chamonix in France, around Mont Blanc to Courmayeur in Italy, from there round to Champex in Switzerland and then back to France. Around a hundred and eighty kilometres and a big climb pretty much each day as the radiating ridges are crossed.

The TMB wasn't my first long distance trail, as I had done all sorts of bits and pieces in the UK over the years but it was my first Alpine walking of any kind. We stayed in the wide assortment of dormitory accommodation, usually mixed-gender, in mountain refuges and *gites* that I also experienced for the first time. (Sensible underwear required if dignity and decency is to be preserved.) Independently and unsupported made it that much better than the adventure holidays I had been buying into.

This is where the difference between thrill-seeking and adventure-seeking comes in. On our trip, no one had done any of our paperwork but ourselves. We had no access to the kind of backup procedure that a large company can provide for things like missing luggage, flights delayed et cetera. There was no one planning the day for us to follow or sort out the domestics and bad weather alternatives. We had to book our own accommodation to match our timetable, which had to remain flexible to allow for changes of route to suit fatigue and that weather.

I think this difference between the two factions can be better explained using my mountain-biking history as an example. For years I had been an endurance cross-country mountain-biker and drew enormous satisfaction from overcoming the obstacles such as grinding away up long hills, or indeed carrying the bikes up them, pushing them through deep mud or at times snowdrifts. I also enjoyed the easy and fast downhill stuff because I had worked for them. I had earned those rewards. The way I did it called for strength, fitness and commitment.

Then along came the downhillers. Not for them was any of that. They only wanted the downhill bits. The whooping rush of adrenalin as they hurtled down…and then perhaps get back in the cable car to go up and do it again. Thrill seeking. The rush without the work.

I have since expanded upon that to include anybody who isn't prepared to work for their rewards by giving up on a few luxuries like washing, clean clothes and a varied diet. To cater for such people the adventure holidays now spend more space in their brochures detailing the food, accommodation and transport links than the primary objective of the holiday. The adventure element has gone. A big fairground ride where you just go along for the ride but are no part of making it happen.

Okay, each to their own. That was beginning to show itself more clearly to me on our TMB trek. Owen spoke fluent French and German, so he took care of the phone calls to book accommodation and anything else requiring those skills. As a person, he is a social animal and will freely go off to talk to strangers while I am one of those who waits until they came to me which meant he also ensured that we met all sorts from all over the world.

My role was route-finding and keeping us on track. I carried the extras above personal gear that we could share, such as first aid, gas stove and brewing tackle, emergency survival bags, maps and compass, along with the food for the day's walking. (Also worthy of note when wondering what old age may bring is that Owen was walking around Mont Blanc when he was older than I am writing this now.)

It worked. And I got an extra little buzz whenever we encountered an adventure holiday group. All they had to do was walk. It's nice to be that carefree and I can't fault them for making the most of it, but they had no real freedom. We were free to make it up as we went along. They couldn't even choose where they walked because it was a group and the leader made those kinds of decisions based on evaluation of the group. If we wanted to dive into a café for a break we could, without having to see what the rest of the party wanted or worry about whether it would have an adverse effect on meeting transport that might be waiting.

I later learnt that this freedom can only be improved from mine and Owen's trip by going solo. Yes, they got the thrill of walking the TMB but for me it falls a long way short of adventure. Their uncertainty has been removed and taken on by others. The risks, an essential ingredient for adventure, had all but been removed and the decision-making minimised to choosing what wine to have with their dinner.

Having recognised these differences, for many years I bounced between the two. I still do.

When I wanted to get away for Christmas one year for a change, I booked onto a walking holiday in Mallorca. A few years later, I did it again but that time in mainland Spain. I raise this here because it's worth noting that on both occasions I did go off a few times to do my own things. I was still finding my feet in the wider world but a whole lot better and more confident than when on Kilimanjaro. My intention, when booking these holidays, was to have a break from the group to go exploring at my kind of level and if possible try for some of the loftier, more challenging mountains, but still within a day's walk of the accommodation. Interestingly on every single trip I did like that, there have been others who have wanted to come with me. Sometimes there could be just one taker and on one particularly gnarly adventure, on the holiday leader's day off, I led a party of eight. They would have learned of this breakaway, as I discussed my objective with the holiday representative or walk leader so that they could cover their backs with the parent company back in the UK if I got in to difficulties, along with being a logical safety precaution on my part. I don't usually have anyone to tell, so nor do I turn away such luxuries when they are available. The awkward bit is that I often change routes and plans as I go along, which makes that a bit of a nonsense.

Once my secret was out, it would travel around the group quite quickly because, unlike going to spend the day mooching around the villages and sitting in bars, my plans were audacious. Positively scary for some!

Here I will admit to another reason why I won't give up on adventure holidays completely. I harbour a vague notion that I might meet someone else, like Owen, who may want to share an adventurous trekking holiday with me. Someone who is perhaps trapped by their lack of experience or insecurity and needs company to take those steps into the more adventurous levels. The holiday companies, try as they may, will never be able to do this efficiently. They have no choice but to target their product to particular groups by grading their holidays. And all that can ever be is a very crude guide in a sales brochure.

The walking grades usually start with the 'easy' or 'moderate', both of which suit thousands of people but by that very definition both the adventurers and the thrill-seekers will be avoiding them because of those low grades. 'Easy. We don't do easy,' will be the reaction of both camps, but as soon as you move it up a notch, it starts to go wrong. The holiday companies also need to attract us more demanding customers so the 'adventurous' grade thus makes its appearance. A higher altitude is automatically deemed to provide their take on adventure for most people so if it's high, it must be hard, so to speak.

It has to be remembered that at the time they receive the holiday application forms the companies do not know their customers' capabilities at all. There is no test to pass and it relies on trusting the customers to know their own abilities when selecting their holiday, with a built-in safety factor in case they don't. It isn't that much of a worry for them because the difficulties actually remain minimal to any average hill-walking customer that will be looking for that kind of holiday. Naturally, if they can walk up a hill or two on their weekend walks, then they quite rightfully think that they are 'adventurous'. But in the real world of adventure, the vast majority of them aren't. The only risk that they have overcome was one of having to give up because it was physically too difficult for one reason or another and their holiday budget has been wasted. Technically, at that level, for the adventurous in the true sense of the word it is still easy with a very low risk factor.

'Challenging' is the next grade to appear in the scales of difficulty. The level of fitness remains at average. The challenge is nothing more than an element outside of the companies' control. Altitude sickness being a prime and possibly the only example of this. But the all too important factor that should never be overlooked is that under holiday company supervision and leadership, they aren't going to let you walk on a mountain trail that's life-threateningly dangerous without the added protection of ropes and harness. Nor will they let you cut your path through an avalanche-prone slope.

Unforeseen accidents can happen at any level but they are nothing to do with a challenge stated. If there is an uncertainty on a route because of weather or trail conditions, or indeed hostile locals, then you can almost guarantee that alternatives will be sought. The number of hours walked each day, or the ascent climbed, could be described as challenging but it isn't really. The walks are all described in the brochure and the customer can see what it entails before they have parted with a single penny and they should know their own capabilities. If not, and they still decide to go on booking the holiday, then that's down to stupidity again on their part and the real challenge is with the company that has to deal with it. So 'challenging' gets stuck in there to try and deter people too dumb to know what it means anyway so there is no way that they can get their money back for misrepresentation in the brochure.

A challenge could also be described as an invitation but that can only apply if there is a built-in plan for failure, as there was with my Kilimanjaro trip. If there is no backup plan, then what is the challenge? They don't leave you there, so it automatically shifts the challenge back to the organisation to resolve it and not the individual.

The thrill-seekers will buy in to a challenge without ever having been challenged in their lives because they can. You just fork out your wad and go with no questions asked. Those who can do the easy 'adventurous' grades with no difficulty may also want to move up. Once this relatively straightforward walk has been done, these folk can now say they have nailed a 'challenging' walk – without any input other than physically walk, step by step, one after another along a predetermined and tested route where the risks have to be minimised again to cater for the weakest members of the party. But it isn't challenging at all unless you happen to be that weakest link. It's still, for the Walkers with the big Ws, easy. For the adventure-seeker, it will have its rewards but they will be laced with disappointments. All around them will be constant callings for a journey into the unknown.

Having ticked off the 'challenging' so easily, it's only logical that some will want to move up to 'strenuous', where it all begins again. The thrill-seekers are getting their kick because they are going on something 'strenuous' with the probability of some fantastic views as a bonus, otherwise it would have no attraction to sell it. When they have achieved it and the adrenalin flows, they will be even more buoyed up because for the majority of them it will have been easy enough.

From my experience, they are not strenuous. Many of the participants couldn't undertake a strenuous walk by my definition, and wouldn't want to. Strenuous is strenuous and nothing less. Gut-busting, soul-searching slogs that test your resolve to the limit with no guarantee of fine reward. Adverse weather, difficult navigation, airy exposure, primitive camping and meals scraped together out of packets. Normal people don't want that. Why should they when adventure holidays can offer so much more, for so much less customer input, with their fantastic holiday deals.

There's no real solution to this in any commercially based adventure holiday because, while I find the grading a waste of time, not everyone is like me and sooner or later a divide will get crossed. They could even read this and go away thinking, 'He's nigh on bloody seventy and if he says they're easy, then they've gotta be a piece of cake for me.' Or it could be the opposite where in fact someone's 'moderate' will be another's 'strenuous' and the real troubles begin.

The holiday companies are not going to sell their product by listing the number of failures, injuries and deaths, so there can't be any. Nobody wants any. Not even me who gets irritated by hype and blurb in the sales pitch. But if you cut to the crux of the issue: imminent threat is the baseline from which adventure works. For paying customers it has to be removed, so the only alternative for a true adventurer, at any level, is to do what I do. That is to buy in to these kind of holidays, if the objectives suit me, because they provide a relaxing break from the real thing. If it turns up with someone who wants to share my trails for a while, that will be great. If not, it's no big deal. I will just carry on as

I did before. And moan a lot. Especially when I get blacklisted by any disgruntled companies that may read this – or for being too old!

Although I claim to be adventurous, that has to be viewed in the context of what I do. I went on an adventure holiday trip to Jordan and really enjoyed it but I wouldn't want to do that independently. The language difficulties wouldn't faze me too much, because I found that English was a very common language, but the politics of neighbouring countries and general unrest throughout the region most certainly would. I believe it's fair to say that my adventure spirit is limited to meeting the challenges of the natural world and not those created by people.

That Jordan trip also showed how my attitude to the surrounding wonders of places like Wadi Rhum and Petra differed from my companions'. I will milk these opportunities to the maximum because I'm very unlikely to be going back. Others will be content with what the sales brochure offers, where there are no unexpected surprises. An example of this came to light during our camping stay in Wadi Rhum.

We were spending the night in our five-star Bedouin camp, which is so far removed from the real thing that I can only shake my head in wonder. We had seen the genuine thing as we drove the length of that country. In the UK there are people, including some of those that I may have been travelling with in Jordan, who would call these ragtag collections of squalid camps that pop up by the UK derogatory term 'Travellers' – or in other words that undesirable element of our wonderful island that blights its beauty.

Our holiday Bedouin tents could be better described as sheds, but covered over with traditional looking, but fake camel-hair blankets that we associate with these nomadic tribes. They had all the comfort of a hotel bedroom with adjacent toilet block, complete with cubicles, showers and hot running water. A fixed base that the adventure holiday companies hire for short periods for their touring clients. Dozens of them scattered about the desert and accessed by 4X4 with the opportunity for short strolls around the best natural wonders along the way.

There's no light pollution that far out into in the desert country so I got up two hours before dawn to walk out into it to watch the night sky fade and the sun rising. There's no danger or even adventure as such. Just a willingness to sacrifice the warmth of the comfortable bed in exchange for the biting cold and a once in a lifetime moment. A truly wonderful, Lawrence of Arabia moment. Wadi Rhum waking up. I have to do it.

The tourist industry provides the bumf, the holiday company supplies the means but the best bits are always the ones I find for myself. Quite often, they come to nothing but the ones that do pay off make them all worthwhile. You don't know until you try it. Back in the villages, others can purchase postcards and paintings of the same thing and not see the need for the discomforts required for the first-hand experience, when down the road, a short drive away, Petra has so much more to offer with little effort or discomfort required. But I did detect a hint of envy in the gaze of one or two of them when it was learned what I had done before breakfast.

Perhaps surprisingly, another country that I'm finding unexpectedly difficult for its people-made obstacles is America. Not just for that clown Trump, or his circus, but because every time I start to think about trips and where I want to go, I get put off by the paperwork. The need for permits to walk in all the good places is made even more difficult by the bizarre way it's disorganised, each permit having to be applied for separately to whatever organisation it is that is controlling the issue of them for the place you wish to visit. Some have to be applied for in advance with no guarantee of issue and others you have to buy when you get there – but the quota of that day could already have been issued. None of which makes it any easier to formulate a vague itinerary for someone like me who must have a flexible plan.

Welcome to America. The land of the free, where you have to pay to walk. They started by hemming in the free-roaming natives on to reservations and now they would herd the tourists as they did with the cattle drives. Obviously this is not the case for anyone with an adventurer's spirit but to expend it on cheating such authorities isn't for me.

I still want to go to America again and will probably end up on an adventure holiday to avoid all that form-filling and mind-blowing bureaucracy, so that I can enter the Grand Canyon, witness Native Americans dancing in their village at night. Every night, it would seem. No wifi, I guess. Where was I? Oh right, day seven, wonder at the cruel beauty of Death Valley and dizzy heights of Mount Witney, experience John Wayne's taste of the wild west on a drive through Monument Valley in a coach. Not a tatty old, bone-shaking, arse-pounding stagecoach being dragged along by six horses throwing up clouds of dust to obscure the views, but an air-conditioned luxury cruiser with tinted windows and narrated commentary through my personalised earphones. Then I can finally relax and enjoy my two free days in Las Vegas!

It's true. Almost every adventure holiday in that area wants me to enjoy my free days in Las Vegas. Is it just me? Am I really the only adventurer or thrill-seeking person in the world who will refuse to go on any holiday that includes a free five minutes or more stay in one of the world's most gaudy eyesores? I can't even begin to see how companies can combine these two extremes into the same holiday.

I guess it's only me, or things would be different. It doesn't surprise me. After all, I have always been a bit odd. Apparently. So it must be time to address that solo issue.

Summit Talks 6

'When you walk through a storm, hold your head up high / And don't be afraid of the dark' – a hit record for Gerry and the Pacemakers in the early 1960s, from Rodgers & Hammerstein, *Carousel*

I walk alone

They are wrong. I have walked through some storms alone and I can tell you from tried and tested experience that holding your head up high is not only nigh on impossible but it doesn't work. Believe me, you'll have to do a damn sight more than that to get some company or help. So get your head tucked back in, drop the corny optimism and get your mind back on the job of staying safe.

Between those organised adventure holiday, I walked extensively alone. With a thousand peaks to climb, I had to if there was to be any chance of success. The odds of finding a companion to do them with was so remote that I couldn't even be bothered to look any further than on those holidays. It was solo or nothing and that is not a hard choice for anyone with an adventurous core spirit.

I have always thought that my reputation as a tough walker was unfounded, because I certainly never set out to earn such an accolade. I merely chased the dream. So what started off as a joke amongst friends was, as I get older, beginning to taunt me. Recently, when I had taken some friends on what I thought was going to be an easy 'social stroll' before dinner at the pub, it turned out to be rated as another of 'Geoff's walks' and was slotted in there alongside previous epics of theirs that are invariably raised whenever the subject of walking with me is being discussed. Yet the bottom line was that they had never been on a Geoff's walk.

Standing alone at yet another of life's crossroads as I approached seventy and found myself, yet again, drawn between art and adventure, I have given that reputation considerably more thought than usual and I came to the conclusion that, when looked at in the right context, it was unfounded. Most of what I do in the hills is done alone and, compared with those others out there who are doing exactly the same as me, then I am probably no more than a good average. However, I'm willing to admit, because of that solo aspect, that it has to be regarded as a hardy group of individuals. Those of any other persuasion simply wouldn't last long enough to be included. Don't forget, this is about wandering the mountains and rough country and not walking the dog through the beechwoods of Buckinghamshire. I would venture to say that for any kind of success at solo walking in the wilderness, then this applies more to the state of mind rather than any physical capabilities.

Think about it. It's not like getting lost in the rural fingers of southern cities where there are always well trodden paths, signposts and people to ask, but out in the wilds where even a short walk alone on an empty mountain or the wide expanse of upland moors could turn into Hell on Earth if you haven't got the head for such things.

Low cloud or fog, which is the same thing to me, is the main worry. That inability to see the safest and easiest options towards safety, I think I've grown used to it and may even be guilty of complacency as the years tick by because I can hold to my line with an accuracy that sometimes surprises me. The discomforts of rain become fairly normal to the veteran as well and always, no matter the conditions when setting off, I carry the gear to deal with it.

Cold is good but can get a bit scary, while heat remains a treat so rare in the upland UK that it hardly ever features in the plans. I've helped people to safety who in fairly clear weather have turned themselves around through a hundred and eighty degrees because of the strong winds that had been in their faces for too long. For a newcomer, for whatever reason, poor weather can be disconcerting enough while in the company of others, but imagine, if you will, that the person who took them up there in the first place had just died of a heart attack. They would have to be capable of both assessing the situation and formulating a plan of action before taking another step. If they can't do that, then they too could end up on the casualty list as well.

It would also be kind of stupid here to start speculating on the correct answer because the scenario presented is too vague, but the ability to strip it back to cold facts would apply to all, or you could end up running around like a headless chicken. When walking alone, that ability is developed over time to become an ongoing process with hardly a conscious thought. Get it right and none but you are any the wiser. Get it wrong and all those online experts have their fingers flying over the keyboard like bluebottles on the corpse.

Your thoughts must be allowed to wander where they will to fill the time but then have to be brought back to the task in an instant when navigation or safe progression demands it. There is nobody to remind you of this or to bounce those thoughts off so, if you can't exercise such control, then you too are in serious trouble. There are two levels that have to work together. While you ponder the universe, your survival instincts have to be constantly reading the land and weather while matching it with your capabilities and fatigue levels. All at the same time. For us blokes who are supposedly unable to multitask, I would just shorten it to 'staying alive' rather than trying to explain it any further. That instinct for survival is an incredibly powerful force of nature that will soon override the opinions of those amateur comedians with a stack of tired old jokes.

How you do it isn't important just so long as you do – otherwise you're running on luck alone. Unfortunately, while you may turn out to be very good at this, there's no one out there to let you know that you have in fact lost that control except one of my travel buddies…the Grim Reaper. He is always ready and waiting to weed you out when things go wrong. If you can't get your head around that as the status quo, then you might want to be looking for a different hobby. That's if your mind is still sound enough to recognise that a choice is needed. That robust sense of humour is useful whichever way you go.

I digress again, this time to explain my two constant travel buddies, this being necessary since I make the boast about being a loner. With the Grim Reaper, my other travel buddy is an oread. A mountain nymph that is always tempting me to go for another peak. These two go everywhere with me but not quite so openly when other mortals gather. I have grown very fond of my oread as I pursued this quest because, like me, I don't believe there is any real malice in her. Just a fun-loving temptress with a fondness for a drink or two who is happy to keep me company, at both supping the wine or walking, while the other guy is trying to remember where he left his scythe. A wonderful distraction when things are not working out as well they could be. Well, she is anyway. I grew up with flower fairies so, let's face it, without trying to be, you know, fairyist, they would be bit too soppy for the job required up there in the rough country. The oread has to be of the feisty persuasion or, like the wimp, she ain't gonna make it either. Mine has quite a famous cousin called Echo, who would endorse this if I shouted it in the right location. The Grim Reaper can be a bit of a bugger, though, always popping up unexpectedly to try and catch me out, but you can't really have one without the other.

Having established that solo mountaineering and the subsequent mind games are not for the faint-hearted, we still find all these seers and shamans telling their customers that a person seeking harmony with the rest of world should be going to these same high places. With some reluctance, I have to admit that I think it sort of works – except that I can't be bothered with words like karma and the practice of searching for one's self. I know where I am. It's all those other daft buggers who have the problem. For the likes of me, such gibberish is far too mystic to mix in there with the harsh realities of traversing over hostile terrain with a mountain nymph in a short frock who's walking barefoot on *verglas*. You need to be concentrating on practical things like whether or not to put on crampons and not have your mind chasing imaginary bluebirds around the pretty icicles; but when you get back down to homes and houses, I suppose that stuff might help you sort out the window cleaner whose ladder is putting holes in your lawn. I wouldn't know too much about that either, since those two buddies of mine have taken to coming home with me as well.

Somewhere, at a less memorable landmark in my life, I seem to have changed a little. This occurred to me during the deliberations about my reputation and I came to the conclusion that while the expert, Maslow, claims that we are motivated by needs, I feel that some of mine are being powered by a souped-up version. An undeniable passion. I don't simply like to walk in the mountains – I fret, plot and scheme for a way back to them if I can't. Even when out there, every summit has to be climbed and skyline walked – and once is never enough. At a pinch, any hill will do and I don't need to know why that is. The really sickening part of it is that I'm jealous of anyone's exploits that appear greater than mine. For me, this is enough to know that ultimately this is what separates the Walker from the walkers. I can lead but I can't be led. I may follow if it suits me but it won't be long before I am seeking the alternative that separates me from the norm. I can't change that and nor do I wish to.

There will probably be a few of those other experts waiting eagerly to tell me that I have indeed found myself but I can live without all that crap as well, because I don't know whether I am entirely content with what I've found. I know my perspectives have definitely been shifted but that may not necessarily be for the better. There are too many 'what ifs?' to be explored before I would dare to make sound conclusions on untested scenarios, but the mind games that I've had to play can be narrowed down to variations of these three core elements: fatigue, navigation and accidents. They hang like the sword of Damocles over every single trip as soon as I set out.

The loner needs logical thinking to sort these things out. Tantrums may release the pressure valve but require an audience, so they're of not much practical use. Next time you pass a grazing hill sheep, just take note of the complete indifference to your plight in their expression. The ravens pay more attention but I suspect they are wondering if there is any chance of eyeballs for supper. Making light of these things is easy for me but it wasn't until I sat down at the computer to try and write this piece that I found out how hard it is to relate the enormity of the task to those who haven't had to do it. After all, everybody faces problems and dangers as they deal with their daily lives. For example, car accidents and breakdowns; club brawls and street muggings; bills and no money; illness and missing relatives et cetera. We all have problems to resolve. That's life. So why do I keep harping on about it?

The only real difference to set me apart that I can see, is in fact the biggest one of all. I have to do it a lot. Alone and a long way from help and a safe refuge. Most importantly it can be avoided by staying at home, so I do it by free choice.

Could someone without such creative imagination and twisted sense of humour do the same as I with as much success? I'm not too sure on this but I don't think they would be the kind of person who would want to. I have to take it seriously but in company I hide it behind the humour and what may look like belittling the dangers to mask any uncertainty. I can't let the doubts show because they may be misread and taken as reason to question my abilities. Those same skills that I rely on to keep me safe when totally alone I get away with because I can appear to do this detachment thing, but the wholly serious person tends to intimidate the ordinary guys of this world. They are thus avoided or held in awe. So by default they too could become loners, yet how they could survive out their without that same creative imagination needed to make their own entertainment eludes me.

If travel in rough country and survival in the rough country are taken so seriously, the mind would constantly be on the task with no distractions being allowed to interfere. There would be no room left to manoeuvre and expand the thought process into whimsical fancies or deviating from a pre-planned route that had been left with a responsible third party in case of unforeseen misfortune – my Grim Reaper and oread being the perfect example of this. This person would deny such an existence because the scientific approach required to maintain an absolutely factual analysis of any given situation would have them deny anything that can't be wholly proved. Without those smouldering ashes of previous creativity, there are going to be no sparks to fly, chase and inspire us to take those steps beyond the accepted norm. So what's left for them to do other than follow in the steps of others, but with absolute accuracy. I will try to demonstrate this in a mountaineering context with the following.

The international sign for hailing a helicopter in your vicinity, if you need help, is to stand with your arms raised to form a Y shape. Posters and mountain safety books all tell us that. The majority of people on seeing it just nod and accept it for what it is. It is a fact. That is the procedure. How many people actually think about what it says? My mind leapt to the following the instant I read it.

If I could do that, I wouldn't need a helicopter. (And a cartoon quickly followed.)

You could say that I thought that as the lot of the loner, so it was automatic. Maybe it is but that's how I think all the time. I look for the hook on which to grab and find the entertainment. Sometimes, as perhaps in this case, the humour could be dark but it's there for some of us and perhaps will plant the seeds of thought on the subject in others. However, the unimaginative would have just accepted it for what it said.

One of my bosses once sized up my lack of enthusiasm for doing more work than my basic pay required as '…too easily distracted'. For which I am eternally grateful, because it confirmed that I wanted to see more in life than I did in work. That constant search process looking at things to see how they can be twisted into humour or an inspiration for a new adventure is essential, so without an active and creative imagination I can't see how that can happen. I might be too easily distracted for the comfort of some of you but nor do I want others to be distracting me from that distraction with their voiced concerns… If you can get what I mean.

At the end of any debate on the subject of solo walking, it remains my choice, so it ought not to be such a big deal that I feel inclined to write about it. However, I do think it has started to influence the way I deal with things back home. So to help explain myself and the eccentricity that surrounds the character, I will dabble just a little deeper because that's where I'm sure subtle changes have crept into my other life away from the hills.

The truth is that I can't survive such arduous demands unscathed. Like a veteran soldier, I carry the scars, both physical and psychological, into the lives of everyday people. Into a world where today, drama plays the biggest role. A world peppered by the fears of the scaremongers, plights of suffering in those least equipped to deal with it, insincerity and corruption amidst our politicians and the double standards of tycoons and big business. All, as Blue Mink once may have put it, glorified into one vast melting pot by a media bent on supremacy in the viewing figures. It's enough to drive any level-headed soul to the hills, where I have now lost touch with some of my ideals that brought me this far.

When at home where I can sink into my pit of humour and art as an alternative escape, I do find myself becoming more intolerant to the fads and foibles that go with the society that I keep running away from. Particularly if they start to follow me outside and into my rough country! The plague of signal-searchers and litter-droppers who blight every landmark are amongst the most annoying but sometimes it is a little less obvious. Try to place yourself in the following situation.

As I keep saying, I wander the mountains alone. Up there, I make decisions on navigation in fogs and bogs, negotiate pathless boulder fields and scree slopes, calculate the risks of crossing streams in spate, work out the potential fracture line of a cornice, and make all sorts of critical decisions to arrive safely back at the car park – where they think I need a sign to tell me that I shouldn't leave the valuables in my car on view! Although they do recommend that, if no one knows my plans, I leave a description of my route and times on the dashboard – so that the thieves, operating in that area, know roughly how long they have left to find them.

Now another sign, closer to home but still in the rough country, on a locked gate tells me that there is No Public Access. After I've climbed over it, a short while later, there is a reservoir and a sign which says No Swimming. Why? I shouldn't be there to read it, so what makes them think I will heed that warning when I ignored the first? On that kind of thinking I should put a sign inside my vehicle to tell the thieves, operating in that area, when they have got in that there is No Stealing. (On that subject, have you ever seen a sign 'Relax, thieves do not operate in this area'?)

I can laugh at it and poke fun at the stupidity of it all. We all do, but nobody takes it seriously because we already know it, and those who don't will not be bright enough to understand the warning. Why do we tolerate it? It serves no purpose and just makes the place untidy.

You shouldn't be surprised at how important these little things are to me in keeping my mind alive when on the dull bits of the walk. I usually choose such idiosyncrasies to explore but I could well be doing politics, storylines for novels, solving global warming. The subjects are infinite. One-sided arguments are so much more refreshing than any other kind and it's amazing just how wise you become when not being constantly interrupted by the trivial interjections of any opposition.

This is fairly typical of my rambling mind when walking alone but as there's so much time to fill, I shoot off into too many tangents for them to be of much use. Trying to remember it all is a nightmare of fragmented snippets and only very few of them come home with me.

Here's one that did, though. The place name and conditions were real but I genuinely forget the subject so I've put another in its place.

Imagine the frustrations if you have pondered all the pros and cons of the financial repercussions of staying or leaving the EU, following the Brexit vote, as you tackle Ptarmigan Ridge in thick cloud, but just as a sensible solution is being reached, your thoughts are needed on a critical navigation issue and by the time you get back – well, it has gone and Britain just plunges into a deeper crisis.

For me, there is nothing like a walk in the hills to escape from the aggravations that threaten to spoil my life and when I do get back down to home, the problems there appear a little easier to solve. I tend to ignore them.

They are unworthy when compared to a serious navigation situation on an icy and narrow route off from a ridge that had to be taken. It's a bit like trying to decide whether it's better to support the corner shop in the community for the weekly groceries or go to the supermarket for the massive saving – when your house is burning down. Except if we go down this road of comparison, then it has got to be remembered, due to the nature of what I do, that you will have to imagine that my house burnt down the week before as well…and could do it again tomorrow.

I don't think my political views have changed but others may think differently. My generalised view is that I just want everybody to be nice to and fair with each other without malice aforethought and mean it. That tends to give me a socialist leaning. Probably more so in the days of my work situation and as an active trade union representative, but now I have retired it gets a trifle confusing.

Up on those hills, alone, I become extremely right wing. Me first. Everything is me. Nothing else in the world matters but me. That is just until I get back – I hope. But I also know that I can get a little selfish in a group walk if my own agenda looks like becoming compromised. Does it end there? Overall, I would say that I don't think my outlook on life has changed that much, nor my politics, but my priorities most definitely have. Those hills are mine.

Nor do I believe that I have become drastically antisocial, but since retirement my chosen lifestyle has become a satellite that circles around the active social lives of my friends and family. Their gravitational pull is a pleasant diversion, but it lacks the same intensity of the wild country that will always unerringly pull me back on course. I may *want* to belong to a particular group or sector within the community but I don't *need* to as a matter of importance. I'm happy to go it alone, which messes up some of the other theories of Maslow's thesis on motivation but not enough to warrant inclusion here. (But it does need its waters muddied on another of my excursions.)

For the present, at least, I enjoy company on a take it or leave it basis. We are what we are. Friendships have to be based on that alone. If that isn't enough, then I will walk away because it's on those same terms that I will spend a fifteen-minute lunch with a total stranger on the side of a hill.

On one of those adventure holidays where I would go off and do my own thing and others wanted to join me, one such person and I struck up a friendship. We walked together for quite a while as I helped them get their Wainwrights. This meant that I was doing a lot of them again but that's no hardship if you love walking as I do.

For several months it worked fine but increasingly I found my judgement was being questioned by someone who wanted to travel with me. At times quite seriously and without foundation. I was helping because I was a friend and had been asked to, but I found that my route choices and decisions were being compared to a guidebook that someone else had written on doing the Wainwrights.

Guidebooks! What kind of nonsense are they? A classic contradiction in ideals that people will buy into without thinking it through properly. Going to the mountains to find an adventure but using a guidebook to do it – that, to me, is madness. It means all you are doing is following someone else's route in which most of the highlights are included to save you looking for yourself. Thrill-seeking at best. The joy of finding your own ways and chancing upon such jewels is all lost.

Conversely, and I will use Wainwright's guides to make my point, if you are an adventure-seeker and decide to write a guide to all the wonders that you have discovered, then all you are doing is inviting an invasion of thrill-seekers along to destroy their beauty. As has happened to too much of the Lake District that Wainwright so meticulously chronicled in his guides.

I have acquired a few guidebooks over the years and will admit to freely using them to find the car parking spaces, but these days even that's being replaced by Google Maps and Street View. They can be useful for when I'm working at this PC for checking place names because the information is condensed, but I can't see any other use for them.

I'll put up with quite a lot of aggravations down in the community to maintain a reasonably harmonious living but very little, particularly people, can interfere with my walking or art with immunity. I walked away from that friend when the guidebook route was chosen as the preferred option, rather than mine, and an argument loomed. I never look back. The friendships can continue if they want but not the walking companionship. I'll say it again: nobody messes with my walking or art. My loner status has earned its capital L from those who thought they could.

> When you walk solo, you are the weakest link and you cannot argue with that or you wouldn't be alone. So why do I still insist on doing so? – The Aimless Rambler

I suspect that I assume too much and that people must know what it's like for me out there because I do so much of it. It's too easy to forget that many, even close friends, have no real idea of what I do. I stick a few pictures on social media outlets now and again, but there are probably a dozen duller walks with no interesting pictures taken between them. They ask to walk with me because those photos do show that I go to many good places and I gear down a proposed walk with them to what I think is their level only to find they are struggling with it. Such is their frustration and suffering that they are unaware that I set the objectives to a lower level than I would consider normal before we had even put our boots on.

The 'Geoff's walk' isn't one of my walks. To elaborate on this, my local ramblers group were doing a walk around my home ground and seeing the proposed itinerary on their website I decided, because it was also near Christmas, to take up the open invitation to join them…only to find that, on the day, the leaders had decided to shorten it. They dropped the part of the walk that would take the group to the high ground (my ground) and we spent the day sodding about on the lower footpaths just to fill the time. A couple of days later, their original plan formed less than half of what I did on spontaneous whim of around twenty-five kilometres.

We have to go our separate ways and once back out there on my own, the rush I get is pure magic. The enormous sense of relief that comes with answering to no one but myself sweeps back over me like a comfort blanket to a toddler. It sounds absurd but I even find myself comparing it with a drug – where I walk with others purely for the massive hit that I'm going to get when they have gone.

The challenges are always calling and each one met asks me for another. And so the wheel turns and at some point a divide from hobby to absolute obsession was crossed. So what? It could be worse. I might have found the same rewards in fast cars and, when I got that wrong, I could have wiped out your family. As it is, I'm only a danger to myself and an aggravating menace to those who want to write the rules and guidebooks for mountain travel.

So, in conclusion, when measured against those who spend the majority of their lives concentrated around the social packages of family, friends and work, I do in fact find that I am a touch unusual – but not unique.

While in my league I may only be average, I'm safe in the knowledge that it's sitting comfortably in the premier division, while lower down the tables most of my walking friends and acquaintances are half-heartedly scrapping in the relegation zone. But to them, I suspect I am regarded as an extremist. A rather good one!

As for the Pacemakers' song, I expect it's been around a bit too long for me to start messing with the lyrics, but you never know. It could provide some amusement as I battle the next storm out in the rough country. When Rogers and Hammerstein wrote their lyrics, I have to assume that they were city folk who were unaware that the larks won't sing in the winter – stormy or otherwise? It's for courting, sex and marking out the new home and not for making us feel good about getting blown arse over tit and wet in the process.

As a footnote to the above, I think it's worthy of note that in today's constant state of media drama, that perspective has to be maintained. Early in 2016 when one of our recently named storms, possibly Gerty or Geraldine, was busy unleashing its worst, the radio traffic news was advising us not to take our cars out on unnecessary journeys. What is an unnecessary journey? 'Oh, it's pissing down. I think I'll go out for a spin.' Anyone who is going to do that is certainly not going to listen to a traffic warning. On the contrary, that could be the only trigger they needed to venture out.

Anyway, I was in Wales and, defying death by driving, I went on to undertake the unthinkable. I sallied forth into the storm-blasted wilds for no other reason than to try and summit six mountains. It was on that wild and wonderful day that I found myself thinking about Gerry and the Pacemakers cheerfully singing with their heads held high while the rain shorted out their electrics in a spectacular pyrotechnic display, the wind dashed their unheard words into oblivion and the larks buggered off to the south of France.

I got my six. It wasn't easy. It rarely is. More importantly, you should know that, as usual, I'm not the slightest bit interested in the opinions or judgement of others for my actions that day, but the reasoning why can be illustrated so clearly here. They were not there or I would have seen them. So they don't know. Nor could they be under the same circumstances. If they were there, then their presence alone would have altered the equation that I had to decide upon. I saw no one up on the hills that day. I don't blatantly ignore warnings but, like everything else on my trail through life, they are assessed for what they are, by my standards. Mine as judge, jury and executioner. So far so good.

I think I have always been a loner. I believe we all are but for some of us it's more important than for others. That need for self-sufficiency in any social structure that leaves others wary. The non-conformist. The oddball. Not a team player. On top of this, I have retained a fitness that isolates me further as adjectives like 'formidable' get added to conversations centred on my mountaineering prowess. Likewise with '...for his age' being added afterwards. Fortunately, when I was awarded an MBE this was all neatly packaged into eccentricity. None of this means that I am antisocial. Indeed, if it does, then I was awarded that medal for being an antisocial socialist!

Summit Talks 7

Why do people insist on telling me to be careful when I go out there alone? Am I really that eccentric that they think I'm prone to leaping about over these high places with gay abandon without such a reminder. Okay, so I may shake my fist at the occasional bolt of lightning, but I'm not daft – I wait until it's gone first.
– The Aimless Rambler

There has be a reckoning

As I see it there always has to be a reckoning. A time to step back and reflect upon what has been done and what there is left to do. There are three such reckonings for me…

The one at the end of each trip where ideas that transpired or lessons learnt are taken on board for further study (that is, a painting, equipment update et cetera). Indeed, I think it's safe to say that it also applies to each painting finished or piece written as well. I do it as an ongoing process.

An annual reckoning where the year is reviewed in terms of achievement and checking out the what has been done and is still left to do, with a view to perhaps see what can be done in the next twelve months.

Then the lifetime reckoning, which in my case could well be this book. That is the time upon which to reflect but with little opportunity left to do anything with it all. Was it worth all that effort? Did I do my bit to make something in this world a little better or easier to endure?

However, for me the most important reckoning is the annual one. This could well be a throwback habit from my civil service days where all staff had an annual review of our year's work, whereupon it was measured, graded and compared with colleagues. I didn't like it much and never took it too seriously because I wasn't that interested, but for my current lifestyle it works just fine.

For me, probably because of that loner element, Christmas is always a good time for an annual reckoning for a number of other reasons. Firstly perhaps it stemmed from being bought up with the custom of making New Year's resolutions. I didn't make too big a deal of it but was always conscious of that practice hanging over me and felt that, if nothing else, it served as a reminder to reboot the resolve into better things.

With regard to mountaineering, the back end of November and the whole of December can get a bit slack unless there is a good dump of snow. Not unlike the Ancient Mariner stuck in the doldrums, after shooting the albatross, looking for action because we are a bit tired of the wet grey days on the high ground and are waiting for an Arctic blast to transform it all into a whole new world. There are also the demands of Christmas, which epitomise the differences between those outdoor folk who will go for the real thing while those back indoors will spray snow from cans and hang tinsel to emulate glittering icicles. Whatever a person's religion or personal take on things, I feel that Christmas is always a good time to catch up with family and friends and as such it encourages that annual reckoning.

I am not altogether sure where I picked up the term 'a reckoning' from but it was probably a well used phrase in a book or film and has been with me a long time. It has that chunky quality about it that befits an active outdoor life. However, wherever it comes from, what it really needs is that first snow of that winter to make it work properly. A good dump of snow will reawaken weary spirits and will have the hardier mountain folk heading for the hills with renewed vigour… While at the same time the nation's media and gloom-watchers will concentrate on disruption and misery.

> There is nothing like snow to symbolise the time for a fresh start. It is like a clean sheet of paper to an artist or writer. The perfect opportunity to get things right this next time round.
> – The Aimless Rambler

A few weeks before one such Christmas there was a fall of snow in the area in which I live. Not too much for us up north but more than enough to make headline news anywhere south of Birmingham. Maybe an inch on the village pavements at the most. It had been messing about with sprinkles of it for several days, so the roads were already gritted and clear of any major traffic difficulties. With low cloud, it was a fairly typical monochrome hill country winter's day with the snow adding just enough to transform it to something mystic.

Although I don't make too much of Christmas because I live alone, I still think it's great for the kids and we do tend to be a bit nicer towards each other for a few weeks. On that day of aimless wandering, I went past one of the most popular and accessible local country parks that sits between the mass of urban sprawls on each side of the Pennines. On the entrance to the visitor centre's car park it told me that the Santa's Dash that had been planned for the next day had been postponed because of the adverse weather. Snow – Christmas – kids. It was perfect…yet they cancelled it.

That spray-snow and glitter has become the real thing for those that make these wimpish decisions. By taking such sad actions, they are teaching unwarranted fear for winter weather instead of respect for it. Their get-out clause being that our safety is their concern. That is rubbish. Safety is *our* concern – not theirs. It always has been and always will be. You just tell the people how it is, that the event is still on and then let them decide on whether to participate or not. Nor can they blame it on the EEC and its health and safety regulations because I have seen an Alpine infant school out walking in over a foot of snow for no other reason than they could. Whereas in the UK, there is a history of schools being closed at the mere threat of snow!

> We are all responsible for making our own decisions – even if that is deciding to leave all decision making to others.
> – The Aimless Rambler

Those safety laws are being misused by the scaremongers and gloom-watchers because they are afraid to stand up to that pathetic and pitiful minority who want to build mountains out of molehills.

The exact opposite to that over-caution applies to me and so many others. Snow demands that we get out and enjoy it and to that end we may even lean towards reckless and daring. No self-respecting adventurer or thrill-seeker could deny the call, and that would include their kids. To plan any kind of outdoor event in hill country in winter without anticipating snow as a possibility is already bad planning. We get so little of it in the UK that we must maximise upon the gift!

Heading for the hills that day, as I got further away from habitation, the footprints started to thin out and the tracks of the wildlife could be seen more clearly. Most of the creatures making them would have been more concerned for their next meal than anything else, which should also remind us of how fortunate we are that it's not just another day in the constant fight for survival. But instead I had that clean sheet and food enough at home for two weeks or more… So, like I said, it's a good time for the annual reckoning.

Inevitably in such conditions, I end up on the hills in the deeper snow because I am drawn ever onwards by such wild beauty and it is often dark when I finally turn for home. While I claim to be ordinary, that has to be put into the correct perspective. I am ordinary in terms of those who seek adventure. My kids would not have even been interested in a low-level Santa Dash around a lake road or car park because on such a day we would have been high up on the hills making the most of it. It's only when placed against those who are taught to be fearful of such conditions that we become extraordinary. That doesn't put us on an equal with someone who perhaps sets out to walk to the North Pole solo or climb the north face of the Eiger in winter but we are perhaps of the same mind set.

Using that cancelled Santa Dash as an example triggered my need to reassert my place outside of their society. I was thinking about it as I headed higher with only a vague notion of where I was going next. It was easy walking 4X4 farm tracks with no serious risk. At the last farm, where the angle of slopes steepened, the tractor tracks also ran out but it was nothing at all to be concerned about. I used to regularly commute home from work that way on the mountain bike and had done so in deeper snow than on that walk. After work in winter, that would always be in the dark as well. There was some ice under it from frozen puddles but it was easy to see where by the lie of the snow. A familiarity that comes with years of encounter and experience.

I got to a junction where I could turn one way for home or another to continue for higher ground and stopped to make some notes before a moment was forgotten. Fifteen minutes or so earlier, on the track before that last farm, a car had come up behind me and passed. I figured it was just some folk having fun in the snow until I rounded a curve and it was back in sight… stopped on the track next to another parked car in a gateway. What amused me was that I had witnessed, out there in the deserted snow-clad hills, a hurried and almost furtive exchange of some clothes and several trays of chicken eggs from one car to the other. Wow! Hardcore egg-dealers caught in the very act.

As I wrote about this and a few other notes that had occurred to me on my journey, another walker, on the same route as me, took my easy way home. That meant I couldn't go that way any more. I had been telling myself that I was an adventure-seeker because I chose such lonely routes as normal while others freaked out in towns and now someone else was already on my route. So I went the other way. The way that other normal walkers do not go – ever. Partly because, although it is a public footpath, there are no signs anywhere to indicate it is one as such. Possibly one in every couple of hundred who pass that junction may use it. That is usually me. If there is an easy way and a hard way, I would normally take the harder, although on that day I had been thinking about going home and would probably have gone the easy way had it not been for that walker spoiling my reverie.

The farmer's track that it starts with peters out after about ten minutes and a single unsigned path has to be found. It's not obvious if you're a stranger to the area, but I know it well. It was nothing more than a faint trod that climbed up a steep-sided clough amongst a maze of other sheep trods. The significant point I am trying to make here is that a slip there in those conditions, with the sub-zero temperatures for the night just starting, that might result in bad injury for any reason, could end up as a fatal one. Less than half an hour's walk from thousands of people.

The nature of the landscape takes away the mobile phone signal. It was almost dark, so there was certainly not going to be anyone who could see into the clough before the next day so the best hope would be the farmer bringing food up to the track end for the sheep, but again it was too late in the day for that. Half a mile or a hundred become equalised by the loss of mobility. The likelihood of being seen by others was as remote as being in the Scottish Highlands. I knew all that before I left the main route. In my view, it was nothing to fret about because I was not going to slip. It's a built-in self-protection system based on my safety being my concern. That adds the necessary caution and any such dangers are passed in a few minutes and normality soon returns. What it does do, though, is turn an ordinary walk into something just a little more adventurous.

There is one more obstacle on that route that has to be overcome which would put some people off from going that way, even on a summer's day, and that's the steps built into a drystone wall that has to be climbed. It's about five feet high and leans over a bit in the direction of the downhill slope – enough to imagine what would happen if it gave way as you ascend the overhanging side of it. I have been doing so for forty years so just add in the extra chance of a slip because of the snow and pulling the top stones off…which might be enough to bring it all down.

While both these two minor obstacles are almost insignificant in real terms, it is the possibility of an accident in such a location, and the time that would be needed for recovery, that make it worthy of respect – but not enough to go the easy way. But down in the valley the Santa Dash fun day had been cancelled whereas, by my reckoning, in truth kids would have loved that adventure with me. Once over the wall, I went on to visit a couple of regular summits and then walked the watershed back down to home in the dark.

The next day, the social media would be exchanging tales of arduous journeys into towns to Christmas socials and at the same time I was up in the hills with not one person having any idea that I had even left home that day. That's the difference. There are those who will chase the glitter of Christmas and may curse the weather that makes it an experience, while those like me will revel in the real thing and, but for relating it in something like this, it would all go unspoken of. The fantastic photos for the scrapbook are not obtained by staying indoors. If you want it, then you have to work for it. That is the inevitable result of the reckoning.

The next bit is a lot harder – and that's deciding what to do next. Not the little stuff at home but the bigger trips where the achievements are greater and thus more rewarding. The peak-bagging would normally fill the gaps between such trips abroad. Or so the theory would have it.

> The hardest part about climbing a Munro is the first three thousand feet. – The Aimless Rambler

I think keeping things in perspective is an important part of the reckoning.

As men have headaches and women have a migraine, then so will the media add drama and sensationalism to what many of us will take as normal. The white-out conditions that they will talk so freely about are not 'white-outs'. There's nothing to see in a white-out at all but white. That's it. Everything in every direction is white. The horizon has gone. The line between falling snow and settled snow has gone. Along with it has gone any angle of slope or sense of direction. There's no sky.

I have experienced it once and that was two thousand feet up and not on a slow crawl in traffic up the M6. I was lucky, because it only lasted about fifteen minutes – under such circumstances every step is a risk so it's better to wait it out. Against such dramatisation by the media and those who are suckered into that way of thinking, then someone like me will always look like an extremist but that's not the case. They have just lowered their own bar to the level of stupidity to gain effect. In a real white-out, you would not be able to see that car in front. You might not even be able to see a companion in any form other than a blur.

As I wander over the Pennines in the snowy darkness, there will be others coming down off of Munros or setting up an overnight bivouac in those very same conditions to catch the sunrise up high. None of us want to die but nor will we be fettered by these scaremongers.

That's the way of the reckoning and inevitably I will be criticised for making it sound too easy and that such irresponsibility could put others in danger should they set out to emulate my achievements, to which I remind you that I am self-taught. Do I care what they do? Not a bit of it. There are stupid people that think they can do this sort of thing without any experience, just as there are those that will jump into a fast car that they can't handle. I had to learn and those who would seek to follow should expect to being doing the same, because if it's worth doing, then it will not come easy. How they do it is up to them but they can't afford to get it wrong. Nature will weed out the unsuitable just as the Grim Reaper continues to monitor my progress more closely as I get older. And I'm happy with that. That is the way of the adventurer.

There's always a lot of press about the number of hours taken and the risks that the unpaid volunteers of the mountain rescue have to put in on call-outs. Particularly the controversial ones that will always make the press headlines. I have to be pragmatic about this. They are volunteers after all and are doing it because they want to. I, like the rest of the mountaineering community, am grateful for the service that provides but, given the nature of what I do, I have to work on the presumption that no one is coming out looking for me. This tends to make me less tolerant of those too wimpish or stupid to be out there and putting unwanted pressure on the emergency services. Partly because I don't want to be branded as 'inexperienced' amongst them.

I will make mistakes. There will always be accidents but by my reckoning I'm an experienced and competent adventurer. Would they think so? They certainly have to understand that there will always be people like me and I do wonder how many think the same way. I don't want to die out there but my current thinking is that I would prefer that to a lingering deterioration in a hospital or care home. If that happened, these rescue teams could well end up expending a lot of man hours searching and bringing me down but let it be said, I know I would do the same for them. There has to be a mutual respect.

I could never be a useful volunteer on any rescue team because I can't be bound by the formality, organisation and training. I would turn out to help anyone in difficulty on the hills but only as a spontaneous action.

That first winter walk in the snow reaffirms the bonds I have with my pursuits. I want nothing more than to be out there being tested by the white stuff. The sheet is clean and it's time to write the next chapter. And it's December with those on the radio expressing concern for the old and lonely this Christmas and the weather forecast is telling me to expect wintry showers. It's bewildering. Aren't all showers in winter wintry? Are we not lonely for the rest of the year? All the usual stuff that we all moan about but still take part in.

So when I get despondent, I would tell myself that, irrespective of where I was in achieving my one-thousand-mountain objective, I had already climbed a thousand. Long ago. Before I had ever started counting them at all. The target was a thousand different mountains but some I had climbed many times over. Snowdon sixteen times, Ben Nevis four, Scafel Pike ten, and so it goes with other peaks that are not so familiar names and are all over three thousand feet. Noble peaks, such as Beuchalie Etive Mor that I have summited four times – once in the dark to watch the sunrise over Rannoch Moor. Tryfan ten times. An Gearanach four times. Then there are some smaller but most worthy peaks, such as the Cobbler three times, the Yorkshire Three peaks at least eight times each and Kinder Scout well up in the double figures. Of those less worthy but closer to home, they will all have had hundreds of ascents each over the last forty odd years. (To keep the less worthy in context, these are the same hills that local walking groups are avoiding if the weather has turned bad but in the snow there will be the tracks made by people like me.)

With those multiple ascents by the end of 2016, I was closer to having ascended two thousand already, without even including many of the less worthy. By that same reckoning, I have nothing to prove but will always go on trying to do so. Yet as part of that reckoning there is the rest of my life that has to be considered. There is far more to it than just grinding my way up endless hills.

I would like a wider recognition for my art and I've always had a passion for writing. Neither of which will go anywhere without addressing the fear I have for rejection after the amount of work that I have to put into the two hobbies.

By my reckoning, time is slipping by too quickly.

Summit Talks 8

Too many demands on my time

By May of 2013, I was a well established peak-bagger. During that month, I logged Rest Dodd as my five-hundredth peak. Typically by 2016, when I was just over ninety per cent done, a confirmed loner, had left my mark that year on the *via ferrates* in the Dolomites, toured the Gran Combin in the Alps, shown some Americans how I go up mountains, I then went and completely lost interest in my UK one thousand.

I didn't mean it of course. I could never give up peak-bagging. I get too much of a buzz out of those last few steps to the top of any hill – no matter how many times I've been up it. These days, that could be put down to the fact that I can still get up them so easily when many of my generation are contemplating electric scooters with fitted shopping trolleys to go about their daily lives. (When I see groups of them, I'm reminded that they were most likely the mods and rockers of my teenage years – what about that for a reunion on Brighton's promenade!)

However, I would have done better to have kept my mouth shut and not told anyone of my intention to get them in the first place so that I was never under any outside pressure to complete them. In saying that, there was a method to my madness at the time. It was the same as when I gave up smoking. A couple of months before New Year's Eve, I told everyone that from when I woke up in 1975 I would no longer smoke. This was to help force the issue. By placing it in the public arena, it invites shame to failure because my commitment would then always be in doubt.

It was a bad comparison, though, because there could be no shame in climbing nine hundred and sixteen mountains. But the logic behind it was the same.

Baring unforeseen circumstances with my health, and measured on my form at that time, I could have got the last of them in less than a year, but I also reckoned I had another ten years left to do it if I took the aged seventy element out of it. Less than ten a year for a decade would see it done with the quiet panache of a stolid champion. That was too long, and panache was reserved for those with style and grace – not the mad artists and mountain men charging through the natural wonders of this bruised and battered Earth looking for new, but elusive, hope and inspiration.

'I only had eighty-four mountains left to climb.' I just loved the way I could say that. Not so many people will have climbed eighty-four mountains, including their repeats, and I was calmly adding 'only' to it and dismissing over nine hundred mountains that I had already done with casual indifference. Mind you, with the job done, being able to say, 'I have climbed a thousand mountains,' sounds a whole lot better. At the time, with the fire burning out, it was never going to be as easy as I hoped. Strangely, it wasn't the mountains that were getting me down, though. It was the driving I had to do to get to them.

I dislike driving and always have done. Although we drove on the farm, I didn't take my test or drive on the roads until I was in my mid-twenties, married and living in London. Until 1972, when I discovered on Kinder Scout that I was a walker, I had only walked to get from one place to another.

While courting Diane, we had lived seven miles apart and I would walk it in the small hours of the night but only because I had to. It wasn't a trial of any kind but I can't actually remember enjoying it either. I was happy to use public transport then and will still use it now where I can. With my old fogey bus pass, much of it is free, and the big reductions I get on the railways with a senior rail card make it a whole lot more enjoyable.

Just after being widowed for a short while, I tried to do without a car at all but UK public transport leaves a lot to be desired. The terrain that I wander is thinly populated so, when the public spending cuts for transport come, those routes are the most costly and with the least users to mount a defence, so that's where the axe first falls. I gave it up when I missed a bus by fifteen minutes after a day-long trek over the mountains, in the rain as usual, and had five hours to wait until the next. I walked some more and when I got home I bought a new motor. If that had been a sunny day, would I have been content to just sit there waiting and still be carless today? I doubt it, because if that hadn't triggered it, the next wet wait would. I was tired of being the eco-warrior and getting splashed by passing cars. I was old, for Christ's sake!

I cycled to work for over thirty years but as a family we always had a car of various sorts. Always cheap and second-hand but cycling suited the budget and my lifestyle, while the cars were saved for best.

During the last few years of my working life in Social Security, I used to go out to visit pensioners in their homes but without fail I walked or used public transport rather than driving to them. This was much to the annoyance of my boss, who was target-driven for his annual bonus and I put that at risk. I could barely achieve my five per day target, which was exactly the same as those who drove, with no hope of exceeding that base requirement, which was what was required to guarantee the bonus he felt he deserved.

One of the things that the whole management chain failed to grasp was that, along with my healthier way of life and greener politics, the difference between achieving my targets and exceeding them was only worth about two quid a week to me. The harder these managers could get us to work, the bigger the bonus they got. To make things worse, some MPs at that time were making more than my annual salary by fiddling their parliamentary expenses! The financial incentives at my level were so pitiful that they only reinforced my policy of working to live and not the other way round.

When that manager planned for me to go out with one of his best target achievers to see if I could find ways of improving, he expected me to go with them in their car because he couldn't ask them to walk as far as I did or use the buses. On that basis, I refused to be driven because any idiot but him could see that was where the time was being saved. That is absolutely true and material for that novel I'm never going to write.

All the worthy mountains left for my one thousand were over a two-hour drive away. That was each way! They always had been but there were more of them when I had started. All I had left were a few isolated peaks that had been omitted for one reason or another and to spend that amount of time driving for a day of bog-trotting to get one nondescript lump was losing its appeal.

I live in the hills and I could have ticked off most of that number required quite easily but then the Robin Hood's Picking Rods syndrome raises its head again. This shortage of worthy targets meant staying away camping or in a hotel to do them but if I was going to do that I wanted to go somewhere decent that I hadn't been before. In short, why would I want to spend a week in the Southern Uplands of Scotland when France has so much more to offer? It was illogical.

This perpetual state of indecision was ridiculous and had peaked in an alien setting. All my life I had been struggling to maintain a home and raise a family on a meagre income and it had dawned on me suddenly that a divide had been crossed. Now, the immediate concerns had been removed and, while not rich, I was able to live financially comfortably in my familiar and basic lifestyle. Hah! A comfortable lifestyle that would have me putting more clothes on before using the heating because that's what I would have to do in my tent up on the mountains. It was how I grew up on the farm. It was how all previous generations of working-class people had lived since time began. I still lived better than billions of others around the world and that tends to prick the social conscience.

I was spoilt for choices. An unfamiliar luxury that I found myself ill-equipped to handle. Rather than make bad choices, I was very slow to make any, while at the same time I was perfecting the art of making excuses. In my case, art itself was playing a big part in them. My art was calling louder than ever.

I didn't like driving but I did like painting pictures. I could walk the local hills from home and, since I lived alone, I could also paint at home and turn the house into a mess without repercussions, so those distant peaks of worthy status slipped just that little bit further away. Indeed, if I was on an arty roll, then everything else, including walking of any kind, could become a nuisance.

We have a family in-joke about the most frequently asked question by strangers we have met on the trail because it's variations of 'Is this the way to Scafel Pike?' (I was once asked twice in the same week! One of those was while on its neighbour Scafel. They had climbed the wrong mountain.) With my art, it isn't a question but a frequently made statement that shares the same fame for repetition. 'You have missed your way.'

> Art! Another art style that infuriates me is minimalism – anything bigger than a dot is, in essence, not minimalistic.
> – The Aimless Rambler

All my adult life I have been surrounded by people saying that my artwork deserved to be on public display. Like me, it speaks in a language for ordinary folk. Recognisable for what it is and not drowning in arty-farty excuses for making a mess or poor delivery. This does not just happen! It takes hours and hours of meticulous application for weeks on end to get the desired result.

What can irritate me more than I would normally like to admit is that, like every other genuinely mad artist, I go through all that same trauma and anxiety that traditionally goes with the job. I can go for months without painting or doodling a thing and then suddenly I have an idea and have to paint. Nor do I want to leave it once I have started it, in case I can't get back into the mood to continue upon return. And I'm not making that up to sound more arty! It's a real problem and there are any number of unfinished paintings around the house to prove it. I kid myself that it doesn't matter because it's just a hobby but it isn't. It's me. Just like going up mountains is me. It's what I do. Neither can be denied but will frequently clash in the demands for my time.

Whether I like it or not, and I don't, art and walking for achievement are both subjective. There's no scoring system to determine levels of success, yet both seek recognition from others. With my walking, I would prefer that to be as anything other than a 'novice' but with art it's the opposite. It has to be genius or nothing. I have achieved that with my friends and most of the ordinary people who have seen my pictures but I can't even dent the walls of the art establishment. This could be because the experts are more likely to tell the truth but that isn't exactly being honest on my part. I don't show it to them. I don't get on too well with experts because I am an ordinary guy living in the world of ordinary people. Arty experts are like sailors in that they talk in a language unknown to ordinary man. It seems to me that unless you are highly regarded as cool and innovative, by those critics' own standards, then comments always feel that they have an inclusive element of condescending insult built into them.

'I know my place' was a familiar catchphrase that dogged my footsteps. 'Keep your head down and you won't get hurt' was another. It may seem odd that a guy who would stand up to management and take them on for the benefit of others should have such misgivings but I was far safer doing that. It was for those others and not me. If you lose, you don't get hurt…well, not so much. Fighting for yourself is a wholly different kind of ballgame. In a peculiar way, the word 'hero' is beginning to emerge, albeit prefixed with 'working-class' to keep it down where it belongs.

Many years ago, I was persuaded by my colleagues to enter an art competition. I subsequently spent weeks painting a bird with as much lifelike detail as I could find, only to be beaten into second place by three shapes and colours. The experts' choice for the coveted first place glory was a canvas with the top half painted orange, the bottom blue, a red triangle in the middle, and that was called *Red Sail in the Sunset*. I could have knocked it up in minutes. We both, that's you and me, could draw it on our computers without any skill involved at all – if you don't count finding the programme and understanding what all those symbols are for…and…er, well, a few other things like technospeak.

Since then, there have been one or two other minor clashes with the professionals that have served to steer me away rather than become embroiled in endless debates. I may go my own way but I still crave that more formalised recognition of the establishment. Even if they aren't allowed to see it.

As with my walking, where I don't want to go into lengthy reasoning or explanations of the technicalities, I tend to rely on you to work my pictures out for yourself. If you want to know more about those bogs that I spend so much time crossing, then I would prefer it if you looked it up yourselves rather than leaving me to fill my pages with geology and botanical data. You don't need me to describe every footfall on every trail to work out that going up and down mountains is difficult. What I do in a day can be written in one sentence and I hope, as with my art, that you are filling the gaps with your own imagination.

With my art, I may give the odd hint but really I want you to take it or leave it for what it is. A light-hearted poke at life, with a leaning towards adventure. The longer you spend time searching it for hidden stories, then the more successful it is. If you can get more out of trying to understand Andy Warhol by staring blankly at his picture of repeated soup tins, then you are far too deep a person to be looking at my work. (Intellectual arsehole! Bugger off.)

Likewise, if you want to waste your time trying to speculate on why I do this, then you are wasting your time on that as well. There is nothing mystic or clever about it. It's just a picture aimed at providing entertainment to ordinary folk and hopefully telling them that if you stop looking at the lighter side of life, then you are on the slippery road to misery. We, those of us who are still laughing, will be going on without you. As with my mountains, I work exceedingly hard to achieve that objective.

One professional art teacher I met dismissed my work as illustration. That one hurt. Gustave Doré is considered both artist and illustrator. How do you tell the difference when he is the same person? But he's dead of course and that counts for a lot. So, really, does it matter? Does the work have to be categorised as anything but a picture before the general public can view it? Or are we deemed too thick to understand? All cavemen are artists by default. Celebrities such as John Lennon are also. Banksy, who does graffiti, is an artist and not an illustrator or vandal.

Then there is the Chinese artist, Ai Weiwei, who doesn't even want to be an artist but is still regarded as one. I use his own words that I once saw quoted in an article about his work to defend that statement. 'I spend most of my effort liberating myself from being an artist to become a real human being.' (This quote can be found with an internet search in an article called 'Enforced Disappearance' by Diane Solway, published 1 November 2011.) So why do we insist on making such a big thing of it when his displays are in town?

Where is that elusive divide now when I need it? The one I can't seem to find, let alone cross. As with adventurers and thrill-seekers, the worlds of artists and illustrators collide. It doesn't make my work unworthy but what gets me is the absolute rubbish that some of those artist produce which have made it into the public arena, followed up by the verbal diarrhoea that comes out of their mouths to match it. I would like to be able to walk away unscathed by their success but the reality of it all is that it pisses me off big-time. Why? Because so many of us ordinary people are saying the same thing: it's rubbish.

So what does it take to make something different from what others see as normal? How do we give it the edge that catches the eye and holds the interest for just that moment longer? Thinking outside the box is one way that is often used to describe it but I'm not convinced it can be taught. I think it's part of the genetics built into that person. They either have it or they don't.

I would go as far as saying that the tons of garbage that's being delivered today as art, and being praised by their cronies, is because these people don't have what it takes to produce something worthwhile. They build a bubble around themselves as a group for defence against the discerning criticism of Joe Bloggs, who recognises it as a pile of shite but has better things to do with his life than waste it arguing with folk who have the heads so far up their own arses that they can only talk crap. Some of these so desperately want to be an artist that they will use controversy to mask that complete and utter lack of talent and the skills necessary to deliver a quality product that someone with a thread of common sense would be willing to have on their wall. Then the wannabe art critic will come in on their side also because it would be seen as intellectually dumb to admit to their inability to recognise the concept of what is before them.

We should be stepping back and asking ourselves what we truly want, or are we, for the sake of appearances, buying what they want to sell us. Be honest. If it's enough to tick boxes like the thrill-seekers in my other world, then that's fine. There's nothing wrong with that if it suits you. If you want more than that, then you will be on a tougher and lonely road with a lot more disappointments along the way, but the rewards for success are immeasurable.

I have no more desire to see my work in the Tate than I have to stand on the summit of Everest. For success at either or both of those requires the help and support of the professionals who are reliant upon income derived from getting me there. No thanks. I will do it on my own.

The same can be said for adventure. There are so many people trying to make their living out of adventure in one way or another these days that it has all become the same. A kind of madness where the ordinary person is almost made to feel inadequate if they haven't achieved great and wonderful things to tick a never ending bucket list of boxes.

I don't care if you have climbed Everest once or ten times, because I'm more interested in the story of Earl Denman who tried to climb it in 1947 with Tenzing (who went on to summit with Hilary in 1953). Their attempt was audacious both in its simplicity and because it was illegal as the Chinese had clamped down on access to it from Tibet. (See *Alone to Everest* by Earl Denman. *Man of Everest*, the biography of Tenzing by James Ullman (1955), is another book that would not go amiss in any adventure-seeker's library.)

The most inspiring book of adventure in my meagre collection is *No Picnic On Mount Kenya* by Felice Benuzzi, the true story of three Italian prisoners during World War II who broke out of the camp that held them near Nairobi to try and climb Mount Kenya and then afterwards got back in again. As we relish the stories of the Brits' escape attempts from the likes of Colditz, these guys had made their own gear, such as crampons, in the camp, out of what they could find to climb a mountain. Not to get out and get back to Italy to carry on with the fight against us Tommies but simply to relieve the tedium and frustrations of interment. The British who held them detained were themselves so impressed with their achievement that a celebration party with friends was allowed before they were off to the mandatory punishment cells. Like Denman, they had not summited either but sometimes just trying has to be enough. Very few people outside of the climbing world will have heard of these guys, though, whereas everyone has heard of Edmund Hilary and Chris Bonnington because of their success.

Art is just the same. I would rather spend two months painting my picture how I want it and shove it to one side unseen and then start another just the same rather than be influenced by the success of the gravy train. Why should I think of the art establishment as anything special? Art is a communication process. I draw something to tell a story. The caveman was the same. He drew a rhinoceros to depict the beast for some reason; be that educational or spiritual, it doesn't matter because twenty-five thousand years later we can still identify what it is.

What does today's stuff tell us? Other than that those creating this meaningless junk are extremely clever, because they have found a way to insult our intelligence and get away with it, because the majority of us ordinary people have turned our backs on to it, while the gullible will fork out millions to finance it.

I have watched two guys in Jordan making a picture in a bottle with different-coloured sands being poured into it. They coaxed and teased it with wires and tilts to end up with what was quite clearly recognisable as a man on a camel. It takes them hours to do each one and they sell them for less than the average person in the UK would spend on their lunch. It's not art, though. No, it's tourist tat! But is it really? It has a recognisable story, it reminds the buyer of their holiday out there and it fits on the mantelpiece, so what more should we be asking of it to make the grade as art?

In the UK, the current household names for Art are all associated with the stuff that the majority of us can't be bothered with, but virtually unheard of there will be other artists equally accomplished as the great masters who will go unseen and unnoticed. My own cries for common sense to be returned will be dismissed, by those who can change things, as nothing more than unintelligent ranting. As with the professional element of adventure, I'm a threat to their income so how could I ever expect to be taken seriously with what I have written here? It could put them out of work if other people started listening to me.

Do I really want to go to Machu Picchu, where millions have gone before, to be herded like beasts to take the same 'unique' photos as everyone else or do I want something I can call my own? What purpose is being served by spending a lifetime of savings to put a household-named artist's work in my house. Do I really like it? Or am I really saying I like the ability to boast?

It's a tricky business and not very funny if your job depends on it, I suppose.

> I do not remember my dreams so how would I know if they are recurring for that dream analyst to sort out?
> – The Aimless Rambler

Nature can get arty and I have some wonderful memories of it to take with me to the afterlife…if it has a gallery for decent art instead of pictures of soup tins. I recently chanced upon some landscapes in an art gallery that caught my eye because they epitomised this failure of humans to do the same. They were supposed to be hills that I have often visited but I couldn't even recognise them for what they were as specific locations, even with place name titles to help me. Just a mess of colour that was supposed to capture the spirit of those hills. My lifetime in the hills, with an undeniable artistic bent, had never seen anything like it.

On the other hand, I have seen two Brochen Spectres, which is as good as winning the lottery, big-time, twice, with about the same odds, although I have never seen a painting of one. Nothing captures the magic of the mountains like those beauties for putting that modern take on depicting a landscape where it belongs, unless it is being on a summit peak as an island in a sea of golden cloud as the sun rises up through it. The Northern Lights are still on the bucket list, though.

Although I don't have a bucket list as such.

The bucket list that everyone and their brother have started to write, since the film of the same name, is not quite as profound as the Battered Box that they all have, but, for the most part, may not know it.

The latter is another little twist of mine that I am rather proud of. The bucket list being the list of things that you want to do before you kick the bucket and die has got a bit out of context nowadays because in the film Jack Nicholson and Morgan Freeman were terminally ill with limited time, whereas today it's written without a care in the world and probably without too much thought. (Now why I am suddenly thinking of those thrill-seekers again?) As you do get older, it perhaps has a little more meaning. Certainly, when I thought about the subject meaningfully, there wasn't a lot I could put on it other than to keep doing what I was already doing, wish for nothing that can be earned and making the most of what I had. And that which Fate delivers unexpectedly.

The following is a slightly edited version of an essay titled 'The Battered Box' published in a chapbook called *From Humble Beginnings*.

Rather than a wish list, the Battered Box is the memorabilia from the things one has already achieved and feel were something special.

It need not necessarily be an actual box but we all have something similar. For example, today's generations are more likely to store it all on their smartphone or computer. For all generations it could even just be personal memories kept in their heads but both of these examples have a distinct shortcoming. Your memories die with you and thus carry no measurable worth.

Meanwhile, that real Battered Box becomes as old and dusty as you are, as it gets shoved under the bed, possibly in the loft or on top of the wardrobe and may go for decades unlooked at. It's what we leave behind in it for others to rummage through in years to come because we don't want to be forgotten too easily. We need – well, some of us do – to feel that our lives have been worthwhile. Hopefully those who are poking about in there will be inspired by our memorabilia enough to push just a little harder in making their own bucket list and Battered Box contents come about as something extra special. That would make our own lives just that little more rewarding.

Apart from two or three photographs, the only thing I have of my father's is his penknife. It's enough to get me thinking about him and life on the farm for a few minutes. Besides all my drawings and paintings of the last fifty years, as a lightweight traveller, who normally has to carry everything in a rucksack, my memorabilia is mostly photographs. At least I thought that way until I realised that my home itself is another Battered Box as it is cluttered with the gear, like my father's knife, used on my travels that I am reluctant to part with for those same sentimental reasons. Tools for the task, as it were. I have my father-in-law's sailing logs and sextant for no other reason than their history. His history, that I only played a minuscule part in but find impossible to throw away. After that realisation I seem to have filled my box with even more treasures. Junk…as some would describe it. They wouldn't know me. I will pick up a feather, a stone or perhaps a conker to put in there with the rest to remind us that even the little things in life have importance and should never be taken for granted.

When I look into my box at what I have done, I realise why there is so little left on my own Bucket List. I have already done enough and the rest is just a bonus. Yet, and this is critical, if I ceased to chase the dreams and thus add a little more to the box, then life would simply become an existence. Therefore my fallback task since retirement was always to climb as many different peaks as I could, with the one thousand target being added soon after. As I have achieved that I am now going to need another. Finding it will be the hard part because it ought to be unique or twisted just enough to make it mine. Writing this book could well be it. Or that novel…

Amongst my proudest Battered Box trophies that helps separate me from the ordinary is my two-hundred mile cycle trip from home to Buckingham Palace to collect my MBE. It restored my credibility as the hardy endurance athlete while, at the same time, enhanced my refusal to accept convention in anything. I have this inner compulsion to apply that twist that personalises the objective. To make it my own.

One of my fondest memories of that particular trip, with an MBE to spark it, was my expenses. The civil service would have paid me twelve pence a mile but the computer was not programmed for anything more than ninety-nine miles in a day for a cyclist. They would have paid me the same expenses rate to do my pensioner visits instead of walking or using public transport. It would have made it quicker too… Alas they had enforced a dress code that would not allow it. Okay so it may have worked in London but not around the Pennines in the constant wet it doesn't. More material thus provided for that novel because I grew my hair very long and untidy solely to offset the professional dress requirement. To some of you that means that I can be a bit of an awkward sod when I choose to be, Yep. I can. The loner again.

At the time I wrote this I was thinking of going to Naples but to make it different I wanted to go by train and then to summit Vesuvius at night to see the night-lights reflecting on the bay and catch the sunrise in the morning. Most people would fly and do it from the Amalfi Coast which is far more tourist friendly than Napoli!

The train journey was easier than expected but the ascent of Vesuvius, even in daylight wasn't going to happen unless I was prepared to fork out a hundred euros for a guide and a geologist that I didn't want. I could see the highest point about a fifteen minute walk away, but you can't get beyond a section of the rim that is fenced in to prevent such adventures as mine without that guide, but notwithstanding that it gives you an idea of how I try to personalise my adventures. Thrill seekers go to the crater rim on the bus or specialised 4X4 on an off-road route, take some photos, buy some tat, and then rush down to see Pompeii and Herculaneum before catching the ferry to Capri. The adventure seeker wonders whether he can kill the rest of the day hiding in the scrub and bushes near the car park until everyone has gone down and then go for the summit.

We all want to consider ourselves as unique but some work harder at it than others. The Battered Box contains the evidence that those others will deliberate upon. After all has been said and done, in the final analysis, it is they, and not you, who will decide upon your merit.

I step out of the box so that I can make more room inside it.

I never did summit Vesuvius because after weighing it up I couldn't be bothered with waiting so long on the off-chance that the park guides would all go home. I suspected that there would be some kind of security left in place at night to protect the stalls from tasteless looters. Instead I got to see something that I thought was pretty good, if not much better.

The hotel owner, on hearing my tale at breakfast the next morning, suggested that if I wanted to see something volcanic I should go to Solfatara, about twenty kilometres out of the city. A couple of hours later, I was standing in a crater and looking at bubbling mud on the other side of a simple rope strung around the pool. I could duck under the rope and walk over to it and die – if I hadn't got the message about how dangerous it was from what I could see. A few hundred metres away I could scald all the flesh off my bones in the one hundred and sixty degrees of a steam vent that had no rope around it at all. Sulphur fumes spiralled up around a score of other lesser vents and red arsenic was collected there in abundance to have with my sandwiches. All for just seven euros.

Outside, on the way back to the station, were Roman ruins that England would die for but were overlooked because of nearby Pompeii, that had been glorified by Vesuvius. It didn't involve much walking or climbing but there was no supervision or tat shops. It was privately owned and did have a campsite worth staying on if you could live day and night with the smell. My kind of place. Am I overstating the dangers? Well, three people died there a couple of years later.

There was a considerable amount of walking and climbing on my initiation to *via ferrates* in the Dolomites a few weeks later. I wanted to give it a try, under instruction, to see whether I would fancy spending out for the extra kit to go my own way on such holidays in the future. Climbing these *via ferrates* was an excellent side trip to my normal mountaineering, with the addition of a stunning backdrop, but, to keep things in perspective, I have scrambled up similar stuff in the past without the luxury of a climbing harness protection.

Indeed I did that on the holiday to climb past one queue when I got detached from the back of our group when a good photo opportunity had presented itself. The exposure was greater than most of what I had done in the past and, to be fair, being novices we only used the climbs in the lower half of the grading system. Exposure isn't normally a problem for me because it doesn't take far to fall to do the damage so I'm always both respectful and practical, but that cold logic of a survival instinct says, 'The longer the drop, the longer you have to think about what it will be like before getting there.' That harness takes away that prospect. I was left undecided on taking that particular line of adventure any further. I think my trial may have prematurely ticked the box and would be difficult to find better. It has earned its place in one of my Battered Boxes.

The best part for me was seeing the remains of the preserved Great War tunnels and trenches where thousands of Austrian and Italian soldiers lived and died as they fought to control the routes and passes from the higher ground. Most of them wouldn't have wanted to be there, and we just go to play. On a sunny summer's day, it takes a very creative imagination, built on forty years of all-weather mountaineering, to even begin to understand just how horrific it must have been. Particularly in the winter when they tried to avalanche each other.

On adventure holidays, the instructors usually get at least one day off to do their own thing. And so it should be. They are at work, not on holiday. This, in the brochures, is called a free day and you usually have to fill it however you choose. There are often recommended trips to help so, when our guides took their day, the group followed the advice, hired bikes and cycled to the next town for a day of shopping and sitting in bars. That wasn't for me.

Bad weather deterred me from going up a big mountain that loomed over the town, so two of us walked sixteen kilometres, and climbed a thousand metres in ascent while doing so, to climb another peak on the border with Austria, and then walked back again. It rained most of the way.

We were the two oldest of that holiday contingent and didn't particularly get on with each other but it was the only chance for a true adventure where we could make it up as we went along. With hindsight again, I might as well have gone up the one on the doorstep because the altitude was little different and lightning is not bothered by borders. On the other hand, I had now been to Austria and another box ticked. About two metres of it, which was even less than my visit to Germany on the bikes!

Adventures don't have to be grand to be good. Lots of little ones, if that's all I can afford, will do the job just as well, providing I can maximise on every opportunity. The day after my Austria excursion, the *via ferrates* climbing was called off short because of rain and lightning. *Via ferrates* translates to the 'iron road'. It's made up of iron ladders and steel hawsers that could also be called *conduttore di alleggermento* (lightning conductor) so, while the group pottered about between bars and museums, I looked elsewhere for entertainment. There were still a couple of hours to kill before heading back to the hotel, so I took the opportunity to try and summit a nearby peak. The guides were okay with it and actually smiled when they told me that I might come a bit unstuck at the top.

I soon found out why! About a hundred feet from the summit height, the entire peak was surrounded with a maze of deep trenches from the war, too deep to simply climb in and out of. With those trenches and rocky buttresses to find my way through, I actually ran out of time and had to retire without bagging the peak. It was an excellent little adventure. I had no map and had gone up not knowing what to expect.

To make it even more memorable, on a level spur at the end of one trench that overlooked the valley below, where a howitzer would have been located, there were three simple wooden crosses made from original trench timbers and held together with barbed wire from the same era. Finding such a poignant memorial, when on your own, in what was once a battlefield, is so much more meaningful than standing with the crowds on Poppy Day or visiting the museum below me. Over sixty thousand soldiers had died around that peak. For nothing as it turned out.

Such diversions, coupled with those concerning my art and dislike for driving, severely hampered the peak-bagging. Nor did it end there. I had been to America for the autumn leaves in New England and come home bubbling with a new idea. During this leaf-peeping experience, the adventure holiday had taken us to New Hampshire, where I had discovered the NH48.

There are forty-eight mountains in New Hampshire that are over four thousand feet high and every one of them was walkable without any additional technical requirements or skills needed. Now that was a worthy challenge!

I had done three of them on that holiday and was contemplating all sorts of things but the bottom line was that I wanted to do them as one single, continuous, through hike. The record had been set at just over five days but I was only using that as a base measurement to work from. I figured that three out of a four-week holiday should be enough. It wasn't just the challenge but the vague association that I could make with the NHS that was begun in 1948 with which I shared my birthday. The NHS48 (S = Summits) for our seventieth year. It had a nice ring to it and also a possible underlying theme for The Trail of The Aimless Rambler if I did it. I had already bought the map.

I cooled off a bit as the weeks ticked by because I had only seen one tiny piece of the US and there was so much more of it out there. (And Trump arrived shortly after, which threw a damper on pretty much everything good in this world!) From it, though, my one thousand became my UK1000. The UK1000 did sound grand. And became another serious contender to replace *The Trail of The Aimless Rambler*. This gradually became the UKM, with a Roman numeral replacing the 1000 because it was easier for a number of technical reasons with writing this book but it also had a rather snazzy sound when spoken as U K M in a code-like jargon. Or 'uckem' if your mind works that way.

What all these distractions never ceased to remind me was the rapidly approaching three score years and ten, and so that too was added to my dilemma about what to do next. I shouldn't be waiting until I was seventy in case I didn't make it that far. Nor should I wait any longer to write the book. Time. There was never enough.

Which throws up another pet hate of mine. 'Relax and chill out.' For me that's an ill-thought out comment to throw my way because it's another contradiction. Relaxing, as most people would define it, is nothing but another term for time wasting. When I'm not walking, there are pictures to paint, birds to watch, tales to write. Doing nothing won't relax me. I become frustrated with inaction. I try to watch TV to unwind at the end of the day but only get wound up even more by the crap, so end up only watching BBC4 – which, being mostly documentaries, means that I can't relax because I'm still learning.

You would think that my love of nature and the rough country would have me perched on some dizzy height contemplating the wonders of the world and my place in it but it doesn't work like that. With no one to talk to, I'm doing it all the time as I go along. Standing still just makes you cold.

As for chilling out – I don't really know what that means for someone like me. If it's feeling good, then I can do that on a two-thousand-foot climb and knowing that I can do it without a break. A good chill out is packed ice and snow with visibility, in the blizzard, reduced to a few metres. Relax and you could die! A gin and tonic by the pool? Pass, but I'll slurp a glass of red to swill down the chilli while I pack my gear for the next trip, if that's close enough.

My life is quite hectic but, as with many of my age group, I'm in the habit of letting a small thing, such as a dentist appointment for a check-up, prevent me from doing anything else that day other than perhaps taking a long walk home afterwards. Once the appointment is made, I'm then reluctant to change it to fit something else such as a holiday. Similarly, if I'm going on a holiday, say on the Friday, I would only walk locally that week instead of going off to Wales or other more mountainous areas. Why this should be I have no real answer but towards the end of 2016 I was beginning to find it had become a bigger problem than I had imagined.

After I had returned from America and was so uncertain about what I was going to do next, I was making excuses not to go peak-bagging while I tried to sort it out. I still walked locally, pretty much on a daily basis, which interfered with my research for new projects, and that sent me out walking again to ease the frustrations. I'm fortunate in that respect because of the hills on my doorstep but, because they are so easy to get to, with some tough challenges if I choose to go after them, some head-shrinker will probably tell you that I'm using that as an escape from decision-making. (They would have to tell you that, because I wouldn't be asking and secondly I wouldn't be listening.)

Summit Talks 9

The winter of discontent

2016 was a very good year and was always going to be a hard one to follow but the annual reckoning was not helped by the complete lack of a following winter. I had three days of stupendous Munro-bagging in the perfect conditions of snow, bitter cold and glorious sunshine, and a brief covering on the high tops of the Pennines at New Year, but that was it. A poor winter for snow. On the Munros I was not alone, so there was little time for reflection. Although on day one we spotted a fog bow, which is supposed to be a rarer phenomenon than a Brochen Spectre. The Pennine trip was dampened slightly by the worry of whether I was going to get my car out from where I had parked it.

Other than peak-bagging, I was stuck for any positive ideas for the next year. I felt that I needed something different but couldn't come up with anything. Adventure holidays were always a good fallback but my disappointments with them meant I lacked the enthusiasm needed to pick one out that I might be able to live with. While swimming in circles in these seas of uncertainty, perhaps because I can't swim, three lifeboats were sent out to me.

The first was someone I'd met in the mountains who'd stayed in touch with who was sounding me out about hiring a guide with the intention of going for the Mont Blanc summit. I was interested but not too enthusiastically so. If I was forking out that kind of cash, I would have preferred to do the Matterhorn as it's a so much more pleasing mountain and a tougher challenge, but Mont Blanc was the highest in what I consider the old Europe of my schooldays. That would do it for me, so I said yes. That was to fizzle out, as do many ideas of such magnitude that get thrown my way, but it didn't matter too much because of the other two.

The second was to walk the Cape Wrath Trail (CWT) from Fort William to Cape Wrath with a friend, Dylan Whittingham. I had said yes about a year before when the idea was first floated for 2017 but I had forgotten about it until the reminder came. Was I still interested? Yes, I was.

The CWT is said be the toughest long-distance path in the UK. Largely because, by what's generally regarded as a path, there wasn't one for much of the route. Just a vague soggy line that picked its way through the remotest parts of the UK with very few opportunities for resupply, which meant carrying everything needed for lengthy periods to prearranged food-parcel pick-ups.

The third came completely unexpectedly out of the emails that I am bombarded with by the clothing and adventure holiday companies that I have used. Like the junk mail, most of it's trashed without a second glance but one had a headline that had caught my eye. 'Your last chance to enter the TGO17'. That is, The Great Outdoors Challenge (TGOC) for 2017.

The TGOC is a coast to coast walk across Scotland that I was aware of because it had been around for a long time. This was to be its thirty-eighth year. Without the email prompt, I certainly wouldn't have considered it but almost out of devilment I sent in an entry. I was, as an ageing and solo entry, actually shocked to have it accepted. I had expected rejection to add to my griefs and moans about the faults in today's adventure-seeking community and it was as if my bluff had been called. In my heart, I knew it wasn't for me because of my wild card temperament but it offered a rather nice finish to my UK1000 that was very tempting.

The TGOC wasn't a competition and the basic rules were fairly simple. There were twelve starting points on the west coast of Scotland to choose from and twelve finishing points on the east coast. You made your choice, picked your own route between the two and accommodation needs for your route and then you had two weeks in which to walk it before making your way to the main finishing post, by any means of transport that you chose, in Montrose. There you collected your T-shirt as job done. That meant I would be picking my own route. I liked that prospect. There are a lot of mountains between that combination of starts and finishes that I hadn't done.

Meanwhile, Dylan's CWT dates were seven weeks later so there was no overlapping to worry about. I had to go for TGOC and cold-shouldered my doubts throughout the planning.

My chosen start for the TGOC would be in Oban, and the finish in Stonehaven. They were selected for no other reason than it included the greatest number of my unclimbed peaks than on any other route. A few years earlier I had climbed fifty Munros in thirty days, so I could see no problems with knocking off a lot of peaks on my crossing. There were a possible twenty Munros for starters and about the same in Munro Tops before starting to count the smaller ones. Plan A for 2017 was that I was going to finish my UK1000 behind the TGOC so that I could kind of dismiss it in conversation, when asked, with a casual, 'Oh, I finished them when I walked across Scotland.' Absolutely perfect.

Of course I knew that I had to reduce the number of summits needed before starting because there weren't eighty-four on the route and I had to allow for fatigue and bad weather which could force me off my high-level routes. I had four months left to pick away at those eighty-four, aiming to get at least half of them.

From that moment it seemed that if it could go wrong, it did.

I couldn't even download the forms for plotting the route because they used Windows and I used a Mac. I don't care what the experts said, for us ordinary folk, those two computers would not talk to each other. I was slightly amused by an advert on TV at the time where a female mountain guide with her Windows tablet and detachable keyboard claimed she could not have climbed Everest seven times without it. She was right. I couldn't even cross Scotland with my Mac!

The route plan had to be limited to two pages but during the conversion it was four before I had even started. I went ahead because I assumed the return conversion process would take it back to the two. It didn't. In the end, after repeated computer frustrations, I did it from Claire's Windows PC. How the hell did we get to a position where we are so dependent upon computers even to get away from them!

Another document that wouldn't open on the Mac was some clarification on the basic blurb that went with the application. The rules and regulations.

> Is one of the T&Cs of the T&Cs knowing what a T&C is?
> – The Aimless Rambler

Being a bloke, I don't bother too much with that stuff but while at Claire's I had a change of heart as it was an event run by other people so I ought to comply instead of doing my usual thing. I retrieved it. Whereupon I discovered that I couldn't even start until 0900 but on my plan I had already walked twenty kilometres by that time and had stopped for breakfast at a café I had found using Google Maps Street View in the last village before heading for high ground. We also had to provide a foul weather alternative (FWA) route if our plan was going high and I found that within these rules and regulations my FWA was still too high! Another rewrite! Eventually, with my plans revised, it was duly sent off for vetting.

They described it as ambitious but, apart from some doubts about a route down some very steep ground on day two and a couple of river crossings if they were in spate, it was thought to be okay. After some more email exchanges to reassure them that I had no intention of killing myself, it was approved. (The hazardous route on day two was the same as the one used by the editor of the magazine that ran the event some thirty-odd years earlier. I had a copy of his account from where it had been included in a book about walking.) What is so frustrating, though, is that they had planted a seed of doubt and it had taken root. Was I expecting too much? Normally it wouldn't matter because I answered to nobody, but on that trip I would be.

The CWT didn't need any input from me. That was Dylan's trip based on his plans and timetable. That didn't mean I wasn't troubled by it. In fact, I was very concerned, because Dylan runs marathons in less than three hours. He had also completed at least one Iron Man competition. Not only that, but Dylan was also over twenty years younger than me. I was going to be the weakest link again. But hopefully I would still be trail-fit as a carry-over from the TGOC.

I have included these irritations here to emphasise that they are the very things that I run away from. Just an ordinary guy taking these things on alone. All in all, it was not a good winter and perhaps a precursor for what was to follow.

However, the year ended with a plan.

I'm not very good with rigid plans…

Intermission

Comfort Break

So far I have concentrated on the history of what I have done to build a picture of how I came to be this solitary guy wandering over the rough country trying to climb a thousand different peaks but have skimped on detail. In other words, an overview of how I, a less than perfect anti-hero, came to be climbing so many mountains.

This second part concentrates on how I use that history and experiences in the decision-making process when rigid plans start to go wrong. You already know that I have achieved the target which, as you may have expected, turned out to be a long way removed from a glorious, trumpet-blowing finale. While the events leading up to it were probably predictable for those experts, it does underline the fact that I am just an ordinary guy dealing with extraordinary circumstances.

The joys of being a loner will be fully unveiled. But first let's go to the loo for some light relief during the remainder of this intermission. It's a dirty business but someone has to do it.

> How come that now I live completely on my own I still feel compelled to put the toilet seat down at home? AND if blokes are so notorious for not washing their hands after a pee, then why should they be the ones who have to lift it in the first place? Leave it up for the health of the nation. – The Aimless Rambler

I have made few references to the somewhat primitive toilet arrangements that will be encountered sooner or later on journeys into the rough country. For far too many people, the facilities, or the lack thereof, can make or break a holiday and are thus worthy of a chapter of their own.

The common denominator of all the mishmash of class, creed, race and gender of all mankind is that, just like the rest of the animal species, the waste material from the fuels that keep us alive have to be dumped. I would then go on to say how one handles this subject in the rough country is a fairly good indication as to which camp they are from – that is, the adventurer or thrill-seeker – but I will leave you to make your own decision on that.

The French artist Henri de Toulouse-Lautrec, pronounced to-loos-la-trek, came from a wealthy background but was hardly able to walk because of a deformity. He plunged himself into his art and the darker side of Paris nightlife, for which he became quite famous and dead. While I come from a poor background and have enjoyed good health as I plunged myself into the mountains, which are another of nature's notoriously hostile, yet beautiful, environments, and I can turn my hand to producing a picture, I am neither dead nor famous. Perhaps this is because I spend my time squinting through clouds to try and find my way, rather than up the frocks of hookers. It would be interesting how we might each have turned out if our roles were to be reversed in another life.

'To loos la trek' – I cannot stop thinking of toilets in that way while travelling in the mountains, particularly abroad. To some, the anticipation of what horrors await can outweigh the holiday objective. What joys are there to challenge the novice! It's more interesting to me than that Paris nightlife.

Toilet jokes being the butt of so much British humour could lead you to believe that I too am now going down that road. Of course I am, but, as the saying goes, 'Many a true word is spoken in jest,' and out in the wild you will need that damn good sense of humour if you are going to get by without shame, disgust or skid marks in your unmentionables. A very sound tip for those new to the game would be – if you are squeamish, prudish or proud, then you would do well to stay at home and not come out and shit in our playground.

For reasons best known to those who want to make money out of crap, the toilet in the home has become the throne room of the English. The term 'throne room' goes back a lot further than I want to research, but it should suffice to say that we were using it with familiar regularity back at school in the late fifties and early sixties. However, since then, when it was just a quirky slang term for the room that was least talked about, it truly has become the Throne Room on which vast fortunes are now being spent. Leaving your soil is now a very big business.

Just stop for a moment and look at the amount of time and money being spent on advertising the toilet products designed to make your visit there that much more pleasurable. Now we can do it with the peace of mind that there is extra strong, double velvet, dimpled, super soft thickness and monogrammed tissue for wiping our bums; anti-bum-smells spray cans to destroy aromatic evidence of a job well done – some of which are on automatic timers or odour sensors; and a whole assortment of wildlife in the form of toilet ducks and chemical turtles to get under the rim and around the bends. We have upstairs toilets, downstairs toilets and en suite toilets. Some older houses still have outside toilets – until they get modernised into a potting shed. But that is far as it goes… In the public environment, they vary from appalling to expensive. You spend your silver to make your choices on spending your pennies.

In UK towns and villages, we can no longer count on finding a public toilet. I know this from years of experience. When I was working as a social security visiting officer, a considerable amount of my time each day was spent on planning my route around town to take advantage of available loos, as I was on foot. If taken short while on my round, irrespective of where the work should be taking me, even more time was wasted as the route had to be modified to try and find the nearest toilet. At least my colleagues using cars had the luxury of speed to resolve the latest challenge but trying to explain my disadvantage to the modern, target-driven, management systems was an even bigger waste of time because they only talked crap as well. Because we don't have plentiful public toilets any more, I had to find supermarkets, nip into pubs and find discreet places in parks to water the flowers. I was a civil servant and on work's time, so I revelled in the knowledge that all that nonsense was 'pissing away the taxpayer's money' being taken to its literal limit,

When we do have public toilets, you have to hope you have the correct coinage to gain access – which at the time of writing was thirty pence worth if you wanted to use the public loos on Manchester railway stations. Thirty pence to spend a penny. That is a rise of 720% since I was a kid. Telling someone that you're going to 'spend thirty pence' doesn't convey the same message, does it? In my day, that would have been six shillings, which does sound expensive, but can you imagine asking to borrow three florins to go for pee?

For the connoisseurs of the I-spy Rough Guide to Toilets, I have to recommend visiting mountain huts and refuges for a lesson in basics. There are rarely two facilities offering you the same challenges. For a start, they don't have the UK hang-ups about separate men's and ladies'. There is often only one. When there is one for each sex, you will usually find that the more urgent users are all cross-dressers anyway. Basically the toilets fit in to combinations of two groups. That is 'sitters' and 'squatters', which are then subdivided into those that lock and those that don't. 'Locks' tend to be subjective and, like gate fastenings on footpaths, some sad bugger like me is in danger of spending a lifetime studying them and producing a user's guide.

The problems of lockless doors that open inwards can depend upon whether it is a sitter or squatter. If it's the former, then you can sit back with your feet up against the door and read your paper – before you need to use it. You did remember to take some, didn't you? Remember, before setting off, the job is never finished until all the paperwork has been completed. With the squatter, it's not quite so easy because when you're off balance, with your kecks around your ankles and trying to keep them out of the line of fire, the last thing you want to be doing is trying to hold the door closed against desperate intruders. And desperate they will be, because nobody goes for pleasure. The mega problems for both sitters and squatters is when the lockless door opens outwards. In these toilets you are trying to hang on to flaky timber with your fingernails, tend to clothing, get your aim right, preserve your dignity and it's minus ten friggin' degrees out there and the wind just vacuumed your paper out from under the door!

Nobody enjoys such challenges but I would go as far to say that the adventurer is better suited to it. For them, it is just another hardship to overcome whereas the thrill-seeker does not do that kind of hardship so well. It may be par for that course but the complaints are more likely to come from that quarter – particularly if they have parted with a lot of dosh for their holiday.

I think this can be demonstrated on a TV programme that I happened to watch where a bunch of celebrities were climbing Kilimanjaro for charity. Not for them the queues and hum of the long-drops. A long-drop is a squatter. A deep hole is dug and then a shed with a hole in the floor is placed over it. When it's nearly full, they cover it over, dig another hole and move the shed. These celebrities had their own portable, chemical, toilet complete with a built-in flush system but there were expressions of distaste for that luxury amongst some of the more finicky participants. I did wonder what happened if they were caught out between camps. Was the toilet placed behind a tree or boulder for them, or was a loo tent put up around it? Okay, so they were raising money for charity and such softeners were deemed necessary by the producers to attract the cross-section of unsuitable people to make it entertaining, but in doing so it separates them further from us and with that, certainly for me, comes a reluctance to support them however noble the cause may be. There is no room for a 'them and us' system in any civilised society – even less on a mountain where only the basics can be provided.

The prudes and squeamish must get it into their heads that, however distasteful they may find the whole business, it goes with the territory so if they don't like it they shouldn't be there. They can't change it without spoiling it, because to meet their need would involve brick-built buildings, hot and cold running water, mains sewers and electricity. Which detracts from what the rest of us are going there for – that is, the wonders of the wilderness.

Number one on my list of loo oddities was a sitter, with lockable door, on a high mountain campsite in Corsica without a service road. Only backpackers use such sites and everything the management of it wished to provide has to be flown in by expensive helicopter or carried up by horses. The bolt for locking the door was on the outside. If it was bolted, the loo was vacant; if unbolted, it was being used. The bolt was on the outside so that the warden could ensure it was locked when not in use to stop his horse from nosing the door open and drinking out of the toilet bowel. Simple.

Part Two

Summit Talks 10

To keep the world in balance there is a yin and a yang, a left and right, a wrong and a right, a black and a white, et cetera. Many people believe this – me included. So if depression can be seen as an illness, then if I am overcome with happiness, in an all-equal world, should I be able to sign off work with it?
– The Aimless Rambler

On the dark side

I deliberately wrote the earlier chapter on walking alone a few years ago as an online blog in a fairly light-hearted, stand-alone piece, and then recently adapted it to fit in this book but, on both occasions, I omitted an important thread because it got a tad too personal for my liking. With the turn of events since that original drafting, I have had to review that omission because I think it's a vital component of my decision-making process.

I didn't incorporate changes in the previous chapter because it detracted too far out of the context I intended, with that mixture of light-hearted humour with a serious undertone, leaving you to imaging much of the latter from what you had gleaned from my previous ramblings. I even said that how you cope with the two mindsets needed to survive in the wild alone and the ability to jump from one to the other was essential but how you did it was up to you. I have now included my darker side because I realised that without it the true picture of how I'm able to walk alone with such confidence will never be complete.

It is currently out of kilter. How come I can claim to have always been a loner when I had such an active family life? To which the answer is unbelievably basic and matter of fact. I've been alone since I moved up north in 1975. I had severed all ties with my past and never wholly fitted into the new. I live in the divides.

From the moment Diane conceived Simon, she was ill with a wide assortment of quite serious afflictions and, having made that move north, I was thus isolated, in terms of immediate help, from the rest of the family, and what little I had in resource and wits was all that remained to hold us together. Other family help was never closer than half a day away and by that time I would have dealt with the worst of any situation.

During the next thirty years, Diane was hospitalised again and again for long spells with problematic pregnancies and other ailments requiring nine major operations before starting on any of the regular stuff. During which time I had to manage the home, job and kids. To complicate it further, she was epileptic and, perhaps as a consequence of all this tragedy and trauma, she suffered from mental health issues as well. Couple all that with lousy wages and my road was not one that could be travelled on sharp wit alone. The Yin and the Yang have to come into play. The unseen other face of the clown was my strength. The dark side.

I have said that when the going gets tough, I walk away. Well, as you may have gathered already, that happens in my head more than in my feet. My imagination will take me out of the crisis to anywhere away from the truth. An island retreat in the proverbial sea of troubles. There, I am all that there is. All that ever was and all that there ever will be. When I die, it's the rest of the world, not me, that will cease to exist, for I am the centre of it. If I'm the only thing that matters, then self-protection is paramount. I don't hide from the truth but have adopted a very pragmatic view of it from my parallel standpoint. One step detached, I will work it through, with a clearer head, starting from the worse case scenario and then looking how that can be improved from there. Pessimism to optimism rather than the delayed grief of the vice versa.

Cold. Brutal even, but that is how I operate. The walk or die philosophy being a case in point. What is the worst that can happen next? I must make what I can from the hand that Fate dealt. I can neither fold the cards nor leave the table but must play it out as best I can. There never has been anyone for me to fall back on and even if there were I would not allow it. To do so would be to lose faith in myself and that can never be, for I am all that I have. For the most part, the stakes are low but each hand won or lost is part of the learning curve. Preparing the players for the big ones to follow, as it were.

There were no conscious decisions involved in going down this road. It just happened that way as, like a ball in a bagatelle, I bounced from one crisis to another. It was outside my control and I could only react as I saw fit to any given situation. I could write pages of examples of this but the bottom line was that it all depended on me. For all intents and purposes, I stood alone as I cared for my family. So alone that for several of the later years when Diane's mental health issues came to the fore, she held me responsible for many of them. I was the hard-hearted bastard who never gave way to her cries for help.

She was right. I didn't. I can give anyone all the physical and practical help that they may need for recovery from a critical situation but I refuse to even acknowledge the existence of many of today's mental health problems on the basis that they are a luxury of selective escape from the harsh realities of life.

Primarily the most common of them all – depression. I can't yield to this because as an illness, in my hard world and all that matters to me, it cannot be. Depression is a state of mind and not the bloody sickness that so many would try to make me believe that it is today. We all get depressed at some time or another but some of us cope, we have to, while others seek to dump it on others. Instead of getting their act together, they allow themselves to slip into a pit of despondency waiting for salvation from the outside.

I have no time for any of that.

My world was made up of taking the action to do whatever life was demanding for the whole family and not the expectations of any individual. I padded this out with lively banter and bad jokes to hide any misgivings. Take it for what it is or leave. Your choice. Thus the image of a me as callous bastard could be confirmed.

Those who would call me as such have never walked in my shoes. They have no idea what they are talking about or the harm that they may do. If these people knew me, they wouldn't even think it. I stuck by my wife and never flinched. Not once did I ever consider deserting her or seek solace in the affections of another. I could not. I was the rock that had to hold firm for the rest of the family to cling to in the maelstrom of troubles that never offered respite. This was not just with Diane because I applied those same rules to everyone – and still do.

Although Diane had taken a different route from the rest of us, life went on. The only price that I demanded, and took full payment of, was that I would not allow any of it to change certain aspects of my outdoor life. The hills and mountains were my only physical refuge. My solid island to partner the imaginary one. Out there I had some semblance of control, for I am the mountain man.

None of it was easy for anyone involved. Whatever is read in minutes here, or elsewhere, doesn't begin to capture the living of it. It's all day – every day. Diane was not helped by the children, who were following in my footsteps. Sickly mother dependent on so many or a solid adventure-loving father? It wasn't a choice for them either. The gap grew wider as Diane reacted to what she saw as complete indifference to her plight on our part. The professionals could listen to her and sympathise but they couldn't change the facts or get my take on things. Interestingly, I was never asked for it and you can make of that what you will.

That indifference as she saw it, and as many others may too, is also what I call flatlining. That's levelling out the peaks and troughs to maintain an even level of emotion. When knocked down, I don't get wholly up because before very long I could be knocked back down again. Likewise, every low could see a rise to follow so I don't waste time wallowing in its misery. Don't react, but level it out instead, that is my code of practice and not just talk. Over the years, it was honed and hardened until, like my humour, it was my armour. My way of life. No ducking and diving for me but just a steady and unstoppable plod. Ever onwards.

If I'm wrong, then it's your next move, not mine. It's you who will have to adapt or move on because, for me, for every positive there has to be a negative to make the current flow. I have no intention of changing that attitude because that's right for me and can be seen throughout the natural world. To expect or even just to ask me to change is a betrayal of the self-reliance that I depend upon so much. It's the backbone of my strengths and I fear old age because of its inevitable decline. (And will fight that off too.) I can cope with most things but only on my terms – which doesn't include playing the mind games of the attention-seekers.

This can be summed up succinctly with the following adage: You can earn respect but demanding it will only buy you grief.

In Diane's case, I was proven to be right. I wouldn't wish to change a thing. Call it selfish if that helps you to understand but I really don't give a shit! Those who know me better gave me an MBE for proving to be the exact opposite of what the doubters of this outlook of mine may want to imagine. (Passive bullying they may try to call it.) I do what has to be done, if I can, and then I take to the hills. I always have and always will.

The Yin and the Yang. Does it work?

When Diane was diagnosed with terminal cancer, I went on, as always, flatlining. Always there. Always solid. Always coping. During those last few years, Diane came to recognise the true value of such inner strength and climbed out of her depressive state. She actually blossomed and was very much the Diane of her teenage years during that short period. The trust in me was regained.

Afterwards I was thanked for that unyielding fortitude by so many that for a brief moment I almost got visually emotional about it. The flatliner had hiccups and the clown quickly stepped up to cover for it.

Of course I feel emotions. I just don't let it get them the way of what has to be done.

So when you tell me you can't possibly go another step further, then you will have to be asking *yourself* why that is because I won't be – unless I can see that you are physically unable to do so. Walk or die.

Once I had been widowed, and the kids, being no longer children, had all moved out, I had become the loner that others could see for real. That took it for a slightly different twist. Now there really was just me. Nobody at all was dependent upon me any more. Financially or otherwise. In addition to a secure income, in my pension, I had good health and was absolutely free of responsibilities.

Free. Totally. One hundred per cent FREE. A phenomenon enjoyed by so few and I had been trained hard for it. A time-served apprenticeship far too valuable to be wasted on the unappreciative. Stretch the goodwill, as a few have done, and I really will walk away – and not just in my head.

In Mallorca, on one of those Christmas breaks, when the tour leader was having his day off, I went for one of the bigger peaks. Word of my intentions had spread and I ended up leading a party of eight onto it. The criteria were simple. I am not a qualified leader. You come in the knowledge that it will be harder than anything else you have done or will do on this holiday. This is my day so I will be going on, no matter what – so don't spoil it.

Sure enough, when we got to the trickier and hairy stuff that I had warned them about back at the hotel before we had set off, there was one who told me that they didn't think they would be able to cope. Then another said the same once the ice had been broken.

I told it how it was. 'Suit yourself. You know the way back.' That was it. Any one of the other six could pick up the pieces if they wanted to. That was up to them also, because I most certainly wasn't going to. This was my day and my mountain. I went on and all eight reached the top. If there had just been the two of us, my conscience would not allow me to be quite so hard. It would have been modified to, 'Okay, you wait here. I'll be back when I've done it.'

A nice little twist for me was that at the end they were all saying, even the doubters, that it was their best day of the holiday. I believe that is largely down to the uncertainty of an outcome when setting off. With the tour leader's walks, they all know it had been tried and tested on other holiday groups before them but on this one even their leader was on new ground. They didn't know if my navigational skills would match the strength of my walking, which was never in doubt. We had discussed the grading of the walks in holiday brochures at various times and as a matter of interest I asked them what they thought that walk should be graded at if it was in the itinerary.

Adventurous was the general consensus, but I would say it was that same uncertainty element that made it the best walk of the holiday. For me, 'exciting' is the word that would be better used to describe it under those circumstances. For us it was all new and untested so the word 'pioneering' can also be brought into the equation. It was an adventure. As for the difficulties, yep, you've got it, 'easy'.

There you have it. I don't play head games with anyone but myself, however bloody stormy it gets. Just because I haven't risen to another's panic, doesn't always mean what it may seem. I may be flatlining or I could be ignoring it as attention-seeking. Reading the difference becomes the problem – but the way I see it, that's not mine either.

On Mallorca, the problem for the doubters was a fairly steep and loose slope with no defined path, At worst, a bit of a slip and slide could happen and that can be addressed with thoughtful progression to suit the individual's own capabilities. It wasn't impossible because others had ascended it before us. It was the normal route of ascent and it was those thousands of feet before us that had loosened it all up the first place. If a person can't cope with that, then they shouldn't be there on my walk. Not one of the holiday's planned walks…but mine.

> This man or mouse thingy – it's only the mice that squeal about this as a matter of importance – The Aimless Rambler

And it's a man's world where I walk.

When the caveman's family were relying upon him to kill the next mammoth for food and shelter, he would be putting them all into hardship if he '…really couldn't go hunting today because she was having such a bad day'. If they want us to 'man up', then they, which may include you, can't expect us to be selective with it. You get what you pay for. No guarantees and certainly no refunds given.

This is why I get rattled with a lot of the attempts to equalise everything in the harsher environments as they would in the workplace. It takes a tough and gritty breed to take on such elements and it should go without saying that they will not suffer fools gladly. With that comes a crusty look upon the world where the newcomer has to adapt to suit them and not the other way round. If that individual isn't up to it and cries unfair, their case may win approval from those who would think they have the power to decide upon such things, but a fact of life says that nothing will ever change. The alleged offenders, because of their very nature, would simply exclude them as nothing more than another obstacle to overcome in their hardy lives and a thread of humour which could well become ridicule may ensue. The only equality demanded being – don't hand it out if you can't take it. If you don't like that either, then get out. You don't belong here.

This isn't gender-specific but delivered in the everyday language of ordinary people. I was desperately trying to word this in a way that avoids saying that a man's world is only for men but that is our language. It is only a man's world when we talk of the strength in mind and body required to endure hardship but by that token it means that the person has to man up to have any hope of being a successful part of it. That means the ability to ride the rough with the smooth alone. Just as there may be bitter cold meltwater in a river to cross, and balmy days off sun-kissed slopes with wonderful views, then there will be people. Some you can get on with and others you can't but you can no more expect to change them in that brief encounter than you can with the land that you just crossed.

You deal with it all in exactly the same way and that's on your own without third-party support. In the idealised, civilised world, they may say that you shouldn't have to but this is the rough country where that person has gone to seek an adventure. Only the laws of nature apply to such conditions. Would they tame the land as well? Yeah, such people would if they could. Thrill-seekers.

Before long, it all comes down to the basic law of life itself: the survival of the fittest. It applies in every social structure on earth because, no matter what attempts are made to equalise it, the fittest will find a way to rise above it. The weakest will perish first. They always have and always will and you won't be hearing the rich shout 'unfair' because they trod on a few less fortunates on their way up.

Fortunately, the loner doesn't have to bother about any of it. There are no rules other than their own but whatever their gender, race or creed, the fact that they can and do stand alone makes them all men. When the rest of the world is still trying to decide which toilet to use, they will have already pissed behind the tree and moved on.

Unlike the gregarious, they move to the outer circles of the herd. More noticeably so as they get older. The security once offered by the herding instincts has gone and out there they are more vulnerable to the predators and nature's worst elements. Some will stare ever hopefully back looking for a way to return to the herd, while others, once clear of the throng, will see the distant and empty horizons and say, 'Bugger that lot for a game of conkers. I'm off.'

In the case of either of these two outlooks, there is actually nothing left to lose. In the centre of that herd will be the richest and most privileged, while the protective wall of those seeking that heart will be forever circling around bitching and squabbling with each other to gain an advantage – or shouting unfair if they lose out. Yet all they are doing is strengthening the security of those in the middle. The ones in there who live longer because they can afford the very best in everything from food to healthcare. Nor is there any Shangri-La left for the disillusioned to escape to. If there ever had been one, that lot would already have found and destroyed it with package deal holidays.

But like I said, successfully wandering the outer fringes of these herds is a man's world. Not only is the terrain a lot rougher but, because you are the loner and are comfortable in such conditions, you could be deemed a threat. After all, who in their right mind would chose to live like that?

Okay, so that reads all a bit fanciful, the rambling mind of the solo mountaineer, but strip it right back and see if you can find anything different. I'm damned if I can.

That is my dark side.

Another of my fond memories was at the end of a hard day pub crawling, linked by off-road biking on the high tops to celebrate a friend's fiftieth birthday, there were eighteen of us in the back-room bar of a moorland pub. We were enjoying a meal and a lot more drinking, as any group of hardy men will do, before retiring for the night to a barn accommodation that we had hired.

Amidst all the banter and noise, a woman appeared in the doorway. She had guts, I will give her that, but it was a pity she didn't have the brains to go with it since she pointed out that, while we were clearly celebrating an important occasion, her and her friend were offended by some of the content of our revelry.

'So a shag's out of the question then?' was the fastest and most memorable reply.

She had been offended and felt she had to do something about it, but to expect anything different from a bunch of inebriated, hardcore adventure-seekers was an act of gross stupidity. These things happen in life. It doesn't make it right but nor does it make us wrong. Although I know morally that she had the right to voice her objections, she was very wrong for trying to do so in that environment. We were the majority and too far into alcohol to get a sensible response from. I wouldn't mind betting that had she asked if they could join us instead of complaining, the language and content would have been toned down automatically because we were just ordinary guys anyway. Fifty-year-old office workers, schoolteachers, a gas-fitter, a gardener and at least one shirt and tie engineer who travelled the world with his job.

I had to include all the foregoing because it perhaps gives an insight to my behaviour under duress. The bottom line is brutally simple. Man up or get out. In other words, you will walk or you may die.

It's your move, I believe.

Summit Talks 11

What's a foot?

By 2 January 2017, I had reduced by one the number of mountains needed to leave the TGOC with a realistic target to obtain. But not the one I had set out to do. No surprises there then. I'd left my friends after our New Year celebrations in the Lake District with the intention of doing Great Shunner Fell in the Pennines on my way home. There was too much snow on the higher roads crossing the Pennines to guarantee getting to the start by car so, unbeknownst to them, I abandoned it and went for Nine Standings Rigg instead. That's what I'm prone to do and that's why I should stay well away from the plans and good practices of others.

Although I may not have known it at the time, something about leopards not changing their spots was being written by my tracks in the snow up there. I didn't change my spots but I did try to change my boots.

Whether it's the TGOC, Dylan's CWT or any other backpacking trip, the biggest killer of our dreams isn't the heights or distance but the weight on our backs. As I got older, that was becoming ever more important.

It first became a problem for me a few years earlier on the GR221 across the mountains along the top of Mallorca in late winter. I normally backpack and camp these days because without my friend Owen, with his language skills to make the phone calls and book accommodation ahead, it doesn't get done. I simply don't have the courage or patience to do it. What makes this an even more absurd idiosyncrasy is that they nearly all speak English. It's an irrational fear that I overcome by knocking on doors when I get there, with the backup of a tent if they are full.

The GR221, unless it has changed significantly, isn't a through trail that I would recommend for a number of reasons but I will stick to those that contributed to my first ever foot problems other than athlete's foot.

The first of those is that wild camping in any Spanish territory is not allowed so, if that's your intention, how far you may have to walk is determined by where you can do so without being seen – if you are to abide by the rules of rule-breaking, that is. That out-of-sight camping is normal practice for me anyway but Mallorca proved more difficult than I had anticipated because, even though mountainous, the villas of the rich, and thus influential, residents spread all over them in the quest to distance themselves from the peasants and the heaving tourist beaches far below. This meant in real terms that, while waiting for dark and searching for secluded spots, I walked huge distances.

The second reason is those residents. They have no respect for the rights of way across their land. If they want to close a recognised route, they just do it. With no consultation or offered diversion, they will throw up barriers to block our way.

On the second day of my walk, I was forced down off the mountains because one of these landowners had blocked the path. I had known about this before starting off so had allowed for it and prepared myself for a long road walk. The battle with that landowner had been going on for some time and walkers were being asked by the authorities not to sneak away round the barricaded path so that negotiations to reopen it would not be hampered. It was late in the afternoon when I had arrived in the area which meant, because of the more built-up areas of the low-level diversion, there were absolutely no suitable places to hide a wild camp. It was well into the night before I found somewhere to get a couple of hours' sleep and my aching feet kept waking me up.

I was gone from there before daylight and back up over the high tops again before breakfast. My early start backfired because I was hoping to stay at a hostel in the next town where the GR221 descended to cross a valley. The hostel was full and there was nowhere to camp. I had to go on. Again, it was late into the night before I could find somewhere to sleep. It wasn't a big enough spot for a tent. Too tired to go much further, I decided to bivouac on a narrow ledge that I had found on the start of the wooded climb to the next high ground. I could see the lights of houses not far away through the trees. I got into my sleeping bag, wrapped the tent's flysheet around it to keep the dirt out and used my rucksack for a pillow.

I lay awake for quite some time with a repeat of the previous night's aching feet but I had walked three very long days on roads and hard-packed trails. When I finally dozed off, I was soon woken again by voices and I could see a torch beam flicking about as two people came down the wooded path. My planned excuse if someone was to discover my impromptu camp and took exception to the law-breaking would be that I was not camping, just sleeping. I need not have worried, as it was a courting couple who didn't even see me. I just hoped they wouldn't stop for other reasons. It was almost impossible to get back off to sleep with the constant dull ache in the soles of my feet. For hours, all I could do was try to ignore it and recapture the sleep. I did eventually get an hour or so and when I set off again there was not so much as a twinge from either of them.

Late in the afternoon, I approached another area where the landowners had blocked the route but again I knew about it in advance. I followed the recommended detour but soon after I found that too was blocked by a very big and new-looking wall. I should have climbed over it but I didn't want to spoil any talks, so retreated again and followed the road to the next town adding about three hours to my journey.

As I passed through the town, the shops were all closing up but an outdoor suppliers reopened the door so that I could get some more dehydrated foodstuffs. During that brief exchange, I mentioned the wall. They got maps out and asked me to both show my route and describe it as precisely as I could. I believed that I had followed the diversion exactly as detailed by the website before leaving the UK and they agreed I had. The wall was another new obstruction.

It was dark when I set off again, heading for high ground. I walked for over an hour along cobbled paths zigzagging up through terraces of walled allotment gardens that climbed like the steps of mountain paddy fields. I eventually bivouacked again. This time it was in one of those allotments near the top that the moonlight showed me wasn't being maintained.

I dozed fitfully but spent most of the night with my feet screaming in protest again. I moved on in the early hours, again with no feet or angry farmer problems. I took it easy that day because I was so far in front of my proposed itinerary and, around midday, back up in the higher mountains, I found a sheltered and secluded spot and slept the rest of the day away with just one or two complaints from my feet.

As I waited for the last of the daylight to pass so that I could put up my tent, I worked it out that I could finish the GR221 with a determined effort the next day. Less than half of the recommended time!

I knew the hotel that I had spent my first night in on my arrival on the island had vacancies because they had told me if I finished early I could stay there. I worked it out that if I walked through the night I would finish by midday and that would give me time enough to get back to the hotel, across the island, on public transport. The glorious moon of the previous night made that a very doable prospect if the clouds stayed away and allowed it to repeat its showing.

It did. The thrill-seekers would die, but not work, for such a night as that. It was pure adventure. Me, alone on unknown mountains, in glorious moonlight picking my way through the rocks and shadows. For the first time since starting off, there were no villas or houses of any kind and I could have camped anywhere. Although it was overlooked by the huge military base that occupied the entire top of the island's highest peak, Puig Major, and I imagined them watching me through night-vision optics and playing war games. It had me thinking that the no wild camping rules and blocked access could be overcome by walking at night and sleeping by day as I had done. It appealed to my sideways thinking.

I felt a kindred spirit with the feral goats that checked me out as I passed. Apparently, according to that shop I had called into, these creatures were the reason for the landowners denying us access. They liked to hunt them as 'big game'.

The downside of this night walking so high that early in the year was that it was bitterly cold and as I started the descent I realised I was going to lose the moon so tried to bivouac on a grassy patch too small for the tent. Protesting feet and the cold said otherwise. I continued down carefully for a couple more hours until I reached the complete and utter darkness of a wood. Using my torch, I found a leafy hollow and made another bivouac but this time covered it all with a generous helping of leaves. (With probable creepy crawlies that were hopefully too cold to operate.) I didn't wake up until a warm and sunny late morning, when I heard voices of people walking close by.

My chances of finishing the GR221 that day were blown because of that lie-in. It was still twenty kilometres to the end and there was just not enough day left to do it and then get back across the island. However, I knew there was both an official campsite and a hostel not far away. It was worth a try.

A couple of hours later, I checked in to the hostel. It was so cheap and in an area still rural enough to offer much better prospects for days out than the hotel in the city had so I stayed for the rest of my holiday. I walked each day, and at night my feet let me know of their disapproval of such action.

The hostel had free wifi so I used it to find out what was wrong with my feet. Contacting my friend Simon (Five Countries Five Days), who runs a specialist mountain footwear shop (Mountainfeet) with podiatrist support, by email we established that I was suffering with *plantar fasciitis*. He advised me to see a doctor when I got back and if they confirmed his diagnosis to go and see him to sort it out. He had been spot-on, which strikes up one for modern technology and another for his expertise.

Among the things that can trigger this off is age, as the support in the feet begins to weaken. Overweight can be another cause. I had both. The latter being that rucksack on my back, aggravated by those huge distances that I had been walking while carrying it. With Simon's help, we sorted it out with specialised insteps for the boots. I have used them ever since when out walking in the rough country, be that day walks or multi-day treks, and very rarely has there been any recurrence of those sleepless nights of the GR221.

However, it is something I'm very aware of now and include it my decision making. Despite all my mountain activity, I'm not the skinny rake that you may expect. I do put weight on quite easily and will lose it again just as quickly on the multi-day walks where the calories burnt exceed the daily input. What's so annoying is that none of it comes off the stomach until every last microgram has been stripped off the rest of the body. I sometimes think my hair and nails would fall out before that will ever happen.

To make it even more frustrating, they just don't make men's trousers with large waist and short legs. I either end up with my eyes popping out or treading on the surplus at the bottom of the legs. At the price we have to pay for a decent pair, there is something almost sacrilegious about taking scissors to them because my household and domestic skills don't include turning a hem…or ironing…

The weight in that rucksack concerns me a lot more and over the years I have whittled it down wherever I can and have pretty well bottomed out with some of the best specialist lightweight gear on the market. I needed to if I was going to go peak-bagging on my two-hundred-and-fifty-kilometre trek across Scotland. I had to be fast and light and to that end I looked at my clothing as well, including the footwear.

The boots were mothballed while I trialled a pair of lightweight trainers that cross-country and fell-runners used. They worked fine and

I use them regularly in all conditions – except snow and ice, because we didn't have any that winter. Although it has to be said I didn't wear them the one time I should have.

For multi-day walking, I reverted to by regular boots. The reason for this was that at Easter I went to the Brecon Beacons of South Wales with the intention, along with socialising with friends, of getting some new peaks to reduce that number needed to a realistic figure. I didn't want to jeopardise that with the wrong choice of footwear so went with what I knew wouldn't let me down.

I hadn't climbed any of the mountains in that area and had a lot to choose from. The first day, with a few of my friends, I ticked off four. The next day everyone wanted to walk, with some wanting to do a bigger walk along the lines of what I do and others wanting something much easier.

To remain social, a route in the nearby Black Mountains was worked out where everybody who wanted a shorter walk could join us and then return on a different path, described in a leaflet that had been picked up in the tourist information office. Anyone who wanted to continue with me was free to do so but I did notice that there was a lot of map study going on. I was going for every peak that ringed a valley – skylining, I call it. I had checked for escape routes to shorten it if needed later on because, with two or three exceptions, I doubted that any of them could have managed my proposal.

It was a late start and progress was, as usual, slow. It was gone midday, about an hour later than I had hoped, when we split up and I went higher with four others. I had assessed very quickly that they wouldn't complete it all and it was so late that I had doubts on myself for a daylight finish. I pushed the pace as fast as I dared and got two of my intended summits before my friends admitted defeat at the next logical escape route path. It was still a fair way back for them. They asked for clarification of my intended route because they thought there were an awful lot of hills and distance around us for a late-afternoon walk.

'All of them and the one behind that big one you can't see,' I replied with honesty.

We happily went our separate ways but on parting they asked roughly how long I would be. I looked again and worked it out in my head from all that experience and reckoned I would top the last one in three to four hours then two hours back to the campsite where we were staying n.

Three hours and ten minutes to the final summit it took. It was easier than expected and, with an earlier start that day, they could have done it too but my three hours from that spot would have been closer to four and a half or even five for them. They walked quite frequently but not as I do. There was no cloud or rough terrain and I could navigate without the need of a map because I only had to follow a valley around from summit to summit. Nor was I hampered by the delays of group dynamics. It was just getting dark as I arrived back at the campsite.

They next morning, I awoke before dawn expecting a few aches and pains from my strenuous two days but there was nothing. I left quietly, had breakfast in a lay-by, and knocked off another seven. Why I'm telling you this, when you already know that I'm an accomplished walker, is because it's all relevant to the footwear choices.

There's no doubt that lifting those heavier boots at every step expends more energy than the lightweight off-road running shoes. I'm not a runner, so the lightness for speed isn't an issue but I had to weigh up the other benefits, such as being easier to dry. Both my planned Scottish trips were going to result in wet footwear. Probably on a daily basis. There are just too many natural obstacles to expect otherwise in the remote highlands. Soggy wet boots day after day are no fun whatsoever. There is less support in a trainer than in a boot but I have never experienced any foot trouble other than *plantar fasciitis*, which had not shown itself in the lightweights with my insteps in them. Bugger those leopards with a spot fixation, I was going for the TGOC in the lightweights.

Summit Talks 12

Playing to your strengths is all very well…until you lose. Evidently 'cunning' was not one of them. – The Aimless Rambler

The TGOC debacle

The TGO, end of May, start came around too fast and my heart was still not in it. I had a lot of peaks left to do but in theory I could still get enough on it to finish my personal challenge. Theory doesn't count for much in my reckoning because, in the nature of this rough and ready sport, it gets knocked about too much.

When setting out, I always aim high otherwise I know that I will beat myself up for not trying, but with that comes the disappointments. Quite a lot of them. The difference between looking at the maps and the reality of what is on the ground when you get there can all too often be poles apart. Gradient changes are the same no matter what, but the terrain itself can make all the difference.

My average walking speed for the day over all terrain works out to three and half kilometres per hour. That includes all stops. Sometimes it's more and sometimes less but that average is all I use when looking at those maps before a walk. The balance is maintained by boggy sections becoming offset by the well made paths, the boulder fields by the clear ridge walk, slow ascents by fast descents and so on… It works for me but occasionally I can get caught out and that leads to the ensuing disappointment.

In the interest of personal safety, I sometimes have to omit peaks to keep on track knowing full well they could become distant satellites from other unclimbed peaks that may never be reached by me. I have several outstanding Munros on that list for those very same reasons. To go for them when there are so many rewards elsewhere makes little sense when achieving completion of them all is so unlikely anyway. So in theory I could get my thousand while on the TGOC but my built-in defence system was already planning for that failure. It's no big deal. Just do the walk, I told myself.

The TGOC started to go wrong, properly this time, in Manchester. On the Thursday, before my next day's start, I was too early, as usual, to get on my platform for the train to Scotland so I went for a coffee at a station café. There, the assistant on the till tried to give me an old five-pound note in my change when they had ceased to be legal tender the weekend before. She had probably taken it in error and was trying to get rid of it before her employer found out but that was a dirty trick whichever way you looked at it. It was sorted out after only a token protest from her. The problem was that I had already walked away before I had realised and had to go back, whereupon it was pointed out that it could have been in my wallet already and it was I trying to dump it on her.

In the flustering of a wallet search, to prove I had no other five-pound notes, except the one in question, was when I believe I dropped my bank card. The one that I discovered was missing when I went to use it in an Oban restaurant to pay for my meal that evening.

Instead of unwinding from my day on the train with a last stroll along the shores of that western coast before heading off eastwards in the morning, I spent the next hour or so on the phone reporting it missing and working out with my family how to get more cash if I needed it. I still had a credit card and was wild camping all the way so I wasn't too worried.

But I do worry about such things. I can't help it. Not about going up mountains on my own but where was my card and who might be using it with this contactless purchasing that sneaked up on me. I stayed at the Oban YHA, which was also my TGOC starting place, in a dormitory of six, and with the worry and general noises of that many blokes to keep me awake most of the night, I was up with the sun and ready to go three hours before the earliest nine o'clock start time.

Now here's another useful tip that could save you some grief. Don't ever wake me up, or anyone else for that matter, because of snoring. It's not bothering me. For continued peace and goodwill to all mankind, get yourself some friggin' earplugs. It's a dormitory dumbo. What the hell are you expecting – elves with magic dust? And while we're at it, your late night will be offset by my early morning so you can stick that one as well.

I ate as much breakfast as I could. It was fuel and for the following two weeks I was anticipating that it might be in short supply. After that, I moeched about wishing the time away so that I could get going on the dot. Whereupon, at eight-thirty, while nosing at the unmanned start register on the counter for something to do, I saw that three people had already left. I was out that door within two minutes still furious with myself for trying to do the right thing. Had I known earlier, I would have been two hours down the road with half of my twenty-kilometre road walking done. I didn't even stop to change.

I had three sets of clothing with me. The one that I was wearing was for getting there and back, along with the meal in a Montrose hotel at the end and any other socialising – such as breakfast and waiting around in a hostel because I was too self-conscious in a community to wear my walking gear. Tights! (Runners' Lycra in this case.) It had been my intention to get changed with about five minutes to go, pack my rucksack and quickly depart before the jibes. On the hills when splattered with mud they're okay but in town and still clean from the last wash you have to put up with a lot of 'witty' comments if you're nearly seventy rather than seventeen.

I calmed down after about an hour of walking along the quiet roads outside of town and stopped to change at a road junction. At which point another 'challenger' appeared from the opposite road leading to it. We exchanged greetings and a minute or two of small talk before he set off again. Five minutes or less and I was following him. He was now my hare. A target to keep me trying to close the gap to maximise my effort. Except I couldn't close it. He was fast, too fast, and the gap widened until he was no longer a target but a bitter blow to my inflated ego. I don't remember his name so he is now Challenger One.

I consoled myself with the walk. The weather was clear and dry and the road was better than I had expected as it wound its way gradually up a valley. A very tranquil and colourful setting of low hills, woods, flowering gorse (possibly broom) and rough pastures with a scattering of farms. There wasn't a lot else.

Once over the high point, it repeated it down the other side. I wasn't interested in any of it, except the cuckoos calling their names for the whole way, because I wanted to get off the roads. I hardly saw any traffic but in front, like the carrot on the stick, the first mountain was always there. Ben Cruachan with a ridge leading to the next, Stob Daimh. On most mountains, you get a bit of a head start with foothills that take the habitation and its roads higher, but that close to the coast this one climbed straight up from the sea. All three thousand six hundred and ninety-eight feet of it. Cloud capped the top. I was sleeping up there that night.

Just before I got to the village, with the café, I caught up with another challenger. When I say caught up, he was sitting on bench at the time and since I have forgotten his name he is Challenger Two. I figured that, at the pace I had been going, both these two were those early starters. We walked to the café together and on the way he told me that Challenger One was the best in the game. It was his twenty-seventh crossing and he was one of those who did the proposed route vetting of other competitors such as me. He was in the café when we got there and joined him for a quick snack before setting off together. Challenger Three then arrived and joined us. (Relax, there are no more relevant to this tale – leastwise not numbered.)

We crossed the River Awe on a footbridge that everyone was hoping would be there. I had looked for it on Google Earth and it wasn't but I had been told it was. Challenger One was checking because he was uncertain also and needed to know for future route vetting. The rumour was that it had been washed out when the river was in spate. We broke up on the far side because the other three went off to view the kipper smokers at a tourist attraction that held no interest for me. Anxious to get on with my 'ambitious' journey, I continued on my own with a few troubling things to digest and mull over. Plan A was not looking so good to me any longer.

My feet ached but I dismissed it. Too much road walking and as soon as I got off the tarmac they did start to feel slightly better. It had been replaced by a hard-packed track but I found respite where I could walk on the grass and muddier edges.

Challengers One and Three were going for the same first two Munros that I had planned for. Challenger One was exploring a different way up to it so as to broaden his knowledge and Challenger Three, about half my age, was going up the same way as me. It was likely that we would all be reunited where the two pathless routes logically merged and would share the same wild camp area. The weather forecast was not favourable.

I don't normally concern myself too much with weather forecasts because once out in the hills there is no update available and I have learnt to read the weather and adjust as I go along. However, it was this Challenger One who had told me about it and he was part of the organisation team. He was clearly one of those true experts that I try to avoid and I didn't relish comparing my rough and ready skills with his if the going got tough up high. Particularly with that dodgy buttress to descend the next day. I was thinking of dropping those first two of four Munros and taking a direct line to three, Beinn a'Chochuill, and four, Beinn Eunaich. (Which for me will be Chocolate and Eunuch because I can't be messing with all that Gaelic that only one out of every half-million people understands.) I decided to make a decision in the morning and was scouting for a decent pitch to wild camp before going any higher when Challengers Two and Three arrived.

Challenger Two suggested sharing with him a site that he had used before that had more to offer than where I was looking. Challenger Three set off up the ridge that I would have to take if I wanted those first two Munros. I opted to stay down and walked with Challenger Two for a few kilometres to the site that he had suggested. It was excellently placed for the alternative route I was planning on and other challengers joined us a couple of hours later.

We stayed independent of each other but did share the conversations between camp chores, where I discovered that I was in the company of another genuine expert and that his wife was a volunteer on the organisation team. They were both very serious backpackers and remain the most dedicated long-distance walkers that I have ever met. To make things worse for me, though, his route for the morning was that alternative that I had been considering, which by then I had already decided to go for because, if I wanted the first two Munros, I should have been on the ridge climbing them and bugger the gloom merchants, instead of drinking tea and swapping experiences barely above sea level. Unfortunately, I had told him that my foul weather alternative (FWA) was to stay low and follow the Glen Kinglass all the way up to Rannoch Moor. The new alternative I had been considering didn't feature in any way at all on the route plan that I had submitted and had been approved six months earlier.

I didn't sleep well. My feet hurt and I was troubled by the turn of events. By morning as I packed up in the rain, I opted to go for my FWA and get as many miles done as I could on easy low ground to put some distance between myself and these guys so that I was once again free. Looking back now, it makes no sense but at the time I felt trapped. Like one of those workers in my trade union days who I had represented for inefficiency and was having their work monitored.

I had taken part in other organised events in the cycling world which included, particularly in its early years when I took an active part, the somewhat notorious Polaris Challenge, where I had worn out partners faster than bike parts. The Polaris Challenge was the pioneer event for off-road orienteering designed for mountain-biking in the UK, a two-day event that included cycling over this same rough country that I walk today, looking for checkpoints to build a score which decides the winners, carrying with them all that the teams of two needed for a night out on a wilderness campsite. The only luxuries provided were portable loos and beer if you wanted it. Later, as the squeamish squealed and prevailed, that went on to include running drinking water. Before that, it was a nearby stream.

It was an extraordinarily tough event for those who could take it but gradually became tamed by the wimping of thrill-seekers until it disappeared altogether. (Ironically this was at the same time as I had stepped down from my trade union duties to look after Diane because I had to do the same from the organisation team of that event.)

After I had run out of partners, I had volunteered for marshalling work for that event and became a key figure in it. From that I learnt, in practice on the ground and not classroom theory, much about the ill-equipped, novices out of their depth, accidents, missing competitors, whingers, whiners and, in particular, the rule-breakers.

Therefore, on the TGOC, as a first-timer I had all that experience nagging away at me and influencing much of that decision making that was forcing me away from what I would normally have done. The twelve years since Diane had died had made me too independent. I resented anything that threatened to impede my carefree life.

To me, at the time, the TGOC was a test that was being judged by others and I was extremely uncomfortable. Which is all bullshit, I know, because these guys had their own agendas and I was already forgotten, but they were the head games I found myself playing on the long trek up Glen Kinglass, where I only saw two other people – passing gamekeepers in a pickup.

On my own, I pushed on and covered a lot of distance by walking the length of Kinglass instead of across the tops where I had wanted to be. I passed a couple of good wild camping spots because I wasn't ready to stop. When I did stop, I was four hours at least into my next day's planned walk and that created a new problem. As part of the event, I had to phone in on prearranged dates to confirm all was well. As mobile phone signals are unreliable in the Highlands, I had said I would call in from the public phone at the Bridge of Orchy for my first check in. If I was up and walking at first light, which was my normal start time, I would get there far too early. They wouldn't be up.

This forced my decision to eventually stop, and I found myself wild camped at a site I had used before, now on the West Highland Way, and that was about ninety minutes' walk from that phone. It had been showering, sometimes quite heavily, on an off for most of the day but it was dry when I got there to put up my tent.

Wild camp? This needs to be put in its correct context as well. In short, it's a two-star bivouac to get you through the night and not what the guys across the road from where I pitched had done. They had put up a tent bigger than my living room, complete with table and chairs, barbecue, windbreaks and ghetto-blaster. They were abusing the goodwill of the landowners to take a free holiday. Although I didn't like it, I couldn't actually fault them for taking camping back to what I consider to be its roots. A poor man's holiday.

As with the adventure holiday companies that had a niche in the market and maximised on their investment, camping has gone the same way. Today, so much luxury has now been poured into camping that it becomes impractical and unaffordable for those at the bottom end of that market to enjoy many of the today's recognised campsites without a touch of envy. Possibly shame as well.

On many campsites, the prime pitches, those with good views and level ground, are reserved for caravans and money. Those pitches often have a hard standing and electric hook-up so that all the luxuries found in a home can be taken into the field. Central heating, TV, running water (both hot and cold), oven cooking, microwaves, electric kettles, hairdryers – the list is endless. It is their home from home.

Meanwhile, the tent campers are relegated to the rest of the fields, which will be further away from the facilities, such as toilets and showers, that they will need…but the caravans that don't need them will have them immediately to hand. This happens because the service supplies, such as water, electric and gas, needed for those facilities are also needed for the shops, reception, staff housing et cetera. It's both logical and cheaper to have all that in one area – which is normally level for that same reason. There are also the associated vehicle tracks which, when put together, may make sense to the efficient management of the site, but not to the tent-camper when they are traipsing across the fields in the wet because that call of nature has become to urgent to ignore.

This luxury, for the sake of it, was epitomised in a boastful article that I read about in a camping magazine where a personalised trailer tent, with teak hardwood fittings, that cost £47,000 was being towed by a Range Rover that was probably double that price. The two together amounted to more than the total value of my home. Yet on TV at the same time there was an appeal for us to send money to help refugees in a disaster zone that would end up in with less than a hundred quid's worth of tent for their whole family to live in – indefinitely!

I have always camped, because that was all I could afford, but I cancelled my long-term membership of a camping club that I had been a member of for thirty years when it was discovered that an age concession didn't apply to me. As a sixty-year-old backpacker, there was no reduction for me whatsoever on a campsite in Keswick, but a double-axle, monster caravan that pulled up on the site paid exactly the same as me, in my tiny single person tent, because of that age concession.

I then worked out what the club was providing for my membership cost and it worked out to be absolutely zero – except for a monthly magazine that published obscene articles about luxury tents for those with more money than sense. I could go on that same campsite as a non-member for not much more than I had paid and because I used these sites so rarely I would never have got my annual membership cost back in that saving. It's such things that push me further into the world of the loner. These organisations may need my money but I don't need them.

A 'legitimate' wild camp is the same as the basic shelter from the elements as bivouacs, much as I described on the GR221, but uses a tent that can be carried there by the person(s) using it along with the rest of their survival needs. This means it has to be light, easy to put up and capable of withstanding whatever nature can throw at it. Small and expensive are the words needed to cover that…perhaps prefixed by 'very'.

To confuse it slightly, there is no such thing as a legitimate wild camp without the landowner's permission but I use that word because it is generally accepted that for those travelling in mountain terrain there is no way of knowing who the landowner is. Therefore, the rule of thumb to maintain goodwill on all sides is to pitch late, pack early and leave no sign of your passing, (Except for that patch of flattened grass that will recover in a day or two.)

There was no way that the guys with the big tent and cars were doing that, but Scotland also has some peculiar laws of its own that I don't mess with. I don't want a blue-faced Australian storming down my way to kick another Sassenach's arse back below the wall in order to rewrite some more of Scotland's history. (*Braveheart* – I like the soundtrack.) For the backpackers' version of the tent to work effectively in the wet is to do everything outside and only get inside for sleep because, even if you are successful at keeping the rain out, then the condensation that forms inside will become your arch-enemy.

The primary objective is to keep your bedding dry so warmth and thus recovery can be maintained. Which makes me wonder why the hell the homeless of the UK's cities insist on spending their days sitting on the pavements, wrapped in their sleeping bags, in the rain.

In stripping down the weight of my rucksack, I had three lots of clothing – outdoor, indoor and posh. Those worn outside the tent are changed to a long-sleeved thermal top and another pair of tights for inside, with the posh stuff being saved for best. (The same footwear for everything.)

On that basis, I ate my meal out in the latest rain shower, wrapped in my waterproofs while blasted by the sounds of DooBarra Wotzit and his Screeching Anus with their hundred and ten decibels of noise from across the road. I must be old because I'm sounding like my father when I tried to tell him about the Rolling Stones fifty years ago.

Dinner? Five hundred calories of something or other, eaten with a plastic spoon that I salvaged from my brew on the train, out of its foil bag where it had been converted with hot water from dehydrated floor sweepings into mush. Washed down with the luxury of lukewarm brown liquid with lumps of dried milk floating on top. Then it's time to go to bed. A routine makes this simpler but my ever changing thoughts don't make it any easier for me.

On that night on Rannoch Moor, with my thoughts wandering off to the hot dry days of my GR20 crossing of Corsica, I forgot to refill the water bottles for the nightly drink when I can't sleep and for morning breakfast. I had packed everything away and was beginning to get my wet things off when I remembered, so I went down to the river barefoot to refill them. This one little, two or three minute, excursion was to prove critical to the remainder of my TGOC challenge.

In the UK, I have been drinking water straight from rivers and streams since I first ventured out into the rough country. That doesn't make it right or safe to do so. It's like the solo walking and just something that I do. Sometimes the water gets boiled and sometimes not. This is dependent on circumstances and need, determined only by common sense. To add further shock and horror to many of today's fastidious water drinkers, I have to admit that I don't actually drink that much water. I'm more likely to stop and make a brew. Even on a day walk I prefer to use my stove than taking a flask.

I have walked in very hot countries, such as Corsica, where the weight in the rucksack is mostly the water that has to be carried due to the short supply of it. One of the things that never fails to amuse me is when one of those survival experts says that before going to sleep, to keep the jackals off the meat from the dead camel that I have luckily chanced upon, I should pee a circle around it. Pee? There is no pee! I have drunk gallons of water in such conditions but most of what goes in does not come out. Leastwise, not in that form. What does is certainly not enough to piss round a rat let alone a camel.

While on this subject, let's make it absolutely clear that, no matter what that survival guru may do, I have never resorted to drinking it. Although some of that cheap wine at the end of the day may taste like it – or so I am told of course.

I met a hardy Spanish couple on one of my European mountain travels who each took a 500ml plastic bottle filled with wine to have with their lunch on the mountains. Great couple. He was a mason by trade and artist by desire and she was a mountain guide for an adventure holiday company. I tried the wine for lunch on a few subsequent occasions but without the company and hot weather it doesn't work so well.

In a 1951 *Boy Scouts Guide to Travel in Moorland and Mountain* that I bought in a second-hand bookshop to see how things have changed, the drinking of water while hiking is discouraged. I was a Boy Scout of that era so maybe that could be my excuse – but really I don't like it that much. It's a bit too watery for my palate. While no reason is given in that manual for not drinking, it does suggest the sucking of a small pebble instead. I prefer to take my chances with the mountain stream than choking back one of them on my next stumble. The same book also warned of the dangers of escaped prisoners on Dartmoor as a natural hazard if that will help you equate to the levels of teaching that I grew up with.

Once in the dry tent with everything ready for the morning, it was time to do the final job before getting into the sleeping bag: check my feet. They ached a bit but I had walked a fair piece. I was more annoyed by the blister that had formed between my big toe and the ball of my foot. I don't do blisters. But what alarmed me more was the tick. My first ever tick was between that big toe and the next. I had probably picked it up on that barefoot walk to the river.

During removal it is important to make sure the head comes out, otherwise all sorts of unpleasant medical things can happen. I knew this and dug my tick-puller out from the first aid kit – a miniature crowbar that you use to lever and twist the blighter out. With it between my toes, that was tricky but I got it out. I knew that I hadn't left its head in because the skin had come off with it. The extraction had removed the blister. That was sore. There was no point in doing anything until morning, so I turned in for the night.

I went out like a light for about half an hour and then spent the next six hours in a fitful doze troubled by aching feet, noisy rain and the wind which had arrived causing the nylon to billow and flap. Doubts saw the gap and crept in. I really didn't have my heart in the project. I was so used to doing my own thing I couldn't see how I was ever going to get to the end without deviating off route in a big way. Even then, I was thinking that I could get the early train in the morning from Bridge of Orchy to Tyndrum for a decent breakfast and then go on from there. Nobody knew where I actually was, so I could just phone in and tell them anything.

These kind of nights are long. There's no going downstairs to make a drink or watch twenty-four-hour telly. Books for reading are too heavy to carry and lying prone with the tapering tent roof only inches above my head makes trying to write trip notes or draw cartoons on the back of the map an ordeal rather than pleasant relief. The pillow is not some super-soft luxury that a score of geese have given their best down for, but a bundle of those posh clothes stuffed in a dry sack. However, because, contrary to what you may think while reading this, I do have sense enough for an en suite toilet in the form of a pee bottle – if I can find where I've put it before hours of tossing and turning in the flimsy cocoon churned everything into a tangled mess. (Pee bottle? It's truly a man's world all right.)

I don't particularly enjoy camping. It's a necessary means to an end. In the past, when it was my hobby to stay in touch with a close circle of friends who camped, then perhaps it was more pleasurable. They had caravans and for many years, with our tent, it was joked that we were the poor relations at the end of the block. I eventually succumbed to pressure from Diane and we took out a loan and bought a caravan. With her assortment of health issues, it was so much easier for Diane to get some pleasure from it.

Personally I found it too restrictive and alien to my call for the outdoors and it was one of the first things I got rid of when widowed. With a caravan, it's too easy to sit at the table, have another brew and look out of the window before venturing out into the cold and wet. With a tent, there's no point in staying inside. It's no warmer, not much drier and you can't see anything. Now that I am solo, this means that normally when I wake up, if it's daylight, I will get up.

That morning, because of that pending phone call, I deliberately forced myself to lie there for as long as I could bear it.

I packed up at about seven. It was still raining, so I decided to put off breakfast (instant porridge) until I got to the Bridge of Orchy. It would give me something to do if the phone was still unmanned at the other end. I wandered over slowly to kill time. It was still raining when I drifted across from the path to the picnic tables by the river to prepare breakfast. I knew about the tables because I had wild camped there once before after three days of walking the West Highland Way in the rain. You could be forgiven for wondering if it ever stopped.

'Would you like a brew, Geoff?' I thought a female voice said.

Nah, that stuff is for the soppy buggers.

I looked round at a woman who was standing in the doorway of a motorhome. I assumed she was talking to someone inside who shared my name until she asked me again.

It was the wife of Challenger Two. During my lie-in, he had caught up and passed me and met his wife there for breakfast. We shared a few brews and biscuits as we chatted about how we had fared and our forward plans. I had a signal for my phone and reported in. We were going different ways from that point.

Challenger Two was staying low on a route that matched my FWA but despite the rain I was determined, having missed out on four Munros so far, to go high. That meant from there I was going due east to get Beinn an Dothaidh and, if the weather stayed bad, I would consider dropping down to pick up my FWA further along around Loch Lyon.

From a high *bealach*, this Munro is off to the left and another, Ben Dorain, would be on my right. A *bealach*, or col if you are south of the border, is a high point between two valleys or lowest point between two mountains. I have already done Ben Dorain but it became another key element to my decision making because Challenger Two's wife was a peak-bagger. She had set her sights on doing all the Marylins and to that end she was going for those two before moving on.

After an hour or so, Challenger Two and I set off again in our separate directions and without my breakfast. That would be a major problem for most people but not me. I'm notorious for my ability to walk huge distances without food. I guess that it's because I can burn body fat with unusual efficiency but I don't question it. I'm just lucky. What it does mean is that I have less to worry about on that score and will have a double breakfast the next day.

My right foot, with its tick and blister damage, hurt on the climb. Every step was unpleasant and slowed me down as I favoured it. It's at times like this when trekking poles really come into their own. They provide balance while favouring injury. I was just shy of the *bealach* when on looking back through the gathering cloud I saw Challenger Two's wife coming up behind me, much closer than I would have expected but she was fast. She caught me at the *bealach* and was going left to my Munro. Bugger. If she had gone right for Beinn Dorain, I would have still gone for it but as I was limping quite badly I didn't want her, as part of the organisation team, to see me make a risky decision.

The way my mind works, I had already got it into my head that should Beinn an Dothaidh cause me real troubles, then I would have done it and then gone back down to Bridge of Orchy to reassess the situation from there. Over lunch at the hotel perhaps. I made the excuse that the weather and my foot were bad enough for me to go down to Loch Lyon and my FWA…as per the plan with the TGOC organisation. She went up and I started down the other side.

Five minutes later, the sun was out. There was no path and I was back on familiar terrain, grass and bog that was much kinder to my foot. In an instant, the plan got changed yet again. Ahead of me was another of my outstanding Munros, Beinn Mhanach. I decided to go for it and the neighbouring top of Beinn a Churin that was also worthy of inclusion. Thanks to that hour in the motorhome, I knew that really bad weather was forecast for the next day but this plan still allowed for a relatively straightforward descent down to Loch Lyon after summiting them if I so wanted.

A lot of people will measure detail on a map with intricate precision in order to estimate a time it would take but I only have one measurement that I use both in the field and when looking at a map. That is, 'hour,' shrug, 'hour 'n' 'alf.' And multiples of thereof. It's near enough. I looked at distance, the lie of the land, the ascent and then assessed. Hour, shrug, hour 'n' 'alf to the col, same again for the two tops. Then maybe 'hour', shrug, 'hour 'n' 'alf down. Yep, I'll be down by dark. That'll do me.

I got them both. I didn't time it but wouldn't have been too far out. Probably nearer to three hours than two for those summits. It was a tougher climb than I had expected. There's not a lot of point working it all out accurately if you're going to be doing it no matter what. Standing on the summit of Bienn Mhanach, I looked back west to the lesser summit that I had bagged on the way to it, to assess the weather before making my next decision on whether to stay high or go down to the loch.

Beyond that summit, the most god-awful weather front was heading my way. It was the most threatening that I had seen for quite a while. It reminded me of another day on Moal Siabod when I crested the summit to see a huge wall of horrendous black and purple clouds already discharging lightning as it hung over Snowdon. Two other people were sitting there calmly watching it. They asked if I knew the way down because they had erred off course on ascent. I gave them a simple choice. 'Follow me if you can keep up.' They couldn't but that lightning chased me all the way down. It remains one of the worst lightning storms that I have ever encountered on a mountain. The theory is that you lie down in such conditions. I'll settle for the animal instinct and run like the cows do. I'm not sure about sheep; they don't seem to notice.

Meanwhile, back to reality, I was going down to Loch Lyon. On Beinn Mhanach, in less than half an hour I was being pounded by wind-driven hailstones bigger than peas. The entire mountain side for a short while was white with them. Slippery as hell too. When they stopped, the rain continued.

I had headed down a pathless slope, east, towards Loch Lyon, where I proposed to camp in Gleann Meurain, which will remain with me as 'Glen more rain' forever and a day. The grass got more lush as I descended and the bogs bigger and more frequent. Pulling my foot out of a grassed-over boggy hole was par for the course. I have been in a lot worse. This is what I do best. Not skulking around afraid to break someone else's rules. The problems are real and not speculative. An acronym would appear in the manuals at this point, so let's try one of mine: the 5As. Assess, adjust accordingly and act. Maybe I should write a guidebook if this one works out.

I arrived in the glen as the sun came out again. Perfect. Taking my time, I put my tent up and strung my waterproofs out to dry so that I could enjoy the solitude and pleasant evening after my three troubled days. The outdoor clothes underneath, wet from condensation and bog-trotting have to dry by sunshine, breeze and body heat or wait until taken off before getting into the tent. (And, wet or dry, put back on in the morning.) I thought it was too early in the year for midges but there had been a few at both the previous camps so I was grateful for that breeze to keep them at bay. A couple of hours later, before turning in, I went to the river to get water for the morning and to give my soaking wet and filthy shoes a good wash out. To do this, I reached inside to take out the insteps...

And the world collapsed in an instant.

Nothing existed beyond the immediate surrounds and those empty trainers. My specialist insoles were not in them. Nor were there any other kind! I had walked all that way with no cushioning under my feet whatsoever. I hadn't left them at the other camps because I hadn't needed to wash the shoes out because my feet had stayed pretty much dry. That meant over twenty kilometres of road then more than double that of hard-packed 4X4 tracks, stony single-track paths and boggy tracks. I had climbed a pathless Munro and come down again. No wonder my feet hurt. How the hell did that happen?

I had been trialling the fell-running shoes for months with no problems so decided to get a new pair specifically for the TGOC. Unfortunately, the first pair were a prototype and the new ones had a number of changes that I was unhappy with and after a week of trying to get used to them, before the challenge, I gave up and at the last minute reverted to my tried and tested old ones. But in my haste I had forgotten to replace the insoles.

Bugger.

Washing the mud off my feet, I found a number of sores but nothing too serious that I could see. I needed to dry them out and look again when the wet wrinkles had gone. I couldn't do anything about it until morning, so I went to bed.

I woke up with a start, before it had even got dark, because the ghost of the GR221 had come back to haunt me. My feet hurt. Not just ache but real hurt this time. I reckoned I was in a bit of trouble. Possibly, just possibly, in quite a lot. Not life-threatening as such but enough to force me to abandon my 'make it up as I go along approach' and work out some kind of proper escape plan.

There were two ways I could go. Forwards on my FWA route it

would take me to tarmac roads after a couple of hours but they were lanes most likely built at the same time as the dams for the reservoirs in the area. No villages for public transport to service. A day of walking those would get me to Bridge of Balgie the first chance of help if I needed it. Beyond that, it would be another day, possibly two, over to Loch Ranonch and down the glen to Pitlochry, where I might get some insoles or new boots. I still had my credit card. Those first two days would be remote. No better than anything I had passed already. Phone signal was not a likely prospect in such a thinly populated area. On the plus side, any inhabited keeper's cottage or farm would do if I got into any serious difficulties.

Alternatively, I could go back to Tyndrum on a low-level route that was over twenty kilometres in the wrong direction of solid 4X4 track and the West Highland Way. If I could get my feet sorted there, I would then have to retrace it all to get back on course. A day out and a day back. I had a rest day built into my plan so I would be using that to regain lost ground. Either way was going to be unkind on my feet.

Sleep was not going to happen. At about two in the morning, I gave up trying. The *plantar fasciitis* had calmed down but the sores were not good. There were several tender cracks in the hard surface skin of my right heal where I had been keeping the weight off my tick and blister wound at the front of the foot. My left was sporting a couple of small blisters.

I had double porridge and packed everything up. There was no choice – I had to go back. My foot was too sore to go that extra distance forwards. There was no hope of respite for two or three days that way.

I was carrying cornflour in my pack for drying my feet properly when a change of socks was required so I split the contents into two, like the addict with his heroin, and poured them into each shoe. I was hoping that if I could work it into all the hard crevices it would be easier on my foot. To help, I put on all my socks as well. In Tyndrum, I knew of at least one shop where I could get new boots and socks.

Thoughts of Cheryl Strayed came to mind. When the film *Wild* opens, she is seen pitching her boot over a cliff. The story then goes back to the start of her walk and how she came to be throwing her boot away while out in wilderness. It turns out she had accidentally let one fall and it was irrecoverable, so she bunged the other after it. She goes on to fashion a new pair of walking footwear out of flip-flops and duct tape. Throwing that boot away was dumb. She should have walked in one boot and one makeshift. Then if the makeshift fell apart, which it would, she still had the materials for making a second. Twice the distance. What a load of cobblers – I wasn't there, so who am I to judge.

I have repaired two sets of boots for other people out on the trail before now. On both occasions, the soles had come apart from the uppers. I fixed a young girl's in the Alps, for her worried parents who had become flustered, with a piece of electric fence wire cut from the surplus that I found on a post. Learning from that, I fixed the second, a guy's in America, with zip ties that I had added to my kit. My first aid kit is for fixing gear as well as people, so it's made up of all sorts of things that have multiple purposes, rather than a fancy pack with a red cross on it, filled with fiddly knick-knacks for different things and those damn wipes again. Wash it clean with water, cover it with what you've got to stop the bleeding and get to someone who can fix it properly as soon as you can. It's called first aid for a reason.

Another casualty, again in the Alps, who had crashed her mountain bike, went down the mountain in a chairlift with my entire toilet roll wrapped around her arms and legs held on with bandages and duct tape. No matter how big that purpose-bought first aid kit may be, there is never enough when you really need it. Like then. That woman, with severe gravel rash on all her limbs from a long slide before coming to rest, had become separated from her companions who were unaware of her accident, just bit her lip and winced a bit now and then, while I did the fixing with some help from a passing French couple. When her friends came back looking for her, just as we were getting her to the chairlift, she came apart and was still crying the last time I saw her being helped into the chairlift. Maybe she was embarrassed by my handiwork. The Frenchman was from the same school as me and steered his partner away. Good idea. It was time to walk away.

Bodge and dodge from my childhood upbringing is never very far away from me when I need it. I set off about a half an hour later feeling quite optimistic because the shoe bodge seemed to have worked. I didn't need my torch because as the track was wide and with no trees there was enough light in the night sky to see by. The puddles reflected it back and could be thus skirted. Walking in the Highlands alone at night, miles from anywhere, was the business. The GR221 ghost again but with a much kinder touch. My adventure spirit was refuelled. This was not thrill-seeking by any stretch of the imagination.

It started to rain about an hour later. What we call Terry Pratchett rain from his *Discworld* books – water with slots in. It stayed with me for the rest of that day's journey. This was the bad day that Challenger Two had said was on the forecast. As it turned out, this was to be the last bad weather for a fortnight. That's sod's law! A milky ooze soon trickled out of my shoes as the water got in. So much for that repair job.

I then made a stupid mistake at a junction because the truth of it is that when I had printed off my maps for the TGOC, I had missed that bit with, as it turned out, a crucial junction. I had never expected to actually be going that way to need it, especially in reverse, so I hadn't bothered to print another.

I corrected this error with my GPS (sat nav) when, believe it or not, it didn't feel right, but that meant recrossing the big ford that I had already struggled across. It was over my knees, and a slip on a stone that rolled under my foot left me with just my head and shoulders above water. Oh, don't I just love this…

I swore quite a lot as I clambered out – onto what? Slightly drier ground. A deluge of rain. I was no wetter than I was before I went in… Just pissed off because I had made the navigation error and followed it up with slip on a river crossing that on another occasion could have washed me up bloated and dead on the edge of that loch. Fortunately, it was just a deep ford with no immediate danger of varied depths and currents. Shit. Get your act together and all the other usual self-recriminations they do in the films. Nah. Just walk. 'Walk or die' came to mind on that occasion as I regained my feet and got onto the correct route, but there was no real danger of dying. Just a reminder that there are people who are not as fortunate as me to be out in the rough country playing… Soaked to the skin… A long way from safety… With very sore feet.

There were no more incidents – just a long, dull trudge that got slower and slower as my feet protested. It took me about four or five hours to reach the West Highland Way and the first signs of other people, early starters who were already heading north to cross Rannoch Moor and on to Fort William.

I turned south wondering if they had any idea how bad things can really get. On that path in summer, you are rarely out of sight of other walkers doing the same popular hike. Civilisation is never more than a couple of hours away. I had walked for five hours just to reach such luxuries. This part of the journey was the worst for me, Not just because of the foot problems but I was down to less than two kilometres an hour and constantly meeting cheerful folk going the other way.

Some Americans asked where I had come from because they were worried by the state that I was in and were they going there too. What could I say? I shook my head, assured them that they would be fine and wished I had added, 'If you get shot of Trump, that is.' I didn't, though, so limped onwards rattled for missing that one.

A while later, amongst the scatterings of other anonymous hikers, a Japanese guy wearing nothing but shorts, trainers and short-sleeved T-shirt and carrying an umbrella was all smiles as we passed each other. He didn't even have a rucksack. I noted that as I looked back over my shoulder for a double-take. He must have been used to that reaction because he looked back too and gave me a wave. I was definitely back again in the world I struggle so much with.

I didn't bother looking for replacement footwear in Tyndrum, because I knew my challenge was over. Instead I went to the tourist information centre and checked for the first train home and, with a couple of hours to wait, I went for a second breakfast for my lunch. I phoned in my withdrawal and politely listened to all the suggestions on how to recover it rather than abandon but they couldn't know. You had to be there and walk a mile or two in my shoes! Besides, wasn't I looking for an excuse to pull out?

I didn't take my shoes off until I got home. Which meant I limped across Glasgow from one mainline station to another, for the train change, in my tights. Then later, through Manchester as well – at night. They weren't even dirty because the rain had washed them clean. I smelt a bit, though, now I had dried out, so that might have helped put any hecklers off.

The bank card was in the foot well of my car.

Summit Talks 13

Credibility regained

I wasn't happy for a few weeks but did recover remarkably quickly. Dylan was anxious to know if I was still on for the Cape Wrath Trail but I was torn because I had only got two peaks on my abysmal attempt at crossing Scotland and I had gotten it into my head that I still wanted to finish them that year and be done with it all.

After a couple of weeks, I was back out in the rough country peak-bagging. I had convinced myself that it served two purposes. One, to get my UK1000; and the other, to get back to trail fitness for the CWT if I was still going to do it. I did a six-peak marathon in Wales that was mostly off piste, which almost convinced me that I was happy with recovery but I needed to do a bigger test to see if my feet were up to the repeated pounding of a hard trail. Walking the bogs was no trouble at all, it would seem. The CWT was notorious for being wet underfoot, so I was feeling optimistic. Nevertheless, I decided to give the Yorkshire Three Peaks a go because I needed a speed test as well as an endurance one. Dylan was fast – even when going slow.

What actually triggered the idea for this walk was chancing upon a note in my Battered Box where my last attempt twenty years earlier was achieved in under eight hours. Allowing an hour extra for each decade because of my ageing, I reckoned if I could get round in under ten, with no adverse after-effects, then I would tell Dylan I was on for the CWT. The established target is to do it in less than twelve but if it took me that long, then I reckoned my days as a hard Walker were nearer done than I had ever imagined in my deepest despondency during that recovery period.

Following a recent programme that appeared on TV after I had finished the first draft of this book, I have amended this version here to include my reactions to it because I can use my Three Peaks Challenge to highlight a significant and ever widening gap between the Walker and the walkers, something I sort of joked about but had not realised was so close to the real truth. We walk in totally different worlds.

The programme was called *Britain's Favourite Walks, Top 100*. The Ramblers Association had compiled the list from a survey taken from its members and presented it in ninety minutes of TV. The Yorkshire Three Peaks is a classic walk but did not appear anywhere in that top one hundred. That is utter madness. A stretch of walking the Thames embankment through the city of London features but not one of the greatest UK walking challenges that has been around a lot longer than I have.

It was not the fault of the TV company or the Ramblers Association, because it was based on a vote. Quite clearly, today's walkers do not want to do anything with any great degree of difficulty. In fact, I doubt that there were more than a third of that Top 100 that went up a hill worthy enough to be included in my list. It is partly my fault because I am a member of the Ramblers Association and had the opportunity to vote but declined. I don't have a favourite walk other than the next one, and if I did, I would not risk spoiling it by telling everyone. I just wish they hadn't called it *Britain's Favourite Walks, Top 100*. It was eight thousand Rambler Association members' favourite walks, because that's all who voted. It's not representative of the nation's walking habits. If it is, then thank God that I'm one of those odd ones out.

More people will do the Yorkshire Three Peaks every year than took part in that survey. Most of them are doing it as a charity fund raiser. There were over three hundred on it the day I had chosen to test my recovery against the clock.

I have carried a GPS for as long as they have been around but have only ever used it as a navigational aid, but at the start of my challenge, for the first time, I set it to record my trip. On the TGOC, I said that I had hoped to use Challenger One as a hare if he had not left me for dead, but on the Three Peaks that day I had over two hundred and fifty hares. It turned out that ASDA were doing a fund raiser. I was told this by one of the faster ones near the end but until then they had just been a never ending stream of targets. I need to thank every one of them who was out there on that day for the unknown service that they were providing.

I started passing the back-markers on the ascent of Pen-y-Gent and never stopped doing it of the rest of the day. At times, they were so grouped up that I would take to the rough country to get past. I even resorted to running at one point to reach a narrow footbridge before a couple of dozen of them blocked it up for a group photo opportunity. I stopped twice to make brews. The second time was the longest, about thirty minutes, because I was beginning to flag a little.

Two peaks done and one to go. I knew I would finish but that time was still important to me. It came good as I topped out on the steeper section of the Ingleborough ascent. My slower pace up that climb had given me time to recover and from then on you can do the rest on willpower alone. Psychologically, it's finished. All there is left is the finishing stretch. This is unbelievably long if you're new to the game and tired. Nor is it all downhill as you may have been told cheerfully by me as I hurried past.

The uphill stretch is never that difficult, though – just a long tedious drag – but on that day I was on fire and didn't notice it. My hares had become few and far between. I remember passing a group checking their map asking me where they were and how much longer would it take. 'Hour,' shrug, 'hour 'n' 'alf.' That's what it took me anyway. There were two or three at the finish but I reckoned to have passed most of them and they had all set out before me.

I had only been overtaken by two guys just after the viaduct on my way to the second peak of Wernside and I have no idea if they were doing the same challenge. If they were, they would be incredibly fast, because I never saw them again. My GPS said that I had done thirty-seven kilometres, climbed 1,710 metres of accumulative ascent in a time of 8.49. Average speed 4.2 kilometres per hour. (Moving time 8.07. Moving speed average 4.6 kilometres per hour.) I was very happy with that. To keep things in perspective: if I had wanted to compete in this challenge in the annual Fell Race over it, then the time needed for my age group to feature in the top finishers was 4.08.

Providing I suffered no ill effects the following day, I reckoned I was good for the CWT. I was still fit and fast…for my age.

Although all of this has to be geared down to a harsh reality. There are walkers of around my age out there who will do the entire Pennine Way in less than seven days. I did a couple of Munros with a guy, slightly older than me by a year or two, who I met on the mountains, who was only just short of his thousandth Munro. Joss Naylor ran seventy Lakeland summits on his seventieth birthday. When I first did the Tour du Mt Blanc, a race was going round it at the same time and it was won by a fifty-nine-year-old Italian on my fifty-eight birthday in a time of around twenty-two hours. My own sons will run further over the hills than I will walk in a day. If the figures shown are indicative of the walking community and I am amongst the top ten per cent of UK peak-baggers, this means there are still hundreds higher up that ladder than me and who knows how many more there are who do not publicly tell what they have done. This is why I maintain that I am ordinary. I may be good but not that good!

None of the top ten of *Britain's Favourite Walks, Top 100* would feature in mine and I have done all of theirs. But the Yorkshire Three Peaks would definitely be in there somewhere. It could sit proudly in anyone's Battered Box whatever time they had done it in.

There was not so much as a twinge from my feet that night. Nor aching limbs, so I told Dylan I was still on for the CWT. I still had my doubts, though. It was not the ability that worried me but whether or not it was right for me. Unlike my planned route for the TGOC, there would be no peak-bagging. While for its entire length the route negotiates some of Scotland's wildest country, it actually only goes over one summit. That is Ben Dreavie, a boggy lump in a boggy terrain that does not even make it to two thousand feet – or so the research has told me. Worthy enough for its remote location and status on the CWT but hardly worth walking two hundred miles for.

On the plus side, the trail passes beneath two Munros, Ben More Assynt and Conival, that Dylan was hoping to divert on to and pick up. Except they were no good to me because I had done them both already a few years earlier. In fact, it was the scene of one of my wildest adventures and the closest I have come to becoming a statistic on my solo travels.

I was in the very north of the Highlands Munro-bagging and had been fighting bad weather for a week. The rain would not let up. After two days confined to living in a lay-by just north of Kylesku in my little van, waiting out the high winds and lashing rain, I had decided to head south and perhaps east to get away from that north-west coast and hopefully find some better weather. It had been a rough night and quite early I was up and driving south. The wind had dropped and the optimistic would say the morning was a little brighter than the previous few days.

As I passed Inchnadamph, I saw a car parked at the start of a popular route to those two Munros. Two walkers were just setting off in that direction. I drove on for about another five minutes deliberating before doing a U-turn and heading back. I would give them a look at. With the other two walkers in front of me, I was likely to meet them coming back if it was too bad up there.

The walk in was okay. A bit of a drizzle now and again, but the wind was nothing to worry about. The path was good and easy to follow. I ascended quite fast. At around two thousand feet, I got into cloud but visibility was relatively good, around fifty metres I would guess. There was a sprinkling of snow for the last couple of hundred feet to the summit of Conival. There I walked into howling winds. All the way up, I had been in the lee of the mountain and had been lulled into a false sense of security but, once exposed, it was a full-on gale. I had one Munro and I might have called that enough but the other two walkers arrived as I was thinking about it. They had done Ben More Assynt and back. It was wild but doable, they said.

I decided to go for it. It was buffeting on the descent to the col between the two peaks but not enough to put me off. In fact, such conditions focus the concentration. As I started the climb to Ben More Assynt, the snow started. Icy needle-like snow hurled by high winds so fierce that it couldn't be faced head-on and still be able to see. I covered my face with a buff and put my snow goggles on so that no flesh was exposed and continued, moving from boulder to boulder using my GPS to navigate by because visibility had been reduced to single figures. It was a wild and exciting but the GPS unerringly took me to the summit, where I simply turned around and headed back.

Again I moved cautiously from one boulder to another, with the wind now behind me. Every move was done with deliberation because it was too easy to go faster than the terrain safely allowed if I yielded to that wind. Then all of a sudden I found myself crashing to the ground in a rolling stumble. For the only time in my life in the mountains, I had actually been blown off my feet. It was not a slip. I literally let go of the boulder from which I had been studying the next section for the best route and took one step forward. Then, as if hit by something, I was blown over.

Slightly disoriented, I collected my wits and started to get up. There was blood on the snow but I couldn't feel any injury. Everything was working, so it had to be superficial. Even if it wasn't, I had to get off that ridge, so I battled on. With enormous relief, about half an hour later, I crossed Conival again and started back down the leeward side. Within minutes of doing that, the wind had gone. The snow was a lot deeper than on my ascent and had hidden the path but it was easy going compared with that crossing. The driven snow had also lost its bite, so I pushed up my goggles and pressed on.

I was at least halfway down before I stopped to take stock and rest for a bit. It was grassy again and after the last couple of hours it was quite pleasant sitting there drinking my tea and eating chocolate biscuits from my emergency food rations. I had earned them.

Upon inspection, I found that the goggles were badly damaged from where the strap was attached and around the edge to where it met my cheek. It looked like I must have hit the sharp edge of rock as I went down and the goggles had taken the brunt of it. In the madness of the moment, I had not even been aware of hitting anything. I took a selfie of my face to reveal a cut on my cheek. Superficial as expected.

It is fair to say that had it not been for the goggles I would have had a serious eye injury. Up there, in those conditions, with such an injury, it is highly unlikely that I would have got down. A sobering thought that has not been shared with too many others. We all have our pride and do not want to go around scaring the alarmists until it's too late, do we?

I am not haunted by demons, so if Dylan wanted to go up them, I would still go with him.

Summit Talks 14

The Cape Wrath Trail with the big ask

A few chapters back, I rather glibly mentioned that I did three intensive days in the Brecon Beacons and Black Mountains in my walking boots instead of the lightweight off-road running shoes that I had been trialling for the previous three months. I then came unstuck on the TGOC because of the business with no insoles and all was okay again with the Yorkshire Three Peaks when I used them for my under ten-hour challenge. The one thing I hadn't done with them was the most critical of all. I hadn't tested them on multi-day walks with only a few hours of recovery each night carrying a backpacker's load. I blamed my foot problems of the aborted TGOC on the lack of insoles, which in turn would also have caused the blisters, aggravated by the tick pulling damage et cetera, but that had only masked another major shortfall in them.

Which is why I came to be stranded alone, with two very sore feet, on the most isolated beach in mainland Britain after just two days of walking on the Cape Wrath Trail. They're not suitable for multi-day events for us old farts with underlying problem of *plantar fasciitis*. The soles are just too thin, even with my special insoles, to withstand two eleven-hour days of constant hammering. There are people who use them as such but I'm not one of them. If I had trialled them for that purpose properly, such as at Easter, I would have found out sooner. Or, indeed, had I not forgotten my insoles, I would have found that out on the TGOC. None of which was a lot of use to me on that beach. You deal with what you have. No wishes or finger-pointing to apportion blame will help. Shit Creek and no paddles were springing to mind. A boat would have been useful too.

Dylan had left early that morning when I had told him that he had to go on alone because I knew on arrival the evening before, at Sourlies Bothy on that beach, that my CWT was finished. I had been hobbling – not walking – for the previous two or three hours. Like I had expected, I was the weakest link and Dylan was often way ahead and I just hobbled as best I could to keep up so he might not have noticed the true depth of my plight. We had done what many people would do in three days in just two and Dylan, who went on to complete the trail, later told me that they were the two toughest days of the whole trail. Which, of course, may be to just make me feel better about quitting so early.

The first day had been a mixture of forty-two kilometres of road, 4X4 tracks with only one short section of boggy, single-track path. The weather had been fine all the way, with perhaps just the occasional light shower that had us putting waterproofs on only to take them off again ten minutes later. I knew most of this route from when I had cycled it on mountain bikes with the lads on a previous holiday. It was the one before the French cycling holiday, in fact, so I doubt if James was any older than seven, which should give some idea how straightforward it was. Harder on the feet than the limbs would be my summary. That night we stayed in Corryhully bothy near a lodge a few kilometres north of where Harry Potter, some railway engineers building a curved viaduct and an Italian dandy (Bonnie Prince Charlie), with no help at all from a history rewrite by a blue-painted Australian, have all made their contribution towards putting Glenfinnan on the map.

Bothies are small huts or cottages, usually in remote areas, that were once used by shepherds and other estate workers such as gamekeepers or labourers but have now become mountain refuges. They are unmanned, free and very basic, relying on goodwill and often nothing more than teams of volunteers to keep them barely habitable for a temporary stopover.

Corryhully is one of the better ones, managed by the estate, who wired it up with electricity for a kettle that they provided, along with the luxury of electric lighting. Water is usually from a nearby stream and the toilet is a shovel and a walk into the woods. First arrivals get first pick of the sleeping spots. If they are all taken, you should be carrying a tent to meet such a situation, because there is no booking system. Sometimes you have to sleep on the dirt or stone floor and some have the luxury of a raised platform. Corryhully went so far as to provide some foam to sleep on if so desired. Everything else needed you take in and you take out. Residential rodents usually clear up any crumbs that are dropped and are unlikely to wait for you to leave before doing so.

After our long walk in, we shared that bothy with a guy and two women travelling together. I had slept okay but was very conscious of aching feet for a while. Wildlife foraging noisily for dropped scraps somewhere close by woke me up a few times but with few pickings to be found, I think they went up the other end to see what the other three might have left.

The next morning, we left all civilisation behind and began our day's walking, heading for the peninsula of Knoydart, a good day's walk away. There, the CWT takes another day's walk to cross the mountainous isthmus and then another, also through mountains, to return the walker to Shiel Bridge, a community large enough to have a bus route and the first logical place to quit. According to some, Knoydart is the remotest part of Scotland, and I believe that.

There are no roads going anywhere near this mountainous peninsula so it's a day's walk from the isthmus to the nearest road head whichever way you go. It is then still another half an hour's drive to reach any main roads – if you have a car waiting there. These are two narrow lanes that wind their way as far as possible up glens between the long fingers of mountain ridges radiating out from the very rugged centre. Without a car, there is not a lot of point in walking that way because there are no buses. There aren't any customers to warrant them. There are a few farms and perhaps gamekeepers' cottages scattered about but nothing else. There are a lot of Munros, though, which gives a fair indication of how rugged that country with no roads is. I have ticked a few peaks off on those finger fringes but had never been into the heart of Knoydart itself. But it was close enough to get the feel of the remoteness that waited further exploration.

The only other way into Knoydart is by ferry from Mallaig to the very small collection of houses, one pub, a campsite and a bunkhouse collectively called Inverie. It's for foot passengers only of course because the road that links this community together doesn't go anywhere else. A no through road in all directions but it is still on the UK mainland.

From the Corryhully bothy, we followed the path to the high *bealach*. Crossing over it would take us to down to another glen leading to those outer fringes of Knoydart and back to the sea, to cross the isthmus the next day.

It started as a fairly straightforward climb with the main point of interest being the stink of a dead deer or sheep as we neared the top. This is always the worry about drinking from mountain streams, such as the one we had been following up since leaving the bothy. More so when you can't see where it's lying. Maths could be used in this instance to provide some reassurances by calculating the sheer volume of water pouring over these corpses every minute constantly washing the nasty bits away and then working out the chances of picking one up in your drink further downstream. I have to be realistic about these things and it does help a lot if I don't actually see a dead beast rotting away in the water supply.

Going down the other side from the *bealach*, the good path ran out and the bogs began. They were far too extensive and complicated to avoid going over ankle-deep on any number of occasions. As the river was neared at the bottom in Glen Pean, I was no longer trying to keep out of them, because it didn't make any difference. I was soaked from the knees down.

A forest with the last of the vehicle tracks that headed our way awaited across the bridge, so it was time for lunch and to sort our feet out. (The nearest the public can get to that spot in their cars was a few miles further down the valley by one of the two feeder roads I mentioned above.) Footwear was washed out and dry socks put on. I had wet wrinkles on the soles of my feet but couldn't see any damage to either of them. They felt better for the warm dry socks.

I tend to find that aches and pains walk off in the mornings and the soft bogs also favour them. With me, the *plantar fasciitis* is at its worst when the feet relax at the end of the day and all the stretched tendons and muscles shrink back to normal. In the morning, that has gone as well, so everything is fine if the pain of relaxation has not kept me awake for half the night. On the harder tracks, where there is no give to the footfall, the soles of the trainers were too thin to absorb the constant pummelling of every rock and stone underfoot, so my feet were aching quite badly. This would ease off again as soon as the ground became spongy but then my feet would get wet and start a whole new set of problems.

Walking the CWT there is no respite as you are constantly going across a mixed terrain with hundreds of stream crossings, from trickles to torrents, all the way. I had walked that next valley, Glen Dessarry, before and knew what to expect. A very long walk in a very mixed terrain of bog, streams and rocks. Nothing easy, and thus my first doubts before ever setting off from home were increasing. Not alarmingly so, because I still hadn't done anything I couldn't reverse.

We passed the next bothy on the edge of a forest, with plenty of time to spare, so confirmed our intention to push on. Shortly after, the vehicle track ran out and the path wasn't much more than a muddy line through the trees between bogs. When we cleared the trees and turned west, it wasn't much different underfoot for the rest of the way either but we could now see how far we had to go.

My son Simon and I had done all the Munros to the north of this valley a few years earlier and had to walk back, in the opposite direction, thirteen kilometres from the last one, to get back to our car. Another wet epic!

Most walking groups will find members who will baulk at walking that far on well made paths for their weekly outing but Munro-bagging in that area demands so much more. Each to their own, I will say again, because I don't want to belittle anyone here just for the sake of it, but I do find it so difficult to describe the enormity of walking into the Knoydart area without making such comparisons to more familiar scenarios. It isn't just the distance but the difficulties that earn its formidable reputation. Help, if you need it, because of both terrain and communication difficulties, would be a long time coming. It's most certainly not the place for those who need the assurance of what we associate with a civilised society. But for our more advanced clothing, little will have changed in centuries of living or travelling through there.

Such paths would never feature in a programme about Britain's favourite walks because they are simply too difficult for the kind of people who would vote, while the users are probably not the type of people who would watch the programme let alone vote. So when the presenters of such programmes tell the viewers that they are 'hardcore' because they voted Helvelyn and Striding Edge as their number one walk it is laughable. For me, it also makes a mockery of how it's portrayed in the movies where time factors and communications difficulties don't even feature in the storyline. Where the hell were they getting their blue paint from!

A thread of a path weaved around bogs, through boulders, over countless streams, slowly rising to another *bealach*, but it would be almost indistinguishable from all the other low ground between the increasing number of bouldery humps and bumps were it not for a small cairn to mark it.

The downhill on the other side was much the same but with Lochan a Mhaim to provide a touch more character. We crossed the Finiskaig River before it started its cascade down the steeper ground to the sea and we paralleled it with our own descent. Loch Nevis, which has no connection whatsoever with Ben Nevis, was now in our view.

The end for the day was almost in sight. Without ducking in to the tourist information centres for help, I can only think of one possible claim to fame for it, and that's the setting for Gavin Maxwell's *Ring of Bright Water*. Even that may be over the mountains of North Mora to the south, and at the next loch, dependent upon whether Camusfearna was on salt water or fresh.

Loch Nevis is salt and thus tidal, which can make all the difference when leaving. Tide out, you can start your continuation of the CWT walk on the sand; tide in, then it's a scramble over a rocky headland and then across a kilometre of boggy ground to find the footbridge over another river that drains into it.

The descent to sea level was straightforward on a much improved but steeper path which, at the bottom, disappeared again when most needed. The final half a kilometre was a fight to get through chest-high bracken and bog with a maze of paths made by deer that went in no fixed direction for more than a few metres but disguised what may well have been a true route through that avoided any obstacles. It was quite an annoying ten minutes after so long on foot but the site of the bothy when finally reached was truly exquisite.

It was a single-room cottage tucked back in the ferns against rising ground behind with a carpet of deer-cropped grass, like a suburban lawn speckled with daises in front. They weren't daisies but an assortment of other wild flora that I can't begin to name because I'm a birdwatcher. The limit to my mental capacity for data storage ends with birds and mountain travel; the rest needs backup. After the lawn, a stony beach sloped gently down to the inland sea. A couple of hundred metres across it, the land rises straight back up to the mountains again. It's circled by mountains, in fact, but they do get lower towards the west. A boat was the most logical choice for access for those who used to live in the bothy and other scattered habitation that now lay in derelict ruin.

Dylan had got there about fifteen minutes before me. There were two other guys already *in situ* and since I have already forgotten their names, they are Pete and Fred from now on. I can't be doing with any more of that Challengers One, Two and Three nonsense. They had walked in from the other direction for a couple of days Munro-bagging based from the bothy.

Relieved that my walking for the day was done, I set my sleeping bag out on a raised platform, had a brew and inspected the soles of my feet. The blisters that had formed and burst left layers of skin pealing off them. My water-wrinkled right heel was particularly bad. It was at the same place as the previous injuries on the TGOC walk and looked to me as if the healing had not toughened up enough before being put under severe load again. I needed it to dry out for a closer inspection, so I ate some dinner safe in the knowledge that I was unsafe. I wouldn't be able to do the two more days' walking to get us to Glen Shiel, where we were booked into a bunkhouse, and, if necessary, I could bail out and get a bus back to Fort William. I needed to stay off my feet to give them time to recover. The memories of how quickly they worsened on the TGOC was still fresh in my memories, which meant common sense said it was over for me. I told Dylan that was the way it was.

I couldn't have asked for a better place to rest up than Sourlies Bothy. When I said that I hadn't done anything that I couldn't reverse, I still hadn't. I just couldn't complete the CWT without a break and Dylan's timetable couldn't allow that, as he a working man with limited holidays, was committed to a timetable which involved other people. I had food enough for a week of R&R, a small pair of binoculars to watch the wildlife and twenty A4 pages of one-sided maps to doodle or write on. We discussed the options, with Pete and Fred chipping in with helpful information about the path to Inverie and the Mallaig ferries, which was the easiest and therefore logical way out for me to consider. Then slept on it. Or in my case lay awake most of the night with the song of *plantar fasciitis* to serenade my troubled thoughts and the additional sores of broken skin and flesh of my right heel to chip in with the chorus. Had decades of hard walking caught up with my age, telling me to call it a day, try to slow down and take things easier?

Alone the next morning, I sat on the beach in the warm sunshine annoyed because I had just seen an injured ringed plover struggling over the pebbles a few metres away. So much for taking it easy. I would have to go and find somewhere else to eat what was left of my porridge and ponder upon my options.

That isn't a cruel outlook. The bird was faking it, pretending to be injured in a bid to lure me away from its young that would be even closer. In the fictional world of film and romantic novels, the location was the perfect place. The bird's injuries would be real and the lonesome hero would nurse it back to health and in doing so find a better person within himself. Perhaps a bond might even be formed as with Gavin Maxwell and the otter.

In nature's world, that I preferred to live in, the lurking ravens on the crags behind the bothy would have those chicks the moment their parents were no longer there to teach the importance of staying motionless until danger had passed. They too had young to feed. And those bloodthirsty trophy hunters of mainland Europe could well shoot the parent plovers on their winter migration when they flew over the Pyrenees.

The two deer hinds, with their young that casually grazed around the bothy lawns, were real enough and those with troubled minds would tick all their boxes for a wonderful retreat to spend reflecting upon their values. For them, there would be no unseen nasties such as midges and ticks waiting to feed upon them when they strode naked out of the loch like Ursula Andress in *Dr No* – or an old and scruffy git looking on instead of the perfect James Bond. (So she wore a bikini. That was fifty years ago. Life has moved on. But not far enough for me to replace that image with a bloke to satisfy those equal opportunities champions.)

It would be difficult to find a more apt situation to explode the myths between fact and fantasy than at Sourlies Bothy. Besides the difficult access, when people get there, they have no electricity, gas, telephone, wifi, separate bedrooms, toilets, showers or running water. The artist, standing on the shore, at their easel, trying to capture the scenery and ever changing moods of the weather to alter the light, wouldn't be able to carry their essential food, bedding, kitchen equipment and clothes as well all the paraphernalia needed to produce their masterpiece. Unless they were happy to rattle off a few small watercolours, from a child-size paintbox and crumpled sketch pad for reference, to be explored later back in their studio, they would be going home disappointed. If that's the objective, it's so much easier to use the camera on the smartphone and take a few photos. You could even find photographs on the internet to save going at all if it's just for a painting.

Would those troubled souls searching for peace of mind, to ease their insecurity in the madness of urban life, be able to get there? If they can't cope in an environment where help is all around them, how are they ever going to fare alone in the blanket cloud and the rivers in spate that may greet them on the way? There are no group therapy sessions where the paths run out. They have got to figure out the next move themselves.

There are no twangs of Gaelic music to change the mood from dismal rain to romantic mist, or cinema heating to remove the cold. Delicious roast dinners cooked on a spit over a campfire in the moonlight are pure fantasy. Who caught it? What with? Who carried the axe to get the timber? Where is there timber enough to provide such luxuries without selfishly cutting the little that is left and spoiling the location for those who follow? The mobile phones that can't be lived without are nothing but dead weight. There is no signal to use them with so that a link to the rest of the world can be maintained. They wouldn't even be able to charge them.

How many in that world of dreamers could get there to live for a while without any of those comforts taken so easily for granted? I'm a self-confessed daydreamer but my proposed stay had not been in my plans, yet it was mine to find out if I could. An important difference was that I already knew that I would. It was just an extension of my everyday life.

That's why I was not fazed by Dylan walking away that morning. Not much of a test but it reminded me of the Moroccan muleteers and the Russian bimbo. The rough country has no respect for fancy frills.

Sturdy and practical are the watchwords. Anything else is extra weight that will be the first to go when the going gets tough. It would always be tough.

There is a possibly one exception to all of this but he didn't arrive until that afternoon.

> How on earth have I reached my place in life, climbing all these mountains, without wearing Cocksure 127-hour deodorant?
> – The Aimless Rambler

Dylan had been away at first light. Soon after, Pete and Fred had left most of their gear in the bothy and taken light packs on their day of Munro-bagging. I envied them, as the closest of them, Sgurr na Ciche, was still on my unclimbed list – with the bothy sitting on its toes to continually remind me of unfinished business. I was actually pondering on whether I could get it before leaving if my feet recovered enough for it but not for finishing the CWT. For a short while, I had the place to myself.

I had worked out a plan. I would have a few days rest there to allow my feet to start the repair, then spend a slow and lazy day walking over to Inverie. Pete and Fred said it had taken them six hours. I reckoned to spread the journey over double that to include long rests for my feet. I would spend that night in the bunkhouse, or on the campsite if there were no vacancies, and in the morning get the ferry to Mallaig. From there, I would catch another to the Isle of Skye. Hopefully, there would be buses to Kyle of Lochalsh, where I would get the train to Kinlochewe, which the CWT passes through. We had accommodation booked there and I would try to meet up with Dylan again. If the feet allowed it, after almost a week of rest, I would continue with him. If not, I had the trains to take me home.

The group that we had shared our first night's bothy with arrived about midday. They were impressed to find we had got there in one day, as they had given up at the bothy in Glen Dessery that we had passed. Deliberating whether to go on or stay, they had their lunch. When they told me their plans, I persuaded them to keep going, because they only had three days left to get back to Fort William. That would be tight on the route that they had planned, which involved thumbing for a lift on one of those roads with no traffic that I have told you about.

Mid-afternoon, another walker, bringing rain with him, arrived to stay. One of my cartoons had come to life, the living exception to my deliberations on the facts and myths of an idyllic stay at Sourlies Bothy. If my pack and travelling style was likened to a small van, then he was the juggernaut…with trailer…road train possibly! To carry that kind of load, he had to be either a very lucky novice to get that far or very dedicated to his passion. It was the latter. He had it all.

There were three empty sleeping spaces left in the bothy before others would have to sleep on the floor but, after a thorough inspection of the rafters inside, followed by that of two trees out in the bracken, he decided not to string his hammock up as intended. Instead he built a shelter out on the lawn with his trekking poles, a big ball of string and a tarpaulin. He was not so much a walker but one of the increasing number of survivalists, possibly inspired by the popular TV programmes of that nature. He even carried what he called an estuary net for fishing. I found this out because he was a talker. Not a listener, though.

By evening, I was tired of all his stories but with my foot troubles I couldn't escape. The rain had helped take care of that as well. He was going to sleep outside but the rest of the time he spent in the bothy with me, telling one story after another about his travels with tarp and hammock.

I was also becoming troubled by the absence of Pete and Fred to ease the burden. I would have expected them back by late afternoon, or evening if they had gone for a really big day, but the night was closing in. The other guy was so full of himself that I could clearly see that, for him, if they were not there, then they did not exist as part of his world. Out of sight out of mind. Whenever I mentioned their failed return, he just changed the subject back to himself with what was coming over as a constant clash with authority. I was grateful when he went out to spend the night in his shelter but by then I was deeply concerned about the missing Pete and Fred.

It was dark and raining. All their gear was with me in the bothy. I might be feeling sorry for myself but as the night dragged on I knew they were in real trouble. Not the panic attack of a newbie on a charity challenge, or me on the TGOC with sore feet, but the real thing. Life-threatening trouble by the barrowload. Somewhere out in that vast expanse of mountains, they were either lost or injured. Possibly dead. In the remotest mountains in Scotland, I was the only one who knew that they were out there somewhere with only the direction they had taken that morning and with Munro-bagging intent as my guide.

In that location, faced with such a scenario, every single hope and option has to be examined, and most were ruled out in seconds. A search, even if I was uninjured, in such a vast area would be futile. There was no way that the alarm could be raised from there. Communication with the outside world didn't exist in any shape or form.

Someone was going to have to take the trek to the nearest community to alert the emergency services. For the fit and healthy, that was at least a half a day's walk away in Inverie.

Tarp and Hammock man outside had already failed to even register the enormity of their absence when he had turned in for the night. He was generous enough making drinks and even offered me something of his to eat but I don't think I would have been comfortable having my life dependent upon him. I could be wrong, but you have to call it how you see it when there are no other choices. Injured or not, I was still likely to be faster than him with his massive load anyway. Besides which, he would still be there to help them, if needed, should they return to find that I had left to seek help.

One way or another, this was going to be a very long night.

With my injuries, I could, metaphorically, walk away. I could just sit it out and see what happened. I always had my injuries to fall back on as a sound excuse for inaction. Pete and Fred seemed competent enough to have emergency survival gear and there were two of them. It was unlikely they both would be injured because they were walkers and not tied together in anyway. If one was injured too badly to move, then the other would have to wrap him in as much survival gear as he could and then go for help. (Which could have been out by the way Dylan and I had come in.)

Would I leave a badly injured friend who was possibly dying out there to suffer alone for a day or more? Would I sit it out with them knowing that I could still walk out after they had died? Shit…there was no stopping the clock for a time-out. How could I possibly know if I wasn't there?

Walking away. I boast that when the going gets tough I will walk away. Would I? This was the big test. Possibly the biggest of them all. Lives were at stake. Not mine, but in the absence of evidence to the contrary, that was how I had to think of it.

Alone there is only me to worry about. On the TGOC, I didn't have to walk out. With all the rain that day and the number of challengers who were starting out from Oban over the weekend, there would be at least one going that way as it was the most obvious FWA. Challenger Two had already taken it. I could have just waited in my tent and related my tale of woe to the next person to come by and dump the problem on them. After all, in today's age I have seen so many mountain rescue reports with tales of people better off than me being flown out by helicopter. They wouldn't even have to do that. It only needed one person to drive up with a Land Rover. By today's standards, it was definitely a legitimate emergency call.

Not for me, though. I had food enough for six days without rationing it, all the water I needed and everything I required to keep warm. I chose to walk out because I wanted to. I was doing it for me and my self-esteem. The self-sufficient, solo mountain walker who gives constant assurances to family and friends that they need have no concerns for my well-being as I can take care of myself. In fact, I made it the epic it became by taking that choice of action. At any time, I could have stopped and put the tent up again. I had two days before my next scheduled phone-in (Kinloch Rannoch) and I could do it comfortably in that time.

This was different. It wasn't just about me. This test was the one we hope we will never have to face. I could dump it on the Tarp and Hammock man. Job done. I could wait there in case they did come back and wash my hands of it.

We all know what is morally right in almost any given scenario. Deep down, whatever face we may portray in public, we all do. A clear conscience is about recognising what I can do, if anything can be done, towards achieving the best solution. Whether I do it or not is the harder question to answer. Anything that I do which leads towards a negative action in some way condemns the fate of others to the mercy of chance or injustice. That is living in denial. On the other hand, as I wander the duller stretches of those high places, I have come to realise that whatever I may do as a positive action will never be enough either. There will always be another cause somewhere else that needs to be fought or others to be steered away from because of their avoidable risks.

The only plea for judgement that I can make is that of the ordinary man. That anonymous shape of a human who may have momentarily filled a space in the world of others. I will have done as I saw fit at the time. It's only later, when the contents of the Battered Box are explored, that I will be judged as to whether it was enough. However, that ever constant defence will still hang out there – unless those who judge were actually there with me to see it, then how can they possibly know if they were right in making such a judgement call after the event?

I can see more clearly these days why I was so unsuccessful in those promotion boards at work. Like many things in the social world, I never took them at all seriously. I didn't rise to the occasion but flatlined them as just part of another ordinary day for an ordinary man. At heart, I was never a manager. It was more important to me that I remained as I was. True to myself. No frills. You get what you see. Promote me on the strength of that. If it ain't enough for you, then bugger off.

I claimed that I can lead but can't be led and that isn't quite right either. I should say that I can lead the way but whether others follow me or not is up to them. I can't manage their choices for them. I will tell it how I see it, providing factual answers from my perception to questions asked and the rest is up to them. If they still can't handle the choice-making, then that creates problems for me that I don't want. It complicates things in my simple life. That's when I walk away.

How the hell did I ever end up as a trade union representative voluntarily taking on the problems of others, on top of my own, with such an attitude? I think it must have been a bit like the Pete and Fred scenario, where I saw people worse off than me and I was capable of providing constructive help in a familiar environment.

> Margaret Thatcher is dead. It occurs to me that if a person like that gets to heaven – then I don't reckon it can be as good as it is cracked up to be. I assume she is going that way or why would we be giving her a state funeral. Come on, religion – help me out here!
> – The Aimless Rambler

I also claimed earlier that I was a Thatcher victim as well and that, with further reflection, is incorrect too. You can thank or blame her for what I have become today, though, because she certainly forced the issue. She was the figurehead at the forefront of a destructive force that I saw as a serious threat to my family's welfare. We were struggling enough without any further help from them to make it worse. Fight or flight were the only choices in such a situation. Except I was already on the bottom with my back against the wall. There was no flight possible, so I had to fight. They had forced me out of those anonymous masses drifting along through our lives just to exist into making a stand.

At the time, along with miners, steelworkers and shipbuilders, the civil service, the government's own workforce, was a target for decimation and to then be hopefully sold off to the highest bidders.

(From where I stood, that was to themselves as individuals – for their profit and not the country's good.) The only thing that government disliked more than those costly public services and nationalised industries, in the absence of effective parliamentary opposition, was those industries' only defence – the trade unions. Those who represented the actual workers themselves. Those who could put names and faces instead of numbers into the argument and thus pour shame on the callous actions of the destroyers. That would be me. I was one of those. Not a particularly militant one and I'm not even sure how I got there. Nevertheless, I was there. In the front line.

This is the guy who can recall over forty years of walking in the rough country with so much detail that it gets a little scary, yet I can't remember that life-changing event when it comes down to my place in work. I suspect it may have been when I needed a trade union representative for a hearing because I had broken one of the staff rules by allowing myself to get poor. I may jest now but that was true at the time. It was against the conditions of employment contract to be in financial difficulties, because that made me vulnerable to outside influence. (Another little known fact for the novel.) If that was the case, then I expect that I was better at my defence than the rep who came with me, because I had more to lose. I might have just been asked to sit in at another such hearing as a friend for a colleague and felt I had to voice a mitigating circumstance that was being overlooked, but I am still guessing.

So to summarise, until Thatcher's arrival on the scene, I was just a bloke you might have seen biking past on the way to his very ordinary job as a civil servant and trade union representative, working for the Social Security offices, throughout her term as prime minister, where I witnessed first-hand the price of that dreadful onslaught that was waged upon the less fortunate people amongst us and their right to have a voice. I get a little sick inside when I see people of today, who hadn't even been born at the time, glorify her as a champion of a better Britain. I was there at the lowest ebb for my own family's misfortunes. Diane was in and out of hospital and I was working for nothing. I was receiving benefits to supplement a dreadful wage for paying out benefits to the millions of that government's other victims – or collateral damage if viewed from the safety of a thirty-year history lesson.

My wage as a civil servant, the government's own workforce for delivering their cruel policy decisions, was below the accepted living wage and had to be topped up with benefits. That was my lot for many years. I might have wanted to be an artist or writer but that was the real world and not some romantic film script where from the ashes the phoenix miraculously arises to save the day. I wasn't borrowing money to further some elusive dream but to spread the debts incurred by Diane's dramatic decline from good health and the loss of her job that had been paying better than my own.

In today's world, she would not have been sacked for that long-term pregnancy-related illness, a protection bought about by those same 'despicable' trade unions but is now taken so readily for granted. It was nothing short of a blood sport, with the victors drooling with drunken power over the broken and twisted vermin that would blight their Utopia.

Throughout her reign of sweet-talking bullying, and the successive governments with little change in policy, I represented colleagues who, for one reason or another, had fallen foul of the system. The craziest thing is that I can hardly think of more than two or three of them who were not either better placed in financial terms, or free to make other choices, than myself. I did that for nigh on three decades. Thirty friggin' years of additional and unpaid toil over and above the daily grind. Not for the employer but for their employees. The ones who needed those names and faces. I can honestly say that I did my bit to try and make it a better world. It even contributed towards that bloody medal! (A Labour government was back in power by then.) It had to, because that helped shape who I was.

Once I knew it was going to be Diane's own final battle, with no possible victory ever being anything more than a wistful dream, I had to take a step back. And to cut the story shorter, after she died, I never found my way back. I still stepped up to help colleagues when asked to, but the fire had gone out. Even now, over ten years later, no matter how much I poke around in the ashes, I can't get it relit. I will turn my back on the world and walk away.

It was never intended that I take on the might of injustice. It happened, that's all. How? I can't even remember most of it but that's all water under the bridge now. I was just an ordinary guy, the common man, just doing that little bit more than usual and now it's over. New battlegrounds have arisen, the world is still a shit pit of greed and corruption. I haven't got what it takes to become a recluse who can hide from it all in total obscurity, so, like thrill-seeking and adventuring, I will drift between the two. A loner.

Pete and Fred were forcing the issue too. I could dump the problem on Tarp and Hammock man outside. I had done more than many to help my fellow man. He was younger, fit and healthy. He had to be to carry that load. I could lead the way by showing what had to be done but I knew that I couldn't make him do it if he said no. I couldn't manage his decision-making. I didn't have the subtleties or panache required for persuasion. Give him the facts and let him decide. I could walk away as easily as that.

If only things were so simple. Walking away is all very well but it doesn't end there for me. I may have moved on but the repercussions of what I do, and have done, still have to be answered. This conundrum only needs to be answered if one feels the need to justify an action to another because they harbour a guilt complex that sooner or later needs to be aired in public. It would seem, by including it here, that I do have one. Even if, as a habitual loner, it's only me asking the questions, I will try to answer them anyway.

With today's instant communication and social media, I am inundated with reminders of this guilt. So many that I think they are having an adverse effect in that I'm not really seeing them any more. Just skimming. I'm made to be aware of one disaster, crisis or injustice after another but the stream is so constant that, as each new one arrives, so a previous one becomes forgotten. There are so many and they are passing so fast that I'm no longer seeing them for what they are.

It's not unlike watching a TV ad, made by UNICEF with Ewan McGregor, about children dying in a war zone, being jammed between some hardly dressed blonde bombshell with her Jardore Dior and then followed by an aerosol can of magic formula that does not just stink of rose petals to hide dog smells but kills them. That would be the smell and not the dog, my twisted mind immediately grabs, but whichever way it goes I can live without it. I haven't got a dog!

Even without the additional distraction of my own thoughts continually distorting them, these messages alone all run into a meaningless blur – where the real horrors of this world are drowned in a constant slurry of glittery shite aimed at using our vanity to steal the money better sent to help those kids. I am shutting down their receptors and the fanatics are stealing the day. Trump and Brexit have become a cue for reaching to the off switch. I don't want to be part of it. Sadly, that becomes all of it. The problem is just too big for me to deal with so, like so many others, I no longer try.

So, just as I don't have what it takes to be a team leader, then nor can I sit comfortably in any team.

I once had a politically hard-left friend who fell out with me because I admired the tenacity of a well known explorer they knew was a UKIP supporter. I didn't know that at the time and nor did I care when I found out. Same bloke. Same remarkable achievements. That's it. I can separate the two issues when that friend couldn't. I recognise the fact you can't achieve greatness in the mountains without that same selfish drive. A group can only do so much but from it those with the most determination will rise. Remember what I said right at the beginning – mess about with my walking and I will dump you. That requires a passion that I and that UKIP member, from completely different political camps and ideals, have in common. A passion that others find difficult to understand because they don't have it.

This reminded me of an observation of mine that I had recorded in my notebook. (Probably because Rolf Harris was headline news of that day.)

If someone you regarded in the past as a good mentor later turns out to be a criminal, does that make you wrong as well? If the rest of what that person did was right, then why should you be ashamed to say that they inspired you? But we are made to believe that we should be.

Hitler was an artist. Does dictatorship automatically make him a bad one? Or is it because he was a dictator, and thus a celebrity, that his work, which may really have been bad, became collectable? A BBC documentary on music in war propaganda told me that *Carmina Burana* was written for the Third Reich's war machine. I'm not sure if that is correct but whether it was or not, it was used by them. Doesn't listening to it now give credence and condone their actions?

It's still a bloody good piece of music.

> I am ordinary. I make decisions and mistakes. I shouldn't have to throw my total support behind once particular faction of the headstrong to retain credibility. I don't expect you to change your politics and views to match mine before you read myrambles or share a night in a mountain bothy. I may not agree with your beliefs but that doesn't mean we shouldn't be able to walk the same trail together for a while. I have an MBE but that doesn't make me an ardent Royalist…although I do sometimes wonder if Thatcher's lot had still been around when I was nominated whether it would have been sifted out. (The notification comes from Number 10 not Queenie.) I see the MBE as a thank you from my colleagues for being a good guy as a go-between in an unfair war of attrition.
> – The Aimless Rambler

Should I be thinking about what political persuasion Pete and Fred were before worrying about them? Right at that moment, they were more real than starving children. How can anyone even think of prioritising – yet if you break it down to basic ideals, that's what belonging to any team is doing.

Most of us are just ordinary people living ordinary lives. We may not want to be but that's the way of it. So pull your bloody horns in, let's kill off a bottle of wine or two and then see what tomorrow brings.

But still the guilt will linger.

Beneath it all, even as I write this I know that other ordinary people, no different from me, but living in different circumstances, are being killed. Slaughtered as the cannon fodder of the power-hungry, or starving to death because the seasonal rains didn't come. Not car theft, power cuts or a knock back on a promise but a life-ending tragedy. No more aspirations about climbing mountains, painting the sunrise or taking the kids to school but a shock horror headline story in the newspapers. Prioritised for maximum effect. This is how one newspaper dealt with it after a headline told me children were killed in a bombing incident in Syria:

CHILDREN DIE IN HORROR BOMBING
(Go to page 7 for full story)

That was it. They needed the rest of the front page for a picture of some other bimbo and the latest Hogwarts offers. When I got to that inside page for the full story, they had to limit it to an eighth of the page (yes, I did bloody measure it), with five short paragraphs and two loosely related stock photographs because their reporters were not actually out there themselves but in some office where they got it off their computers from some live news feed or other.

This shocking horror story fizzled out to nothing more than a vague round-up of minimal facts padded with standard reporting rhetoric as it competed for space with three other stories for half a page – and Tesco's had bought the other half for a Christmas advert. There was no news. No first-hand factual account, just sensationalism, and the victims of the atrocity just became another statistic before the ink had dried on the adverts that I had been steered to.

A few months later, the same paper filled their first eleven pages with news of Prince Harry announcing that he was getting married. Of which only one and a half were displaying adverts. This was followed by an update on a crisis in TV's *I'm a Celebrity Get Me Out of Here*, and there were no horrifyingly maimed or dead at the hands of others until page fourteen.

To rub this in, the next thing I know, there will be a grand TV charity fund-raiser where a line-up of rich celebrities, between a couple of songs or comedy sketches which they are doing for nothing because they are such nice people, will beg me to donate as much of my money as I can afford, plus a bit more, so that the relatives of those ordinary, but almost dead, people will know it is Christmas.

Now let's get this straight. While unscrupulous accountants for some of these wonderful people are busily shifting their customer's money to tax havens abroad, the ordinary person from that lower-income bracket is being asked to help clear the nation's conscience because it's a season of goodwill to all men… And we'll pretend that killing of kids in other countries is an unfortunate act of war by ourselves, or terrorism if it's the other lot, and never happened to real children, I suppose.

Of course we will because here's an advert for a wonderful cough mixture that knows the difference between the five kinds of cough that until then we didn't know existed (and I still don't) followed by another for the latest surround-sound, 196-inch, curved-screen TV, with HD and an additional, exclusive, on request, simulated smell function. Meanwhile, during my frantic channel hopping for something I can almost bear to watch, someone else wants to sell me this new 'Bad' deodorant that's so cool it will compel pretty young maidens to rip their knickers off whenever I pass by. I sincerely hope that it's so high-tech that it doesn't work on them until after their sixteenth birthday.

Is a person who donates all their spare income to an animal charity lesser than one who would give it to children in need? In turn, are they better than someone who gives nothing? Why, oh why, is it me with the guilt complex because I can't save the world? How can I ever be part of that? It's no real wonder that I will walk away. I am an angel in comparison with those who really do hold the power to make a difference.

I know this and I know it's wrong but like so many others I was kind of hoping that they could sort it out without me this time. I also know that ain't gonna happen, so once more I may have to rise up and take my place on the barricades. But if I could just get my UK1000 first, that would be kind of neat.

After any brush with the civilised world, I have immense gratitude for that rough country where I can regain my freedom for a short while. For that is what it is. The freedom of choice without the influence of social niceties and politics. There is only me. The tougher the terrain becomes, then further away the rest of the world slips, thus making my next encounter with it just that little bit less of a struggle.

That is, until Pete and Fred chanced my way. Somewhere in all that history and madness is the reason that I chose to walk. Not away, but to Inverie for help. I had to do it for myself as well as Pete and Fred. Who knows, I may have done it to mask my other failings. I don't think I care that much. The decision was made and that was it. Right or wrong, that was what I would be living with. My contribution to making the world a better place, if you like.

One way or another, I could get to Inverie, that was never in doubt. How long it would take most definitely was.

I also have to relate it to you in this almost disjointed manner because that is also me. That's how it works. My mind under stress still refuses to accept the enormity of a task with the severity that the dramatists would seek to apply. It's just another walk, so the usual distractions will always apply. Most of the time on that last day of my TGOC, my thoughts would have been bouncing all over the place and very few would have been directly focused on my plight.

There was none of that Hollywood drama about thinking of home and loved ones to feverishly focus on. No determined gritting of the teeth and forcing myself on against near impossible odds with my subconscious stare fixed on a monochrome image of Diane wishing me on with her encouraging smile. The reality of it is trying to drag from my mental knowledge of birds enough information to determine whether that was a winchat or female stonechat watching me from its perch in a stunted blackthorn: I ought to have a pee before I get to the West Highland Way and other people, but the thoughts of battling with waterproofs, tights and underwear in the rain would be putting me off: I wonder if I should use these injuries to cry off from doing the Cape Wrath Trail and head for Europe: I could do the GR54 before Claire's baby is due instead. That was a stonechat after all, there's the male: If there is any shelter down by the railway, I'll stop and make a brew, I'm not sitting out here for one…

It was just another day and another walk. A bit grimmer than most – that was true. But that's the nature of the rough and why I don't come under duress on the adventure holidays. I truly have done the strenuous – alone and unsupported.

> Like one that on a lonesome road,
> Doth walk in fear and dread,
> And having once turned round walks on,
> And turns no more his head;
> Because he knows a frightful fiend,
> Doth close behind him tread.
>
> 'The Rime of the Ancient Mariner'
> – Samuel Taylor Coleridge

It would seem that STC's pathways were also dogged by the Grim Reaper. Unable to sleep, I considered setting off in the dark but too many alarm bells were sounding on that score. Unlike on the TGOC, there was no broad and clear vehicle track to follow or the moon of the GR221 to light my way. Navigation could be difficult if the path was as faint as the one we had arrived at the bothy on was anything to go by. There would probably be low cloud with all the rain that I could hear pounding the tin roof and some very rough country for the first two or three hours, if not more. I was of no use to Pete and Fred lying on the side of a mountain with a broken ankle, because I was looking the other way with my head torch when my foot found the hole in the darkness.

I wrote a note in the visitors book of the circumstances and my intent for any other traveller who might pass through in case they could help in any way that I had been unable to see. And then left another note on their gear in case Pete and Fred had turned up fine and well to find mountain rescue teams looking for them.

After a last hopeful scan of the lower slopes of cloud-enshrouded mountains for them, I set off at first light. I was apprehensive. Unless I was very much mistaken and miracles do happen, then the TGOC sequel was in the making. Except this one was going to be so much tougher. My feet were in a worse state to start with. It wasn't a low-level walk on a vehicle track. Navigation might be a problem. My biggest concern was that I had to cross a mountain ridge. Walking up would probably be okay but down was going to hurt. Feet move more inside a boot or shoe on the downhills. When the boot stops, the body weight behind the foot causes it to slide fractionally forwards inside at every step, causing abrasion on the sole of the foot. Under normal circumstances, my feet would have been tough enough to cope with that but the damage had already been started.

It was still raining and the tide was high so the easy option of the sandy walk round the headland was not even on. The injury-faking ringed plover was still at it to see me off. I scrambled over the headland and down to the mist-enshrouded estuary flats. Crossing the bogs to the bridge over the River Carnach was kind on my tender feet but had soaked them before halfway over. A sign nailed to a post warned me not to cross the bridge. It was in desperate need of repair. They all are. The landowners put up the signs and leave it up to you to make your own choices. I had been over worse and crossed without pause. (The bridge was taken down in January 2018 as too dangerous to remain *in situ*. You had to wade the river instead.)

Very shortly after the bridge, the paths split. The CWT headed north up the glen, my path went left towards Inverie. I had a two-thousand-foot climb to take me over the mountain range that separated me from the phones that I needed.

I learned years ago that there is absolutely no point in getting het up or fazed by a climb if you're going to take up mountaineering as your hobby. There are different theories and practices on how to best do this and all you do is find the one that suits you and apply it. Then hone it until it becomes a routine that is applied without much conscious thought. It works – for me anyway – as I have very few unpleasant bad memories of arduous uphill slogs…even this one with sore feet.

I set my thoughts to the task and just climb, steadily and relentlessly. Grinding ever upwards. Machine-like, some would call it. Perhaps it is but I'm still the one looking out of the windscreen. Once settled in to it, my mind will then wander off somewhere and leave my body to get on with the job without much thought. Just as a bricklayer will lay bricks, as a Walker I will climb hills. I set no intermediate targets to reach before a rest stop, or stare hopefully for any tops because in practice there are always too many false ones. On that day, the cloud had taken everything more than a hundred metres or so away. Visibility reduced to thirty to fifty metres as it started to level out.

Over the top, I descended a short way, found some rocks to sit on and got out my stove to make a brew. I had no map, because it was no longer on the CWT route, but I had my GPS if necessary. I had also taken time before setting out to study a map that belonged in the bothy. The brew was so that I could stop and collect my thoughts about what I was going to say before dialling emergency numbers on my mobile phone. I had a theory. Looking at that map, I figured a straight, uninterrupted line could be drawn from my high ground to either Inverie or Mallaig, so there was a possibility that I could call in from there.

'No service' greeted me. So much for Plan A. Plan B was that in another theory if I dialled 112, the international emergency number, I would be switched to any service provider with a signal and redirected to the emergency services. I dialled it, then made and drank my mug of coffee while waiting. Nothing. I dialled 999, just in case I was wrong about that theory, and packed while waiting for a response. Nothing.

There was to be no easy finish to my mercy hobble, as I was beginning to think of it. Somewhere out there were two guys in dire straights. Dead or dying perhaps. Not just unknown figments of a creative imagination but Pete and Fred, whose real names I couldn't remember, and who I had talked with just thirty-six hours earlier about the path I was on. Possibly right at that moment they were hoping like hell that I had been bright enough to join up all the dots and was out trying to help them. It made me a touch guilty for stopping with the reminder that it was not a game. What now of my walking away policy when things got tough?

Inverie was still a long way away for me and even when I got there I didn't know exactly where they were. Even if I did, helicopters were no good in that muck. I could have stayed at Sourlies bothy and walked away by continuing with my R&R while Tarp and Hammock man had the final call. But I hadn't. I had set out to get help. In the bothy, I had written down on a note what I was going to do. Could I have really done nothing? I don't think it was ever a real option. There, but for fortune, it could have been me out there.

Now, with only that grit I am so proud of to rely on, it *was* me out there.

I hadn't actually spoken to Tarp and Hammock man in my decision-making. That troubled me a bit but I had assessed, adjusted accordingly and acted. I ruled him out of the equation. He would see they were still missing. He would see that I had gone and he could read the notes. What he did, if anything, was his call. If I had included him, he might have shown my assessment was wrong. I couldn't change it. The decision was made and that was it.

I walked on. There had never been any real doubts that I would but my mind will wander and speculate on any whim that it may find. That 'walk or die' philosophy of mine became 'walk or they may die'. A couple of hours later, it became a slightly more desperate 'Oh shit, walk or we may all die.' It kept me amused if nought else.

I would be a liar if I told you that I didn't sometimes seriously think about what it would be like to die out there alone. On some wet and soggy mountainside, like that one, with the cold soaking through to chill me to the marrow and leaving me wondering how long it would take. Then I think about that forty-ton lorry with its sleeping driver crashing over the central reservation of the motorway heading my way. Or that next aeroplane flight in the gloom to somewhere more exotic than the UK and the loose hydraulic connection that got missed on the last dull routine service. The same old job – servicing aeroplanes by a mechanic whose children are keeping him awake at night. At least that final mistake would be mine and not a total stranger's who was distracted for a moment. It wouldn't make it any nicer, though, so I'll look to my oread instead.

I really ought to give her name.

I called one of my bikes Tinkerbell when I was a kid. The craze was to convert your racer into a tracker – which shoots all that garbage about the Americans inventing mountain-biking down in flames. We had them at least ten years before. The smooth road tyres were replaced by the best nobblies that could be found, the drop handlebars changed to wide and high motorbike cow-horn bars and the thin narrow saddle by something more forgiving. Flames and stars were painted onto the frame and names like Fire-rider added. Then it was time to go tracking which is hurtling around the woods and dirt tracks as fast as only fearless kids can. My racer had been lime-green and bought by weekly instalments with my paper-round money. No fire or stars were added but I painted Tinkerbell on each side of the crossbar. Don't ask me why, because I have no idea.

My oread could be a Tinkerbell but it kind of makes me a bit soppy.

Random thoughts like that would be popping in and out of my mind throughout the journey. It was still just another walk and Pete and Fred would be forgotten for long periods because, with them, there was nothing more to think about.

> Toothpaste. My current one is Oral B Complete. Would I have had still bought it if it had been Oral B Half Finished?
> – The Aimless Rambler

The downhill was a path of running water. It was loose, it was stony, it was boggy, it was torture on my feet. It was going to take a damn sight more than the six hours it had taken Pete and Fred to do the same route in reverse. Periodically, I tried in vain for a phone signal. Once out of the cloud, the angle of descent eased and Gleann Meadail stretched out before me. It was better in the cloud when I couldn't see what I still had left to do.

As I reached the floor of the glen with its better made tracks and paths, the dull trudge began in earnest. All the risks that keep me alert had been left up on the mountain. My skills were now obsolete and all I had to do was walk. Anyone could do that last bit. Amateur runners can be seen doing it every year towards the end of the London Marathon as they limp along encumbered by fancy dress that seemed so cool five or six hours earlier.

There were no farmers or gamekeepers with quads, no inhabited properties to shorten my journey. There were dippers in the river, though. It stopped raining somewhere along the glen and I took my waterproofs off to try and cheer myself up and stop feeling sorry for myself. As with the TGOC walk, I was soaked through with a mixture of rain and condensation but there were no cheerful hikers going the other way to swap greetings with. Like that descent from Ingleborough to Horton-in Ribblesdale, after the Three Peaks for the novices it went on forever. Every hope for a finish over the next rise or round the next corner was dashed with more of what had just been done.

With the TGOC, it was those last few kilometres that were the worst but on the mercy hobble it was the arrival itself. It was unfamiliar ground and, with no map, it was all new to me. Inverie was hidden by trees until right into the actual buildings and for those last few hundred metres I followed the signs for the bunkhouse because that seemed logical, as I was hoping to stay there and they would be more used to walkers and their associated problems.

Until then, I had sort of blanked it out but now, as with the stop on the *bealach*, I needed to concentrate on what I was going to have to say and how. I also recognised that I had been carrying the burden alone for too long, and now it was nearly over for me, I was beginning to come apart. I couldn't really think straight. That familiar detached element that came before my hypothermia and altitude sickness was back. Quite frankly, I was too drained to care any longer. I just wanted to dump it and run. To hide away somewhere and drown myself in my sorrows. I had trashed my feet again and needed a bottle of wine and a decent meal. It had taken close to nine hours from Sourlies bothy to Inverie and I had done all that on a sachet of instant porridge and two mugs of coffee.

I hadn't seen a single person all day, even from a distance, until I finally arrived at the bunkhouse and saw someone working in an adjoining yard. There had still been no mobile phone signal, so the owner of the bunkhouse had to hear it all. I will admit that I was choked up and almost crying when I related the crisis to another for that first time. Not quite, though. Bottle it up and hide it to preserve dignity. I don't know whether this chink in the armour was the relaxation of last reserves with the relief of the battle end, or the incompetence I felt for being unable to supply anything but those sketchy details described here. I didn't even know their real names. There were too many variables. Too many questions that I had no answers for. And I was hurting myself but making light of that so as not to detract attention from the real emergency, which, upon refection, may have backfired by lessoning the enormity of what I was passing on. But, like on Kinder

Scout after pulling those two guys out of the river, I had done all that I could and the problem now belonged to others better equipped to deal with it, however they saw fit. I didn't possess the means to do anything more. My job was done.

Game over.

I checked into the bunkhouse for the night. Less than an hour later, I learned that Pete and Fred were already safe. They had been helicoptered off the mountains the day before and flown to an Inverness hospital.

There was wifi at the bunkhouse and I caught up with news from home. Claire was in hospital also, with pregnancy problems, and that gave me something different to worry about: Diane's long-term sickness had begun with pregnancy problems from which she never fully recovered.

Pete and Fred had turned up at the bunkhouse shortly after I had learned they were okay. They had spent their day getting back from Inverness. It turned out that one of them, very high on the mountain, had fallen about fifteen metres and was on a ledge with a number of injuries, too worried to move. The height had given intermittent phone signal and, while not enough to call the rescue services, it was sufficient to get a text out after about four hours of trying, and a coastguard helicopter picked them up shortly afterwards. The faller had a number of injuries which all turned out to be minor, but collectively, they had knocked him about quite badly.

We exchanged these tales over about fifteen minutes, discussed how they could recover their gear from the bothy, shook hands on it and moved on. Like me, I think the 'what ifs…' and the 'should haves…' were for those who weren't there to waste their breath on.

That evening's meal was another packet of dehydrated something or other washed down with a mug of indifferent instant coffee. The five hundred metres to that pub was a prospect far more daunting than I cared to take on. *Plantar fasciitis* had no respect for my noble gesture either and kept me awake much of the night to remind me to take better care of my feet if I wanted to continue with this walking malarkey.

It is fairly safe to say that I was a very battered and broken man when I limped out early the next morning to get the first ferry to Mallaig and then the train home.

My granddaughter, Chloe, was born by caesarean section the next morning.

I like to think that with my 'mercy hobble' I went some way towards earning that MBE they had given me for pushing papers about seventeen years earlier. There had been some blood as well as mud in the basin when I had showered that night in the bunkhouse. It made me kind of proud to put one over on the increasing numbers of those who will call upon the emergency services for trivia because they are caught up in the constant drama of modern living. But it was sod's law that my walk was all for nothing, for which I am grateful yet left thinking about what might have happened if it hadn't been. Would I still be an ordinary guy just passing through?

Summit Talks 15

You can steal my belongings. You can break my heart. But you'll never take away my achievements. – The Aimless Rambler

Done and dusted

There are some things more memorable than others and that's what I have to look for to keep this entertaining while at the same time providing the information needed to make the point intended. For example, I found it particularly difficult trying to describe the mercy hobble because, apart from the circumstances behind it, I don't remember enough to single it out as anything more than a sore-footed trudge. A bit of underlying drama that is difficult to milk for my lighter touch.

Whereas I can distinctly remember a five-minute section of the West Highland Way from about ten years earlier when I had to push my way through a packed herd of cows that were blocking my path. They were about a foot deep in mud near a farmyard gate that I had to go through and clearly had no intention of moving because it was too much hard work. It raises a smile, picturing the hiker with poles and rucksack trying to push his way through unyielding, shitty-arsed cows. Now if they had been in Knoydart blocking my journey, I would have had a decent counterpoint to work with. Yet, as it was, they were just the high point of another rather dreary day.

There are whole days that slip into obscurity like that. From it, I have to salvage the bits I would like to keep and set myself triggers to help find them again. They are those mountains or walks, big or small, that are on that list that goes into the Battered Box. This, the only account ever told in full of my mercy hobble, will go in there too.

When setting out to write about my mountain experiences from the outset it had never been my intention to seek the sophistication of the eloquent but to wander those same routes with the harder dialogue they deserve. The cold, brutal disregard the rough country holds for a person's suffering, in both mind and body, is what separates those like me from the romantics who seek to make something illusory mystic. We will be hunkered down and getting a brew on while out on the hill their poem remains unfinished and rigor mortis is already setting in. That is how I see it.

Anyone can go to the mountains and enjoy them in their own way but those with their heads in those metaphorical clouds will be taught, sooner or later, that same lesson as the rest of us who venture out there frequently. Practicality and logistical analysis, when that time comes, are what you will need and not being good with words. Anything else is dead weight and counts for nothing in the crisis that lurks hidden to unexpectedly test us.

I have found that with most accounts of rough country travel I read, the authors are often making their personal dramas out of what I, and many others of the mountaineering fraternity, would consider to be just another normal day. I hope I have addressed that. My own life on those Scottish treks was never at risk. The walk or die is just the bottom-line reminder like the spare wheel of a car. It is there but you may never need to use it. The rest was just what I saw as the most practical solution to a pending crisis at that time.

> I have always felt that I am one of an endangered species BUT now I feel like I am one of a dying breed. Possibly the last.
> – The Aimless Rambler

Life after the mercy hobble just picked up where I had left off. Get better, walk a bit, paint a bit and write a bit more than I was doing before. As part of my recovery, I backpacked two days of the Pennine Way from Edale to home without any trouble, although it shot down any last illusions I harboured about doing it as a through walk south to north. It was too easy to go home for the second night and restarting again would be no better. I have done too much of it already in bits and pieces, including all the tops except those in the Cheviots towards the northern end.

A second test for the recovery, and to introduce my son-in-law, Paul, to my gritty world, I did the Yorkshire Three Peaks again with him in the September. I wore my faithful walking boots. Probably to the dismay of Paul, who works in the manly world of the building trade, I had kept the tights, though. They're so much more practical than wet trousers around the ankles. Gaiters to prevent that are okay, but not as good as replacing the two with tights that dry so quickly if the sun comes out. Tights and walking boots – another cartoon coming to life.

As usual, there were a gaggle of charity walkers out there in front to serve as target hares. A lot less than on the ASDA day and these were much harder to catch. It was a slow day, though. Too much rain and mud to keep the pace up and we did it in 9.59 or 10.14, depending on whether the false start and returning to the car for forgotten items is counted or not. I know which I chose.

I was the weakest link again but still only about half a dozen people passed us – four of them while we stopped for a brew and retaken when they topped the last steep climb and rested while, as it turned out, waiting for me to check the way off after the summit, as they were unsure. Paul, who had already caught them a few minutes earlier and was now getting used to my ways, had told them that I wouldn't stop. His prediction was absolutely spot on. They got their directions as I walked on. 'I'll show you,' and left them to tag on behind.

The day before, I had taken my UK1000 total to 993 with a nondescript Marylin in the Trough of Bowland. I knew I was going to finish the UK1000 in 2017. I had even set the date to coincide with a group of friends for a camping weekend around Bonfire Night (5 November). A new problem suddenly appeared. An almost laughable one. I was worried that I would peak too soon!

It was somewhat fitting that those last six needed before that date were slightly tougher than expected. I only got five and one of them wasn't in either plan A or B. They were the last I was to get solo and worthy of little more detail because, as opposed to the Scottish treks, they typified much of what I have had to get used to in my quest. They were like me – not as ordinary as I would have liked them to be.

They took me to the Arans, a mountain range to the south of Bala in North Wales. There's a wonderful ridge rising from the south of that lake, running parallel with the A494, roughly towards Dolgellau. It fairly bristles with rugged peaks and cliffs that have long been on my jobs-to-do, even before peak-bagging became the primary objective. So I didn't go there. I wanted to but couldn't.

There were more of my unclimbed peaks amongst that lot than I needed and I didn't want to leave satellite peaks that I would probably not go back for. I would save them for another day. I could have lied if I had got my thousand before the date arranged, and none but me would be any the wiser. The truth might get bent a bit for humorous effect but not on something as important to me as those thousand peaks. Being true to myself has served me well so far and there is no point in spoiling it that close to the finish. Instead I went for some other lumpy hills on the eastern side of that same range. The beige and boggy ones that have featured so much in my life. Just like those at home but slightly bigger.

I parked at a high point on an unclassified road at Bwlch y Groes. Pass of the Cross… Damn. Look, a *bwlch* is another name for a *bealach* or col but might not always be spelt like that. I certainly have no idea how to say it. This one is also known as Hellfire Pass but you'd best be getting onto Wikipedia if you need more on that. The important thing for me is that it's high and gives, in theory, an easy start to the day.

Before leaving the car park, the first thing I noticed, after the litter, was a fence. It followed the high ground towards my first peak, Llechwedd Du. I couldn't see that top, though. It wasn't raining but threatened to all the time with the shifting cloud that had blown across the ridge and hidden it. An indifferent grey day, I think of them as. The all too familiar normal mountain weather that I have come to expect in a UK summer or winter alike.

I like fences. There was no path on the map but a fence is like a handrail and a trod has often been formed alongside it by people like me and animals that may want to be on the other side or, like us, are using it as a navigation aid. There was a bit of path for about two hundred metres and that was it. First boggy stretch and it was gone. There is always an optimistic start to paths from popular viewpoints where the sightseers, inspired by the vista, set out to stretch their legs for a bit, until the first nasty obstacle is encountered in their street footwear. Then they turn back. Funnily enough, the litter thinning out can mark the same spot.

The bogs were worse than I had expected. A route through or round was always having to be looked for. Every now and then, there was a vague trod running parallel with the fence, so it was used where possible, but the bogs would force the route wide again before too long.

At the beginning of the walk, more care was taken than towards the end in an attempt to keep my feet dry. If I had done the walk the other way round, there was a good chance that I would have ploughed straight through some of them. Not all, though. There was a nasty feel of depth about two or three of them. It just needed a little more poetic licence to add the skeleton of a hand reaching out of that flat, leafy pool to finish it off. The ground got firmer as height was gained and the trod became well defined where it led to the small pile of stones of the summit.

Others will call these piles of stones cairns but I have become a little more selective. I like to think of a cairn as a thoughtfully built pile of stones for navigation purposes, whereas on some of these remote and rarely visited summits they are often a small shabby heap that says, 'I guess this is the top. I suppose we ought to mark it or no one will know we have been here before them.'

A gap in the clouds gave me a convenient view to my next target, Foel Rhudd. The fence, now a new one by the look of it, headed in the right direction to the next *bwlch*, col, *bealach* or pass but would need crossing as it did not go over my target summit.

Going down the long easy slope, the boggy stretches had returned but were not as bad as the day's openers. Mostly splash-throughs, big steps or jumps to be artfully described in that manual that I'm not going to write either. There were sheep on my side of the fence and one solitary one on the other looking through at its mates. The fence was very new, and I wondered whether when they were putting it up if that solitary sheep had been left stranded on the wrong side. There was nothing I could do about it and the shepherds would sort it out at the next gather.

Then I witnessed something that I wouldn't have expected possible. When those sheep on my side started to drift away to keep their distance from me, the one on the other side ran around in circles for a bit then suddenly, just like an Olympic high jumper, it stopped, looked at the fence and took a running jump that cleared it with spectacular ease. I couldn't have done it!

I climbed over it myself shortly afterwards. Bad call. It was not too boggy but the going was rough with Turk's heads and peat hags. As I neared the summit, I could see that if I had followed the fence further it met another that did lead to it. Slightly longer but easier walking. I could also see that this fence curved round towards my third summit. Too far to see clearly, as the next lot of cloud obscured it, but close enough to get me near enough and then sort out the search for the top when I got nearer.

Determined to stay with the fence, I set off again and ten minutes later changed my mind again and made a good call. Cutting a straight line across the arc of the curving fence line looked a much better prospect, so I left it. And so it works. Sometimes you get it right, sometimes you don't. Esgeiriau Gwynion done, then it was down to Bwlch Sirddyn (Welsh = no vowels or too many). I followed a vague trod down the steeper ground still following the fence. Playtime was over. I could see the lower ground was going to be very wet. There were a hundred metres or so of telltale reed grass to cross. The fence I was following went straight through it and up the other side to the ridge of my next summit. It was steep and with no sign of any trod or path but even on the fiercest of hostile terrain the existence of a fence tells you that man has been that way before – so there is a way.

There was supposed to be a path crossing the bwlch at right angles to my direction of travel but there was no sign of it except a stile over the fence. I had one wet foot by the time I was climbing again. Climbing straight up steep rough grass is tough. That one was particularly so because there were quite of lot of mossy sections that suck the foot in. It's like walking on down pillows, so it absorbs the power needed to push and take the next step up. Featherbed Moss in Derbyshire is named that for that very same reason.

Thick cloud engulfed the summit of Foel Hefod-fynydd and rain came with it.

Plan A was not looking so good any more. I had been thinking that for some time. I was about an hour slower than expected due to that rough ground. From that summit, I was hoping to pick my way across to the big ridge that I mentioned earlier and get the two northernmost peaks from it before reversing back to Bwlch Sirddyn and taking the footpath to the road for an easy road walk finish back up to the car. The cloud didn't bother me but rain, rough going, being late and a path that didn't exist decided it for me. I had four and would call it a day. Plan B was to quit there and go back to the car, then sort out another day's walking before the big finish on the third.

There was also another factor in this decision-making that I was having to come to terms with. I don't know whether it was the Scotland epics or because I was nearly finished with the UK1000, but just like when Diane had died, in those last years of my working life, and I struggled to continue with my trade union work, the fires of my passion were burning out. I was losing my enthusiasm. There was a time, not so long ago, that I would have gone for those two summits and be damned. 'Hour,' shrug, 'hour 'n' 'alf up. Same back, maybe less. *Morceau de gateau.*' Yet looking at it through the rain I just did not have my heart in it.

Back down to the bogs. The missing path did appear as a trod eventually but it was grim. I was knee-deep as I crossed one stream almost completely covered with three-foot-high clumps of reed grass. These reeds can usually be walked on to keep your feet dry by pushing them over with each foot to form a continuous mat as you go but there was just too much water on that occasion. Once your boots are full, further finesse is pointless and the crossing is finished with less care. Then struggling out of another, similar gully, I climbed a bank and was on an old vehicle track. There were lots of reed clumps and puddles but it was easy and fast walking. The best of the day so far.

When the sun came out, having abandoned my proposed walk and now back in front of my timetable, I stopped before I got to the road for the lunch that probably would have gone uneaten had I stuck to Plan A. Some habits die harder than others. I emptied my boots and wrung out my socks while making a brew. I had a spare pair of socks and decided it was worth finishing my day in relative comfort, so changed them. With nothing else left to do, I then got my map out for the first time since leaving the car. I didn't need it to navigate but it is always nice to fit the scenery to the map sometimes as I have to be doing something.

I confirmed the track and path were the same thing. Such tracks will always lead to a road but there is usually a farm to go through before doing so; therefore it's prudent to check that the path doesn't divert off before it and bring about confrontation with an angry farmer…or, worse still, his dogs. While doing all this and enjoying my brew and lumps of cheese and bread that was once a sandwich until being shoved in a bag and spending the day bounced about in the rucksack, Plan C jumped out at me.

The path would bring me out on the road at the bottom of that Pass of the Cross and I was following it back to the car parked at the top. On my map, all the summits that may qualify for inclusion are dabbed with a yellow highlighter pen so that I can pick out alternatives easily when plans have to be altered. There were none on my map that were feasible but there were on my other one. There were always two maps.

On this occasion, I had included my map of the adjoining mountain range, the Berwyns, because I had three peaks amongst them that had been left out for one reason or another. They met at the pass, in fact. One such peak was on the very edge of that map, which put it close to where I had parked. I filled the missing gap with my GPS and found it was less than two kilometres from the car.

The reason for its outstanding status was I had deemed it as unworthy. A single peak, very close to the road, with very little height gain. Its qualifying height for inclusion on a recognised list was because it was a Nuttal. Over two thousand feet high. That unworthy tag was removed because from where I would join the road it was actually the longest continuous ascent of the day.

I had a Plan C. I was slightly annoyed because I hadn't seen it before leaving home but then again it was only one and I did need two in order to leave myself just the one for the grand finish.

I use Ordnance Survey (OS) maps with a 1:50.000 scale, which for the non-metric is about one and a quarter inches to the mile. They also do a 1:25,000 scale which, compared with the smaller-scale version, seems to sound better when saying it in the translation to English, 'two and half inches to the mile'. It has much more detail and has become so increasingly popular that I may be in the minority with my preferred option.

I have stayed loyal to mine for a number of reasons: (a) I have always used it and read it so much quicker; (b) I went metric long ago. Each grid square is the equivalent of one kilometre across and therefore much easier to see than on its somewhat cluttered brother – I can estimate a crude distance a lot faster; (c) when I was biking, I would cycle off the larger scale map too quickly; (d) I have the whole of the UK at OS 1:50,000 on my computer and print off my maps, A4 size, as I want them – cheaper and easier than buying all the maps; (e) most importantly, I need glasses for reading but not walking and there is so much detail on the larger scale that I can't read it without them, whereas I can glance at my maps and see enough – sort of.

I do get a tad blasé about it, though. Particularly when walking with others. On my own, like on that day, I didn't need it. I could, for the most part, see where I wanted to get to next and go for it. I have looked at the map before setting off, pictured it in terms of hills and valleys, remember what I need and go. With others, I am the same, but when asked where we are in relation to where we want to be, I read the land, picture that map in my head, make a guess and throw a few figures in the air that invariably featured the 'hour,' shrug, 'hour 'n' 'alf' formula. To me, it makes no difference. I don't need to know how far it is to the top because I'm going there whatever.

It usually ends up with me being precise in the end because this habit of mine is no longer a secret. If it gets really nasty out in the rough country, I will always have the GPS charged up and ready for backup anyway. At 1:50,000 scale of course. And I'll not trust the judgement of anyone who doubts their accuracy. The only time mine faltered was when I had let the batteries run down to critical and could no longer pick up the satellite signals.

The GPS had shown a county boundary running over that ridge top to that chosen summit and, while walls and fences are not included on my chosen scale for maps, such boundaries are often matched with a wall or fence. There was no path marked but there could be a trod. I set off again slightly cheered. That road climb was steep but the traffic negligible. I had cycled up it once many years before with the kids, for no other reason than we could. I was right about the boundary. Another fence and a good trod. The best of the day.

When the fence is easy to follow like that one, my thoughts are free to wander, but I have two that often recur. One is associated with Johnny Cash who 'walks the line', which is about not erring from the straight and narrow in marriage, and nothing to do with the 'Wichita

Lineman' by Glen Campbell, who rode the line of fences to check for breaks made by pesky rustlers and Injuns. The other is the film *Rabbit Proof Fence* about runaway Aboriginal kids in Australia, where, I am told, the painting of faces blue is not a common practice, who were following the fences as they tried to get home after being forcibly removed from their parents to be trained to work in service for the white population – because we knew what was best for them. And we have people today who think they have it tough when petrol prices go up or the trains are late. Johnny and Glen I can live without but, like my oread and the Grim Reaper, those kids are never far from those fences if I start to feel that I'm hard done by.

Apart from cars on the road, I saw only one other person while out walking that day. That was another walker about five hundred metres away in a side valley at my lunch stop. No path there either, so they were probably a bit like me. It had clouded over again before I got to the last peak and the red kite drifting about up there was the best bird of the day, while that woolly jumper after peak one would be my fondest memory. It could only have been better if those Aran mountains had been where the Aran sweaters originated, so that I could make an even better joke out of it.

And that is a typical day in the hills for me. With a two-hour drive home left to do.

I was so nearly done with the UK1000 and with this book. I just needed to tidy both up and finish them off. Bung them in the Battered Box and chase another dream of the oread with my rambling thoughts trying to keep up with her. She's a bit of a bugger, and that's for sure. I hope we go somewhere warm.

This book may contain what may read as a dramatic and adventurous lifetime but that's not entirely a true reflection of it. The incidents referred to are some of the landmarks of a near fifty-year journey condensed into a few hours of reading. That leaves an awful lot unsaid. The ordinary bits of ordinary lives that us ordinary people live. The dull and the bland that we seek to escape from, not to find ourselves reading about when trying to get rid of the day's troubles and the mind rested before sleep.

For it to have any link with reality, perspective has to be maintained. I just chip off the gloss and polish of those higher flyers to tell it how it is. Not the shiny impression put over by the journalists of outdoor-orientated magazines or on our TV screens by articulate presenters and celebrities lapping up new work.

Not for me are there any invitations to the preferential treatment that they show in their documentaries on any given subject. I don't get a private tour of the Sistine Chapel to savour the art. I, like you, have to queue for hours for a ticket or alternatively get an advance ticket and be shuffled through on a lightning tour of the entire Vatican Museum when twenty-five minutes of jostling in the packed chapel is all that I'm going to get.

Out in the rough country, that role gets to be reversed. I have the advantage. I am on my home ground. I'm free of backup crew needed to make that programme, where there are no directors and producers to satisfy, no inane interviews to carry out with quirky local traditions, no repeated retakes because someone, like me perhaps on their way to their own agenda, just walked across the shot. Yep, did that. No one messes with my hill-walking. I was actually asked if I could go round a summit rather than over it because of the filming. Not on that occasion I couldn't. It was a new one.

Solo, there is no noise of conversation to scare off the wildlife, and in the pre-dawn glow of a three-thousand-metre pass I have stood face to face less than five metres from a big-horned *bouquetin* (ibex) while we each weighed up who should give way. I've enjoyed eye to eye contact with an adder basking on the rock step that was to be my next objective on a scramble.

While descending a ridge in the Pyrenees, I once came as close as you can get to a griffin vulture without one of us being dead. Oblivious to my presence, it glided the thermal around the large boulders behind me, which had hidden me from its sight, so closely that I felt the breeze of its passing. It then circled, without a wingbeat, and came back to check again that I wasn't ready for eating. (It was using the thermal to gain height most likely, but that's boring.) Ten minutes later, some French walkers who had witnessed the close encounter were shaking my hand too because they had never seen anything like it either.

There have been days of glorious sunshine with Alpine meadows in full flower against a backdrop of snowy peaks and glaciers. Natural ice sculptures that the human artist could never hope to emulate in both the Cairngorms and Snowdonia. Perfect reflections in mirror-like lakes and no one to share them with and spoil the moment.

You have to walk through hundreds of ordinary days between these grand landmarks and tests of fortitude. They are what make the others so special but should never be dismissed or belittled because they all offer something for your efforts providing you are willing to look for it.

Finishing the UK1000 almost epitomised that. Just another mountain on just another day. Two friends joined me for it and others might have done had I not deliberately chosen to do it on a working day so that they couldn't, as I didn't want to make a too big of a deal out of it. And it was no big deal because I will go on to do more. Like those walkers in front on the charity walks, my UK1000 was a target and not a limit.

To finish on the right one, we had to do another unworthy for 999 but justified it by doing a bigger one before that. That one I had climbed before on a glorious, bitterly cold winter's day when the snow was crusted with ice. Wind-blown freezing rain had transformed the fences into a line of giant ice waffles two kilometres long. It was so magical that I had dawdled and finished the day descending in the dark. I remember them all.

We faked a champagne-drinking photograph on the thousandth to send over the social media for friends to view and be told the task was finished. It was far too cold and gloomy up there to be drinking fizzy pop when there were flasks of hot coffee to be had. Besides, in our ordinary world, I still had to drive back when we got down. I may not like driving but I never mix it with my drinking. On my own, I might have stayed at the summit for a little longer than with those other two companions of mine, because I owe the mountains more than I can repay, but they won't mind waiting. They will know as sure as night follows day that I will be back.

There were also two more smaller, but not so worthy, tops that I could have got if I had gone a different way back to the car. Just there, 'Hour,' shrug, 'hour 'n' 'alf, tops.'

> Getting older. Sometimes you just have to stop, look and enjoy the moment. You might as well, because you could well have forgotten it by tomorrow – The Aimless Rambler

Ordinary people doing ordinary things. I refuse to go very far past that concept. We all do it in our own, sometimes peculiar, little ways. My only desire, beyond the entertainment value of this work, is that you may go away, ignore the celebrities, the reality TV, and hype and blurb of the media and attention-seekers, and do something ordinary but, unlike the easily satisfied thrill-seekers, try to make it personal by adding your own stamp of approval to the twist you give it. It makes us just that little less ordinary if it is only to ourselves.

I will go on climbing mountains for as long as I can but as far as everyone else is concerned I will always now be going for my thousandth mountain. As each new one is added to my list, I will feel just a little better about some of those Robin Hoods Picking Rods that will fall off the bottom. It could end tomorrow and I would be happy because I still have my wild card. The Joker. That's all those foreign mountain tops that I have reached, most of them bigger than any UK peaks. They remained uncounted in my reserve to be used should the task fall short of the objective. There are enough to knock each and every one of those dodgy UK ones off in a single swipe with one simple change in my rules. In fact, with an absolutely clear conscience, I am going to do exactly that.

I have climbed over a thousand different mountains.

www.ingramcontent.com/pod-product-compliance
Lightning Source LLC
Chambersburg PA
CBHW030904080526
44589CB00010B/132